WARRIOR'S CREED

WARRIOR'S CREED

A Life of Preparing for and Facing
the Impossible

ROGER SPARKS

WITH DON REARDEN

ST. MARTIN'S PRESS ❧ NEW YORK

First published in the United States by St. Martin's Press, an imprint of
St. Martin's Publishing Group

WARRIOR'S CREED. Copyright © 2019 by Roger Sparks with Don
Rearden. All rights reserved. Printed in the United States of America.
For information, address St. Martin's Press, 120 Broadway, New York,
N.Y. 10271.

www.stmartins.com

Designed by Omar Chapa

The Library of Congress Cataloging-in-Publication Data is available
upon request.

ISBN 9781250151520 (hardcover)
ISBN 9781250151537 (ebook)

Our books may be purchased in bulk for promotional, educational, or
business use. Please contact your local bookseller or the Macmillan
Corporate and Premium Sales Department at 1-800-221-7945, extension
5442, or by email at MacmillanSpecialMarkets@macmillan.com.

First Edition: July 2019

10   9   8   7   6   5   4   3   2   1

Dedicated to our struggle
and the hidden salvation within

CONTENTS

ACKNOWLEDGMENTS

To the artists, writers, filmmakers, and healers who have entered my life as I grew beyond my military experiences: thank you for helping me express what's in my heart and helping me find my way. To Joe Yelverton for turning his attention on my work and to Don Rearden for enabling this book—you have both been powerful affirmations to the direction of my life. To Bobby and Sara Sheehan: your virtue and grit make a special kind of magic I am lucky to know well. To Debra and Don Yarian for trusting and mentoring me—thank you for making us feel we are one of the family. To Scott, Casey, and David for making that trip and changing my life—you all represent the mercy, love, and grace I was unable to accept for myself.

It doesn't seem right to thank everyone I served with, but I would like to thank the officers or supervisors who put up with my bullshit. To the Reconnaissance Marines, Pararescuemen, and Aircrews with whom I've experienced the limits of ability and resolve, our language doesn't contain the words to capture the trust and raw emotion we've shared over the decades.

My father is no longer here for me to thank. He taught me how to live in this world and take it on the chin. I can't articulate how much I miss him. There is only one person who misses him more than me, and that is my mom. She's an amazing woman, and I can only imagine what it must be like to have a son like myself who has made a career out of risking his life. She's given me unconditional love my entire life, and I've repaid her with decades of worry. I'm sorry about that, but grateful for your steady and constant love that saw us through.

To Orion and Oz, you are the two stars in my life that have guided me home and taught me more than I'll ever be able to teach you. I love you both with all my being.

To Jennifer, who has given me the gift of our two incredible children, and a lifetime of love and memories that I've never felt worthy of and can never repay. You've seen my soul, the best and the worst of me, and stood by my side through it all. We are each other.

AUTHOR'S NOTE

The events detailed in this book, and the many I've left out, were done out of desperation. I've taken grave risks for others not because I was trying to do something valued by society, but because I was trying to save myself. Extraordinary acts in combat are born of subconscious desperation, not heroism.

We pick our heroes in an attempt to propagate our belief systems to the rest of the world, and in a way become our own Greek tragedy. I do not want to be a hero, nor would I ever claim myself to be, because as I see it, a hero's future exists only within his demise.

This book is my attempt to make meaning of what I've survived through circumstance and choice. Some of these stories were hard to tell, others just too difficult or sensitive to print. The details have been changed to honor those involved who risked their lives or saved mine. I have always been mesmerized by what we can learn from the events of our lives.

People have their own version of a story or an event. What follows is my version.

There are many people I love and respect who make up parts of this story. I tremble at the thought of upsetting friends, family, and my peers with the wording or stories in this book. I am indebted to the events and individuals who helped me become who I am, and who sustained me through this crazy and, at times, surreal existence. I hope in telling my story I am as much honoring them, and their contributions to my life, as I am trying to share what I have learned on the journey. I am still trying to save myself.

For most of my life I have tried to make myself stronger and more capable, not truly knowing why or what for. When we are young we are taught by the reflections of those around us. The emotions between the movements and words find their meaning. Early in my youth it was apparent that real truth and growth are found in the gray areas of life. Black and white are false ideas that attempt to govern us. We head out to shine light on the dark and gray, to test ourselves and develop our own sense of the shadows. If we are lucky we will find deep exhaustion and reflection. It is only at the end of a voyage that we can attempt to sail home to ourselves. Writing this book has been challenging for many reasons. Staring at yourself is difficult. Often our experiences isolate us. The more surreal the experience, the more severe the isolation. My effort is to close the gap, share some colorful stories in an effort to find perspective, and connect deeper with my humanity, and in a way to yours.

The flower blooms not because it seeks beauty, but because nature must express itself. This is a story, my expression, and that is all.

WARRIOR'S CREED

I have no parents
I make the heavens and earth my parents
I have no home
I make awareness my home
I have no life or death
I make the tide of breathing my life and death
I have no divine power
I make honesty my divine power
I have no friends
I make my mind my friend
I have no enemy
I make carelessness my enemy
I have no armor
I make benevolence my armor
I have no castle
I make immovable-mind my castle
I have no sword
I make absence of self my sword.

ANONYMOUS FOURTEENTH-CENTURY SAMURAI

WARRIOR'S CREED

PROLOGUE

ON THE OTHER SIDE

A real man does not think of victory or defeat. He plunges recklessly towards an irrational death. By doing this, you will awaken from your dreams.

—YAMAMOTO TSUNETOMO, *HAGAKURE*

Out of breath. Frozen, upon a trembling mountain. Wading in the cold wet blanket of thoughts at what is lurking just past my slumber, beyond what I can see. The earth shudders and groans. I hear screaming, percussion, and gunfire. I can feel all these things. I sense them around me and within me. When I allow my subconscious to get out, the horror paralyzes me.

My sons, Oz and Orion, wait for me on the other side of the hill. The enemy is ripping them apart with machine guns and explosions. The mountain fighters tear them to pieces. My boys are being mutilated. There is no mercy, love, or grace.

The vision causes reality to fade.

———

I swim in a nightmare of wails of the dying, of bullets like small flaming angels ripping at the air, the ground around me erupting in showers of dirt and gore, and yet my two sons are beyond my reach on the other side of the hill.

Their cries fill my ears.

Surrounded by the dead and dying. Trying save my children. Crawling and dragging my weapon; slipping on blood, rock, and feces; trying to resuscitate the cold, lifeless body of my youngest son. Reality is irrelevant; only this moment exists. I will not save them, despite my horror, despite my rage, despite myself. . . .

Then . . .

I fumble for a pulse against my son's neck.

Boom!

A rocket explodes.

I sit up. Sweating and out of breath. My heart races and my head gleams, like a runaway train. The fan blows. The house falls silent. The sounds of war are consigned to white noise. There are no screams of horror. No gunfire. No explosions. Jennifer lies in bed next to me, asleep. I turn to check my watch. It is one a.m. I grab my headlamp from the nightstand and swing my legs out of the bed.

Next I move, as quiet as possible, with the green glow of the headlamp illuminating my way through the house. The floor creaks. I work to steady my breathing and ease my way into the room.

The green light forces reality to become surreal again. I am drawn into the back of the HH-60, lit starkly with the green, dim crew lights exposing the harvest of fresh violence. Hours of hauling what's left of human beings back to the hot, humid shipping containers. Fuel, feces, acrid sweat, and blood fill my lungs. Even sitting and holding on to overhead straps, I slip wildly on the gore-covered floor with the g-forces of the helicopter. I am intoxicated with horror.

I sit down on the edge of Oz's bed, and pull up his blankets. I lift the sheet over his face, to cover his eyes, so only his fingers stick out from beneath the comforter. I take his little finger and poke it, trying to disturb him as little as possible.

The green light of the headlamp on the blood glucose monitor's screen reveals my next moves, whether I need to grab a needle and syringe and give him a shot, or reach for a small box of chocolate milk and slip a straw into the side of his mouth and whisper, "Take a drink, little buddy." Without even opening his eyelids, he downs the milk. He knows he won't be allowed to go back to sleep until he does.

I am so attuned to doing this; even the tactile sense of this nightly operation is routine. Oz has special needs. He is type 1 diabetic and has cerebral palsy.

He's twelve years old. Sometimes I check his sugar eight times a day, so it is just automatic. We don't want him to have a seizure at night. We've lost him once before, and don't want to lose him again.

Then it is back into bed. Quiet as I can, to not disturb Jennifer. I lie down and begin counting my breaths until I fall asleep, and the process repeats itself.

I am not afraid of the nightmares.

I am not afraid of death.

I am not a Christian, Buddhist, or some new-age prophet, but I have seen the face of God. I've seen it in the beautiful landscapes and in the contorted faces of dying men. I have heard the voice of the universe.

The fear I feel is not about what I have done, or what I will do. The fear is what I will discover on the other side of the hill, that I cannot protect them from the violence. That I will not save them from death.

1

WARRIORS OF A DIFFERENT CLOTH

*I dream of fighting to the death . . . and as the dream
progresses I grow accustomed to the idea of death and
become comfortable with it.*

—YAMAMOTO TSUNETOMO, *HAGAKURE*

A series of muffled thumps pulled me from my sleep. I was
eleven or twelve, probably dreaming at that moment of big air
on my bike. Perhaps soaring off a jump and flying several car
lengths, and as high as a school bus. Half awake, I realized
someone was in the garage, going through our stuff. The crashing and rummaging drew closer. I could hear movement
in the dividing room between our kitchen and living room.
I sat up.

An intruder was in our house and rummaging through
our belongings. No doubt after drugs and cash.

I heard my dad rise from his bed.

Footsteps outside my door. Rushing.

Hollow thuds against the wall.

Then the terrified voice of a strange man and followed by his screams. Panicked screams.

I knew better than to go running out, so I cracked open the door to my room. Just enough to see.

Wearing only boxers and holding a police baton in one hand, my dad dragged the burgler behind him back into our house. He threw the stranger on the floor, and brought the baton down against the man's shoulders with a sickening whack. Then hit him again.

My dad was a very formidable man. I was a child and naturally impressionable, but my father was powerful looking to me. He always worked out. He was Tommy Chong, from Cheech & Chong, the guy with the glasses, but yoked up, and muscle-bound, as if he did CrossFit for a living. The man standing in front of me with the baton possessed animalistic strength, and I was witnessing his power firsthand.

He looked up, saw me peering out from my door, and very calmly said, "Son, stay in your room. I'm handling this."

I closed my door and went back to my bed and listened. I had little choice.

Dad kept the man out there for a couple of hours, beating him and talking to him in this calm voice.

I can only describe what I heard as vicious.

The guy would lose consciousness, and when he came to, my dad would beat him again, but this time in a way that wouldn't let him pass out. I could hear him talk to the stranger about what was going to happen to his friends and his family.

I fell asleep by the time my dad loaded the man up in our VW Microbus and went and dumped him in the creek down our long street.

In the morning, I awoke to find bloodstains all over the carpet.

In the coming days there were homicides likely related to that night. I have no doubt my dad and his buddies hunted down some of the man's friends and family. He wasn't going to turn the guy in to the cops. My dad and his associates were always working in the shadows of the law. He visited all that violence on the intruder and the others involved as another sort of justice. He was going to force them to remember what they did at our house, but in a very horrible way.

With my dad, fighting and violence were right on the periphery. And from his perspective, you had to be fully capable of dealing with that violence. I was always learning from my dad, and the message I took away from that night was simple. Be ready for absolutely anything life throws at you in any given moment.

Growing up with this way of thinking affects me still. To this day, I'll work out until I'm almost throwing up. I don't know too many people in their forties who, every morning, work out in such a manner.

I learned from my dad early on to live this way. If a monster, right now, might break in to try to rape my wife and hurt my kids, I should be able to solve that situation through sheer will. Even if I have been mortally wounded, I feel like I should be able to project whatever violence is visited on me, right back—and in a very extreme way.

I grew up in a modest gray ranch house in a suburb of Dallas–Fort Worth. The exterior didn't match the interior, you could say. A cookie-cutter neighborhood. Short metal fences. Kept-up lawns. Tiny little front and back yards. An elementary school right across the street. And in our garage, my dad's Harley. Inside there was likely heroin, cocaine, weed, and weapons.

My dad was known as Big Roger. I was Little Roger. That's how the name game seemed to work in our world.

Big this. Little that.

Violence was part and parcel of life in our house, and my early exposures to violence came from being around my dad. I was with him once on the road, and we stopped in our VW to refuel. While he pumped gas this weird trucker walked up to him and started talking shit. I couldn't really tell what they were saying, but I sensed my father's anger.

Big Roger finished refilling, put the nozzle back in the pump, walked over, and dropped the guy with a single punch. Then, like it was nothing, my dad went inside and paid.

When he came out I asked, "What was that about, Dad?"

As he turned the key and we pulled away, he said, "We just had a slight altercation. No big deal."

There was another instance that stands out from my early youth. I was maybe eight years old and having a sleepover with a friend at the house. My mom came out of her room, all gussied up. As she left, I could somehow sense or smell the stress hanging about her. Then my dad headed out not long after her. He wore his leather Harley patrol jacket and his leather pants. He had his nightstick and an SS Luger on his hip.

There's that song Willie Nelson and Merle Haggard recorded about Pancho and Lefty, where Pancho always "wore his gun outside his pants, for all the honest world to feel." Every time I hear that song, I think of my dad. That pistol was there for the people of the world to feel him. He would ride around with it, for all to see. Definitely a junkyard dog.

I didn't know it then, but even at that age, elements of warrior culture were being instilled in my mind. The intruder and the trucker had crossed the lines of respect. In the case of this night, the lesson was about both respect and loyalty. It turns out an associate of sorts made the misstep of hitting on my mom. The guy was really disrespecting my father with his behavior. That was the line the man had crossed, and he would pay.

One time our neighbor's cat bit my sister's hand. I was around six at the time; she was a couple years older. I don't know why it was such a big deal, but I sensed my mom's stress over this. She waited for my dad to get home, to see if she should take her in to the emergency room for a tetanus shot.

It was always a grand arrival when my dad got home. He would ride up into the garage, his Harley rumbling. I would yell, "Dad's home!" When I heard that chest-shaking motor purring, I'd take off at a sprint for him. His return always marked one of the highlights of an afternoon. I enjoyed this race to greet him so much, but on this day Mom reached him first and told him about the cat. He headed into the house and came out with a can of opened tuna fish.

I'd been down the street. I raced up on my bike in time to see him swing his baton. *Whack!* The cat made one quick spin of fury, claws scratching the concrete, and went limp. He picked up the dead cat, carried it over to the neighbors, and shoved it into their mailbox. He started toward our house, then stopped. He returned to the mailbox, lifted the small metal red flag, and walked home.

That was the way my father handled life. An eye for an eye, of sorts. The fact that he would have to take my sister to the doctor's office and pay a couple hundred bucks pissed him off. In his mind, the neighbors and their damn cat had crossed the line.

There you go.

I look back and realize how smitten I was with my dad all the time. As a kid, dirt bikes and BMX racing gave me a sense of freedom. Ever since I was little, I was really into working on my bikes. My dad and his buddies would tinker on their motorcycles in the garage, listening to Steppenwolf on an old record player and smoking weed. My dad built me my own little workbench, but he wasn't bullshitting with a kid's pair of pliers for me to work on my bike. I had real tools. I would completely disassemble the entire bicycle, down to the pedals, and put it back together. My father was always turning wrenches, and I was his helper. I possessed a rare skill at that age. I could look at a nut or bolt and know instantly whether it was standard or metric, and the exact-size wrench or socket needed. Just by sight.

I loved to hang out there with my dad and his friends. The bikers were mostly Vietnam vets; without knowing it, they romanticized my notion of brotherhood. I grew up in that world, so it wasn't a contrived thing; this was more of a very sincere culture that chose to be disenfranchised from mainstream society. They lived a life that they felt was more truthful. Of course living outside of the law, with drugs and criminal activity, is destructive to our society, but these men who I grew up around had significant character. They had values they lived by, but those values were not the norm of what America was at the time.

I spent countless hours around these men and their stories, and witnessed a certain amount of violence. But also I think, more important, I grew up around a very structured set of principles. The way they lived was very real and tangible, and to be around this culture of men who had been warriors for our country in Vietnam, and had returned to become warriors of a different cloth, had a lasting impression on me.

I fondly remember sitting on my father's motorcycle. When I was really young I struggled to climb up on the tall metal horse. Once, carelessly, I touched the inside of my leg to the exhaust pipe. In that instant a doughnut-size patch of my skin sizzled like a piece of bacon on a hot skillet. I'd burned the soft young flesh of my leg on that hot steel.

This might have my first experience learning to swallow swords. The white-hot pain hurt worse than anything I'd felt up to that point in my life, but I bit my lip. I didn't cry out. I was worried. I worried he would think I'd shown my incompetence around his motorcycle, a machine so intimate to him. I told myself, *You can't let Dad know this happened.*

I melted the inside of my leg but didn't say a word.

2

FEMININE BEAUTY

Everyone says that no masters of the arts will appear as the world comes to an end. This is something that I cannot claim to understand. Plants such as peonies, azaleas, and camellias will be able to produce beautiful flowers, end of the world or not. If men would give some thought to this fact, they would understand.

—YAMAMOTO TSUNETOMO, *HAGAKURE*

You would think that growing up in an environment like that would be somewhat neglectful or harmful to a child. I guess in some capacities it was, but I always felt loved and I always felt safe. In terms of rules, we had a pretty open house. I could do whatever I wanted. For a young boy this was pretty cool. I could kick-start my dirt bike and rip through the neighborhood, ditch the bike in the woods, and then slip into the mall and steal Mötley Crüe cassettes. Then tear ass home. I was twelve and racing as fast as that Honda CR 80 could go, maybe a hundred miles an hour. I rode the shit out of that thing. The motor of the CR 80 at the time had a wide power band. They were two strokes, and fast with a lot of get up and go. Big Mike bought two of these motorcycles. One for Little Mike, one for me. Any time Little Mike got something, Big Mike made sure I did, too. The man took care of me like that. He might have been my dad's boss, but he was like a second father to me.

I was no saint, but my older sister was a wrecking ball. A real wild child. A real fucking wild child. I have many fleeting thoughts of my youth, and looking back it was a weird world, for a kid growing in the midst of biker culture. But this was normal life to me. My sister was another story. She was involved in all sorts of rebellious activity, and to come from such an environment and be thought of as too rebellious? That was as caustic as you could really be.

This was the era of Black Sabbath and jean jackets, and for my sister: trouble.

She started selling—in *junior high*. In many ways we were more worldly, more adultlike, than high school kids in this day and age. We might have only been in junior high, but the life we lived was intense. We had to grow up fast.

My sister ran with a tough crowd. I was always impressed with that about her. We played football across the street at the school. I would watch the older kids, including my sister, play. I know moments like this were impressionable because of that younger-sibling relationship. Sometimes they would have me join in, perhaps just to hurt me.

Sometimes I would be forced into the game. I had to play, because if I didn't I would be looked at as weak, called a pussy.

The out-of-bounds consisted of a gnarly wall of thornbushes, which I risked getting tossed into with each snap of the ball. The big kids didn't take it easy on me or my two buddies, Little Mike and Joey.

The one thing I had going for my well-being? My sister. She always had my back. She was protective. If someone messed with me, they messed with her.

My sister was tough, but not butch, and not a tomboy. She was beautiful, beautiful *and* tough. A deadly combination. Where the rocker women of the era, like Joan Jett, postured as if they were dangerous, my sister might really pull an ice pick and put it in your kidneys. She was that kind of hard. She walked that cutting edge of feminine: lethal and tough at the same time. She reminded me of my dad, though I, more sensitive, took after my mom.

My sister wasn't one to be roughed up. One time, a kid named Brandon made the near fatal mistake of pushing her into the thornbushes. This was a chump thing to do during a football game, and in his defense he made the push out of desperation, too, after all, this was street football at its finest. These games were often bloody, with everyone scuffed up, and the game almost always ended in some sort of a fight.

My sister rose out of the thornbushes swinging her fists. Swinging and connecting with full-on punches. She beat Brandon's ass. Beat his face down into the sunbaked Texas grass. Bad. I remember thinking that it was violent and primal.

She gave off this *don't fuck with me* vibe. Forget chicks messing with her. Even guys skirted her path. She took after my father in that violent way. I could see her picking up a brick and smashing someone in the face with it and stand over them, taunting them to get up. She always had a presence with people, and because of her pugnacious reputation, I was always in her shadow. She might have only been two years older than me, but when someone found out who my sister was they would say, "You're Tracy's little brother?" Then there would be this pause, followed by a change in tone and deference: "*Fuck, man.*"

Then they would politely walk the other way.

Tracy was a force of her own. All of my friends absolutely worshipped her. When punk bands like Gwar would come to town, she would be hanging out with them, and everyone seemed to know her. She slowly became connected in a subtle and strange way to these famous people. But this was a rough and unforgiving world.

One of the unwritten rules in the culture I grew up in is that if one of the men my dad associated with sold drugs to us kids, or to anyone associated with our group of friends, and my dad found out, that would be a lethal mistake.

There were clear lines drawn. And clear penalties when you crossed the line.

In many ways I grew up in a lawless land where you needed to be constantly aware, to be present, and to pay attention to figure out what the rules were in order to survive. Paying attention to details kept you alive. I learned this from my father, but also from my mom.

My mom looked just like Cher, when Cher was hot. I got my looks from her; make Cher a man, and that's what I would eventually become, I guess. As a young boy I liked watching my mother paint. She was into oils, and also brilliant with graphite sketching. I loved to sit and watch the paint from her brush create life. I observed how the images would take shape and form, and could feel the emotion and beauty coming out. I was young, and I don't know what sitting there watching her did to my neurons, but I know it affected my brain development. To this day, my mother is very artistic; not only do I look like her, but I think much of my character is derived from her as well. She bestowed upon me the ability to draw and engage with my creative capabilities.

I loved her for her art and her beauty, but I didn't know she was sharing her gift with me then, and showing me a path forward that I wouldn't put in to practice until much later. There is something magical about watching someone talented bring an image of beauty into this world.

My mom and my sister share the same birthday. I was the only one in our family who knew that my sister planned to run away when she turned sixteen. Tracy was horrible at picking men, and she'd found someone to escape with.

The day arrived. To celebrate my mom's special day, my parents and I went out to this Japanese hibachi restaurant where the chef would flip the shrimp and make the little onion volcanoes in front of the patrons. A seedy Benihana of sorts, Texas-weird. Underlaid on the wood counter was beautifully shellacked-over porn, really graphic porn. I can't explain the place any better than that.

I knew that Tracy planned on leaving that night. The

knowledge weighed on me. Finally, while we were eating, I couldn't contain the secret any longer. "I don't want to ruin your birthday, Mom, but Tracy isn't going to be home when we get back."

And she wasn't. Just like that my sister disappeared. Off to an unknown and dark world. The two of us, despite having the same upbringing, were about to head off on very different life trajectories. One thing was certain. I always knew my sister could handle herself; this was in her nature.

Power can be destructive, but I've never worried for her. Ever.

3

OVER COME

Throughout your life, advance daily, becoming more skillful than yesterday, more skillful than today. This is never-ending.

—YAMAMOTO TSUNETOMO, *HAGAKURE*

My religion in my early teens became racing bikes. All Little Mike and I did from sunup to well past sundown was ride, and those hours began to pay off. We were both pretty good on wheels. Our local heroes were the nationally sponsored racers. The two of us would go down where they practiced and build our own jumps. Not little skate ramps, I'm talking dangerous. All of our time before and after school became dedicated to BMX. A guy named Joe Kyle owned a shop called Kyle's Bike and Mower, and Joe sponsored local kids to race BMX. His shop became our home away from home.

I always felt as if I was weaker than the other guys I rode with. I lacked their explosive power. I attempted to overcome that deficit by continually training on the one big hill in our neighborhood. I would sprint up this steep hill two or three times a day as hard as my legs could carry me, until I tasted metal in my mouth. I didn't know it then, but this internal drive and ability to find my own motivation to better myself would become integral to my existence.

I was heavily involved in athletics, racing bikes and running track, and playing both football and basketball, yet I don't think my father ever came to one of my games. It never occurred to me he should have attended, so I never let this weigh on me. My mom would walk to my games with one of her friends, but she never made a show of being there like some parents. My dad had other shit going on. I had my thing and he had his thing. It wasn't that he didn't love me.

Around the same time, my left knee started aching. I wasn't about to go complaining to my dad; he was a loving and tender man, and I was at the center of that love, but I knew what he and his friends thought of weakness. I wasn't going to run crying to him about a little knee pain.

Then the pain became significant, crippling, and sometimes when I was alone I would sob and cry when it hurt. Which was often. This was my junior high era, when I was forming my identity. The early teen years are fragile when you're figuring out who you are in the world, and here I was in horrible pain with my knee hurting every waking moment. A giant knot began growing there, and it grew big enough that I couldn't fully extend or close up my leg. Movement created pressure and pain. I felt as if shards of crystal and needles had taken up permanent residence in the joint.

But I allowed no outward signs of this torment, which forced me to be very introverted. The internal mantra grew. I'd say things to myself like, *I'm just experiencing pain because I'm weak. I'm pathetic. I can't handle this.*

At some point I complained. "Mom," I said, "I can't sleep at night and I'm having pains in my legs, everything aches." In terms of what my body was doing, I was *Teen Wolf*ing out— literally exploding out of the front of my shoes and my pants. I was in the throes of intense growing pains.

"Aw, just stop it," Mom responded. She didn't say this in a uncaring, dismissive way, more like that this was life and I'd be fine. I cared so much about my mom and my dad and how they felt about me, so I chalked up the pain as something I needed to overcome. I said to myself, *That's just me. I'm just a wimp. I'm less if I can't handle this. I just need to buck up.*

The pain went on for another year.

Despite his tough exterior, my dad was a very compassionate man, especially with me. Sure, if I pulled into the garage with road rash all over me from crashing a dirt bike or wiping out on my BMX, he might pour a beer or tequila on my wounds and say, "Ahh, you're fine," but that was the atmosphere I grew up with. When I couldn't bear the discomfort in my leg any longer, I sucked up my pride. I went to my dad, very sincere, and said, "Dad, my knee really, really hurts. Something isn't right."

He took me to a family practitioner. No doubt the guy only needed one look at the tall, lanky body of a six-foot teen growing like a freaking giraffe to make his expert diagnosis and collect a couple hundred bucks cash from my dad.

"Growing pains," he said, and offered up some silly physical therapy regime.

That diagnosis spelled one thing in my mind: *weak*. I couldn't let my dad and his friends think that of me as *weak*. I did the physical therapy and quadrupled what I was told to do. I began to work out incessantly. I powered through the excruciating pain. I began to pack muscles onto my tall frame. But as my muscles grew so did the lump and the accompanying agony.

I really first thought I was feeble or incapable. This injury began to keep me from doing everything I loved. Knowing that we lacked the money for a surgery only seemed to press down on my shoulders and add to the burden, so for a long time I felt too guilty that we might have to go back to the doctor. This worry about health care and money was also my first real exposure to social inequities.

After I got into a little trouble with the law myself, I received a ticket and some community service. That cascade of events landed me a gig at a local hospital to earn some extra money. The hospital was a world apart from what I knew at home. I enjoyed working there and could almost see myself doing a job like that in the future. Almost.

I began to walk with a pretty serious limp. One day a doctor at work pulled me aside and asked if he could take a look at my knee. "You have a tumor in your knee, Roger," he said. "I need to talk to your mom and dad. Right away."

I had my folks come in. I was right there listening to this

conversation happening between my parents and the doctor, as if I wasn't in the room.

Tumor. Golf-ball size. Malignant or benign. They needed to operate.

I was interested in Latin and medicine at the time, so I understood what he was talking about. My mother felt horrible, like she had neglected me and missed what I had tried to tell her. I never wanted her to harbor any guilt for that. But we were dealing with what we had at the time.

They scheduled me for a surgery that we could never pay for. Before the surgery the doctor told me, "Roger. There is a fifty-fifty chance you're going to wake up potentially without your leg, and just to be very honest with you, you're probably never going to walk normally again."

I was only fourteen when he told me this. To an active fourteen-year-old boy, who already felt so feeble in the face of a world of muscle and might, this felt like a death sentence.

Desperation about my nagging knee pain, the gritty nature of that, being young and being exposed to an unfathomable level of uncertainty, forced me to look inward and question life itself. The severity of having everything you loved taken away was unimaginable. The doctor's words rolled like a freight train in my head: "Fifty-fifty chance you're going to lose your leg." "Fifty-fifty chance you'll lose your life." "Fifty-fifty." "This might be cancerous." "Cancerous." *"Cancer."* Words like that were striking to me as a kid. They seared themselves inside me. I needed a path forward. I needed guidance and help.

To me, with this diagnosis the doctor confirmed that I was weak, but not on a personal level, on a DNA level, like the very DNA in my body was flawed. This news pissed me off, not at him, at me. Again I blamed myself for things, as I was never the type to impugn anyone but myself.

I balled my fists up and said nothing. But inside I yelled, "Fuck you!" *You don't realize this*, I imagined telling the doctor, *but this is only going to stoke the fire.* I even said to myself, *If they do take my leg I'm going to be a Paralympic champion, and I'm going to be the fastest runner with an above-the-knee amputation.*

After the surgery, the tumor removed, the doctor said, "I had to take out your MCL and replace it with a cadaver MCL. It's going to be a yearlong recovery. Walking will be difficult, and I'm afraid you're never going to really run again."

Whatever, I told myself. No doctor's words would ever define me.

Every school-age kid has poster board lying around. After my surgery, I dug some old science project out from the closet. I flipped the board over. I had never understood the power of affirmation. I was fourteen years old. But I got a pencil and the biggest Sharpie I could find. I created a grid on the big sheet and gridded out the lettering on the poster board. I wrote one word on the first sheet, as large and as symmetric as I could. I wrote that first word with as much power as I could. Then on the second poster board I wrote the second word. I took the two poster boards and duct-taped them together on the back, so they fit together seamlessly. I took thumbtacks and mounted the poster above my bed. Right over where I slept.

The phrase became my mantra. The words were powerful, a direct affirmation I would constantly tell myself. Constantly tell myself. Constantly. That poster brought out something overwhelming within my being, something that I wanted to bring into my life.

The two words:

OVER COME.

4

CREATE YOUR REALITY

No matter what it is, there is nothing that cannot be done. If one manifests the determination, he can move heaven and earth as he pleases.

—YAMAMOTO TSUNETOMO, *HAGAKURE*

Despite the strange nature of my upbringing among my dad's associates, I had some powerful mentors. My dad, for one, but also a few of his friends. One was a real badass Vietnam veteran named Jack. This guy was very experienced and mysterious. He seemed larger than life, with an energy and presence that exuded strength and confidence. Jack owned a room when he walked in. The way he spoke commanded attention. I like to think that the warrior in Jack sensed my desperation, or my need for inspiration, while I struggled with the finality of the doctor's words about never running again. At one point I posed to Jack a single question. His answer would transform my future.

Naively I asked, "Who are the toughest guys in the military, Jack?"

"Easy," he said, without even hesitating, "Marine Recon. Toughest bastards on the planet. Spookiest, grittiest guys I've met and ever seen. And I've seen 'em all: Rangers, SEALs, Green Berets. You name it." Jack went on to tell me all about the Reconnaissance Marines he'd seen operate in Vietnam. While at the firebases the men slept on the ground, while their gear sat ready on the cots. When he shared his tales of these unique men he added something strange, something that didn't fit with his story: "You won't understand what I'm telling you."

But I did. At that young age, I somehow comprehended what the man was sharing with me. In some way I understood that Jack was showing me a way out from the clear path of violence and uncertainty ahead for my future. Jack was revealing to me there, in my dad's garage, that there truly was a place for men seeking something more of themselves and the world around them: Marine Reconnaissance.

The only thing I didn't understand at the time was the experience of war. How could I? No one can grasp the weight of combat until they've seen it for themselves. I don't know if Jack understood the influence his words would have on the trajectory of my being, but he was setting me up for my future career, and in a way for my life.

What he told me about Marine Recon would be important, but that larger-than-life man shared with me something much more powerful. The greatest thing Jack ever taught me was when he said this: "Roger. You create your reality. Whether it is your hell or your heaven. You create that." It was easy to see Jack had been through the grinder. On hot days he would break out in a bright rash where he'd once worn his flak jacket. He would tell me of getting sprayed with the defoliant Agent Orange, and how it burned in the summer heat of Nam.

On multiple occasions I would blunder into more intimate ways that his experiences had affected him. Jack was a Marine medic or corpsman in a grunt platoon. One day they were on an extended patrol in tall elephant grass. Jack decided this was an excellent opportunity to have some quality time with his favorite *Playboy* mag. He was midstream to having his way when his platoon was ambushed, with grim results. As a young boy I walked into our bathroom to find Jack, his junk in hand, by candlelight. The subconscious is an overwhelming force within us.

I don't know how, but I understood what he was saying. I don't mean to toot my own horn, but I very much knew that religion was what we made it, and for me, if heaven and hell exist, then they exist right here, right now. Whether they exist in my head, or what I'm projecting or interpreting or internalizing, it's right now. I felt that way early on.

Jack put those thoughts into words, and empowered me through them.

Words and thoughts at the time were all I had.

I stole a book from our high school on yoga and meditation, and I dug into it. Fourteen years old and I dove into yoga, trying to rehabilitate after my knee surgery. I tried to understand the mind-body limitations. I wondered if I could do what Jack said. Could I create my own reality? Could I will

myself to heal? Or could I will myself to be strong in a specific way?

There was only one way to find out.

I started a process of intense yoga and rehabilitation. I lived
in the gym. In no time I found myself back on my bicycle. If I
couldn't run, I would bike. And soon I was with my buddies
and racing and riding again—in love with and feeling the mo-
mentary magic of weightlessness and flying.

I was behind Kyle's Bike and Mower when I crashed.

This was a huge jump, serious air, the width of two or so
cars. I miscalculated. I can't remember exactly what I did
wrong when I launched. What I do remember is eating it. Bad.
My bike had this sweet old school DK gooseneck, with razor-
sharp graded aluminum, and that gooseneck, the stem below
the handlebars, hammered me right through the knee. The
same damn knee the tumor had been removed from. I could
see the inside of my kneecap, my patella fractured. With a
mouth filled with dirt and blood, I crawled toward Kyle's shop.

The pain was horrible, but nothing like the sting of shame.

Kyle called my mom to come pick me up.

Mom took me to the ER, where I received minimal care. Looking back on that day, with the medical knowledge I have now,
I realize I'd received what I can only describe as appalling
medical treatment. Worse than what I've seen in Afghanistan.

They irrigated the wound, sewed it up, immobilized the
knee, and sent me home.

If I thought my athletic career was over with the tumor
and the first surgery, this new knee injury spelled the end.

It was just fucking done.

One miscalculated jump and I'd ruined everything. Shame and defeat hung in a black cloud over my head. That ER visit was only six months after my initial knee surgery. I could have given up hope then and there, but giving up would have shown my dad and his friends that I was weak. I dove back into physical therapy, even though I was really disgusted with my treatment.

My dad must have sensed my need to recover quickly. He spared no expense. He took me to these really high-end physical therapy places, paying cash for my treatment, and at each place the therapist would offer a weak home-exercise program for rehabilitation, saying, "Do these exercises once or twice a day."

"That's it?" I'd ask. Then I would do those exercises, as prescribed, and then do them tenfold, adding weight, then adding more weight. I was driven to get my knee back. That poster hanging above my bed spelled out the mission: OVER COME.

The second knee injury brought me to the weight room and an obsession with lifting iron. I think there was some subconscious thought at play there, where I thought I was weak. I became hyperfocused on both diet and exercise, spending less and less time with my friends and less time in my dad's garage. I asked my dad to take me to different gyms. I didn't know it at the time, but I was searching for something, or someone.

With my dad's help, I found what I needed after a twenty-minute car ride from where we lived. Iron Horse Gym, a steroid-bodybuilder gym. A serious fucking gym. This place was the real deal; it looked like a run-down garage. Spartan. Flickering fluorescent lighting. Motivational quotes handwritten in black marker on the walls. Iron Horse was intense by any standards. Which was why I wanted to be there. I enjoyed the stripped-down reality of what was really happening inside.

I established a relationship with Ken Frisby, the owner. Years later, Ken would go on to be the best man at my wedding. Any time bodybuilding or weightlifting competitions were in the area, Ken would sponsor them and I would attend. I was enthralled with the heavy lifting. I knew that the weightlifting-bodybuilding world was the perception of strength, but I admired the seriousness and dedication of those guys.

One of the writers for *Flex* magazine, a major magazine of the time, wrote this piece called "The Mental Set of Greatness." The story captured how the lifters would meditate before each set, visualizing everything before lifting. I loved their level of devotion.

I was by no means some physical specimen coming out of there, but I got really strong at that gym with those men. I would work out with some of the greats of the time.

I'm sure they didn't know what the hell to think of me, this tall skinny kid, but they saw my work ethic. My resolve and intentions were on a par with their own. I would be using a fraction of the weight they were using, but I wasn't afraid to work out with them. I would walk into the gym on a Saturday morning and Ken would say, "Hey, Roger," and point me toward some monstrous dude to go work out with.

I was sixteen, and the men at Iron Horse were my peers. At the same time, my buddies were doing drugs and stealing steaks from Safeway. I didn't like the path they were headed down. So there I was working my legs with one of my heroes, desperately trying to get stronger and rebuild my knee, while the guy is preparing for a bodybuilding competition the next week.

My days at Iron Horse, added with the desperation of how I would heal, tempered with the grittiness of the environment at home, made for some nitrogen-rich soil for self-reflection. At the same time, as I worked so hard, and made something of a miraculous recovery, I realized two things:

1. Jack was right. I could create my own reality.
2. No one gave a shit.

5

THE CONTEMPLATION OF INTENTIONS

In troubled times . . . one knows that by a single word his strength or cowardice can be seen. This single word is the flower of one's heart. It is not something said simply with one's mouth.

—YAMAMOTO TSUNETOMO, *HAGAKURE*

In 1992, I graduated from high school. I was awarded a grant with the potential to pursue medicine at Rice University in Texas, but I had a different plan. When looking back, I realize I never spoke with a school counselor. It was palpable: no one cared. While the majority of my friends found themselves joining the Texas Department of Corrections as inmates, I enlisted in the Marines. My dad drove me off to boot camp, and I left behind Jennifer, the outgoing raven-haired beauty who had hijacked my heart.

Before I left for the Marines was a time of wild late-night parties. I don't want to embarrass Jennifer by sharing this moment, but it's a memory I cherish from when we first began dating.

Early evening, and the Texas sun had just set. We stood alone together out by her car. I really liked her and didn't want to screw things up. This was one of those awkward moments very early in a relationship when you don't know what to say or do. I asked her the classic question a guy asks when he only wants to be the presence of a woman, and doesn't care where they go or what happens as long as he's with her: "What do you want to do tonight?"

Jennifer walked around to the trunk of her car, and she opened it up. This was right in front of my house. With a huge grin, she took out a bottle of Mad Dog 20/20. She twisted off the cap, and lifted it to her lips. I watched in awe as she downed the whole bottle. When she finished, she smiled and smashed the bottle on the ground.

And I thought to myself at that very moment: *Roger, you are going to marry this woman.*

As we got older, the parties only grew crazier. A friend of mine came from a broken home, so we would use his house to get wild. Dry ice parties. Strobe lights. Everyone dressed up in costumes. Plenty of alcohol and no shortage of drugs. One night when it poured rain, everyone stripped naked and ran around the school.

I never got high, or did any of the heavy drugs, but I went along and had a good time. I was dedicated to lifting weights and taking care of my body. I was committed to that culture of the Iron Horse, making myself stronger.

Jennifer and I went to prom together. I guess we were

serious from the start. Perhaps that night in front of my
house with the Mad Dog solidified it for me. She was a woman
of action. I was leaving her behind, headed off to the Marines,
and I knew she loved me. But headed off to boot camp, I had
no idea how strong of a woman she actually was, or the extent to which she would be there for me.

My dad drove me to the Marine recruiter collection point at a
rundown strip mall with a Target. The car was a shitty old
four-door Volvo, rust colored and squeaky. He was proud of
me. Along the way I thought about a story he'd told late one
night, long before I'd signed up, when he was pretty buzzed.
"I was going to join the Marine Corps," he'd started telling me,
or telling both his buddy Jack and me. "I was in court and
headed to prison. I told the judge I'd join the infantry if he gave
me a reduced sentence." This was at the height of the Vietnam
War. My dad's voice got a little softer for a moment. "The
judge," he said, "told me, 'I wouldn't do that to the Marine
Corps.'"

That story romanticized the Marines a bit for me, but I
wasn't joining for my dad; I was attracted to what that story
represented. That dark comment from the judge made me realize the irony in which we live. While my father wanted to
sign up for Vietnam out of desperation, it would have been the
best thing for him and for the Marines. You want a man like
him doing your dirty work, not wasting those talents in prison.

He was reserved but emotional when he dropped me off
that morning. Some real basic words passed between us. The
standard "I love you." And he was crying, crying with pride.

"You're facing down your future. Facing down uncertainty," he said. There was not a lot of ceremony like that in our family. His tears resonated with me—he was rarely emotional, and I don't know if I'd ever seen him cry before then. He shook my hand, gave me a powerful hug, and off I went.

I flew all night. When I landed in San Diego, it was game on.

I can't say for certain what the instructors thought when I hit boot camp. I couldn't help but stand out at six feet seven and 210 pounds with next to no body fat. That the issued clothes didn't fit made me feel self-conscious, but I was excited to be there. I felt confident and well prepared. I'd been in training for years, so no amount of bullshit the drill instructors dished out seemed all that bad. Thoughts of Jen, and her reliable stream of letters, also fueled me.

One particular image stands out from those early Marine days. We stood in a giant auditorium line waiting to get combat boots or some other gear, in a musty and shitty-smelling warehouse. Marine Corps propaganda was all over the place at basic. The only pictures you could find were Corps photos, and at the time I enjoyed that level of fanaticism. The walls of this weird building were bare, except for a quote scrawled in big red block letters. The phrase read, "If you cannot defend your country, the enemy will kill you and breed a stronger race."

I was eighteen. As I read that, I thought about how real and raw the brotherhood was that I had gotten myself into. I was beginning to get a glimpse behind the curtain.

You can't say stuff like that now. I'm sure they painted

over it, out of political correctness. But there was something in that level of suggestion that intrigued me early on.

After boot camp, the School of Infantry, and a few setbacks—including a snapped wrist, being hospitalized for pneumonia, and a broken foot—I got stationed with an infantry platoon in Kaneohe Bay, Oahu, Hawaii. I checked into my first platoon and the staff sergeant we called Chicken Hawk asked me, "What are your goals with the Marine Corps; what's your future with the Corps look like, Sparks?" This is a very beautiful question to ask a young man because it forces the contemplation of intentions. We become what we envision ourselves to be, and we're constantly becoming what we think of ourselves.

At the time I still had to do two years in the infantry before I could even apply, and I knew this, but I said, "I want to be in Reconnaissance, Staff Sergeant."

The staff sergeant looked up at me and laughed.

"Good luck with that," he said, still chucking to himself.

Yes, the platoon sergeant laughed at me, but I was indifferent to his doubt. His skepticism illustrates how Reconnaissance is viewed within the Marine Corps, a subculture within a subculture within a subculture. An analogy that might be similar is asking some kid who was a cook in the Navy, "Oh, what did you do?" And he replies, "Uh, I was a SEAL." And you know, he's full of shit; I mean it's just completely ridiculous to imply such a thing. However, the people within those subcultures know what it means to be an operator, not just wear the T-shirt. Real knows real.

There I was, a Marine infantryman being introduced to my Marine infantry platoon in all the severities that *that* entails, and this guy is acting like there is no fucking way. He's looking at me as if to say: *You know, you're not going to make it in Recon.* He's just an affirmation of himself. I might as well be saying to him that I was going to study astrophysics and create a time-travel machine. That is pretty much the way that he reacted to my plan for the future, because, in his defense, that is how highly regarded Reconnaissance Marines were.

I knew I wasn't the strongest or the best looking or the smartest, but I was going to sacrifice everything to get there. He might have been laughing, but there was no doubt in my mind that I would do what I said. I would be a Recon Marine, or there was no future or reality for me. I was going to die trying.

To be very frank, the hardest thing I've ever done in the military was those two years in infantry. It almost makes me emotional thinking about it because a decade later I would become a pararescueman—and those young men, those infantrymen, are the men that I'd be rescuing. There would be times when I would feel like I was rescuing myself, because people really don't understand war. The majority of the infantrymen and the people who are actually in combat is very small percentage. Some may love to take the wind, or love the accolades just for serving in the military, but unless you served in that capacity in battle, you have no idea what combat is really about.

Infantry is a thankless job, and those signed up for the job are absolutely the bone marrow of America. If you think about my background, there was no college fund for me beyond a small scholarship, no grooming for any special job opportunities. I had done bloody-knuckle push-ups my entire adolescence. I was where I needed to be.

Instead of Marine Reconnaissance, I found myself in Japan at Camp Fuji. An ocean away from home, I realized that Jennifer was definitely going to be the most significant woman in my life. Despite the distance, we maintained our relationship. We would rack up a $600 phone bill each month, and this was in the early '90s. Half of my paycheck went straight to paying my AT&T calling card, yet I didn't feel like I was a sucker; we were in love. That pile of money for phone calls? I saw that expenditure as an investment in our future.

I spent a year at Camp Fuji. All I did the entire time was work out and talk to Jen. Around this time my dad had a breakdown. After his thyroid died, he lost it. I suspect he possessed an accumulation of PTSD from prison and the horrible things he'd witnessed throughout his life. He took the family car, and no one heard from him for over a week. They found him 530 miles away and placed him in a local in-patient treatment facility. Half-naked, he had tried to jump in front of a semi-truck. Once they got him back to Fort Worth, he went through a local program for mental illness. My mom, who I haven't done justice with my story thus far, was a beautiful and strong woman in her own right, and was working hard to take care of my father and become a flight attendant. At the same time all this was happening, my mom was raising my sister's son.

Jennifer, always there for me on the phone, stepped in and took care of everybody.

All I had to offer her at the time was a long-distance relationship cobbled together with my voice on the phone and letters, but she was a rock for both me and my family. I was all the more in love. She had me. I would learn this strength was in her personality and her nature. Not a front or anything, just there.

We've been married now since February 1995.

6

NINE-SIXTEENTHS SMALLER

When meeting difficult situations, one should dash forward bravely and with joy. It is the crossing of a single barrier and is like the saying, 'The more the water, the higher the boat.'

—YAMAMOTO TSUNETOMO, *HAGAKURE*

I stood in what felt like an oven. Cinder-block walls. Prison-like. I could tell they had hosed it out just after the past group of men had left. We were all sweaty and hot. Hungry. Jet-lagged from a thirteen hour C-130 flight. Exhausted from a heinous run behind one of the French Commandos' young studs, and I could tell the dude had been going easy on us. Treating us with soft hands. Another guy came in and, in broken English, told us, "Time for assemble. On your uniforms for ceremony."

We didn't know what ceremony he was talking about, but we correctly assumed he meant there was a ceremony and for us to put our charlies on. So we got all dressed up with nowhere to go, and stood out in a small plaza. Blue sky. Blinding sun. Stifling, tropical heat.

This odd opening ceremony began. Music played. Flags were raised, and the poor guy, with his one duty to man the flagpole, screwed up: waving above us, in that brilliant blue sky, our flag, the American flag, fluttered upside down. I watched one of the French leaders march straight over to the fella raising the flag and throw one hard punch. Straight into the jaw. Dropped the guy, cold. The officer with the wicked right hook then lowered the flag himself, put the Stars and Stripes facing the direction Betsy Ross intended them, and raised it back up into that big blue sky.

Then the commandant—or whatever his leadership role was, we didn't know—gave a speech in French. We understood nothing. Then he closed in broken English, attempting to be poetic, saying to us something along the lines of "The sides of the mountain are steep, but the top is beautiful."

That was my introduction to French commando training.

Landing a shot at the French Foreign Legion exchange was a big deal. In the infantry I'd been stationed on Oahu, an active duty grunt. The best dudes from the entire battalion applied for the opportunity to do French commando training. *Commando Brevet*, in French Polynesia. Naturally I signed up. *Commando Brevet* was essentially a selection course for the French commandos, paired with a no-nonsense jungle and nautical training program.

To get us prepared, the Marine Corps took the best of the 2nd Battalion 3rd Marines grunts and put us through a three-month death session. Intense. They couldn't send a bunch of soft losers to be trained by the French commandos, so they made us endure a Marine version of pre-scuba/indoctrination training. We could not let the French show the Marines up. We put twenty men from 3rd Marines on the plane. I was one of them.

Once that interesting opening ceremony with the flag snafu was over we went back to our prisonlike barracks. After the long day of travel we were all starved, but didn't know where the hell to eat. Someone asked, "Where is the fucking chow hall?"

The answer wasn't what we expected.

This was the French Foreign Legion. Their motto could have just been: Your Mom Doesn't Work Here.

Basically, a guy comes in and throws some bread and a few jars of jam at you. That's what you eat. If you want milk, there is a cow grazing over there, and some chickens laying eggs. Go get yourself something to eat.

This was our first introduction to the French Foreign Legion. Become self-sustained. And get used to it.

Having to find our own food was just the beginning.

The whole experience was, in one simple word: brutal. In retrospect, it was harder than the pararescue and Recon courses I faced later in life. We would have to evacuate a couple of guys for medical treatment. And we thought Marine instructors were mean, but these instructors didn't give two shits about any of us. We were worse than the lowest life-form. Even as American Marines, guests to the French, we weren't being given any passes through their program. There would be no special treatment.

Some of what we suffered through could be deemed insane by any standard of military or warrior training. Calling our instructors bloodthirsty maniacs wouldn't at all be a stretch. They would scream at us in French and set out a series of impossible tasks. The training and the rigor of what they put us through really opened my eyes to the world of what the human body is capable of, what we can endure.

The experience is a book unto itself. Surreal, from the strange remote tropical location, to the language barrier, to the deathly scary training scenarios and impossible workouts. The French commandos were hard-core. We bounced around between three or four different islands, these little atolls, where we would do training for jungle and water insertion. The French take all political correctness out of the military and allow NCOs to beat subordinates, and I mean serious corporeal punishment. We didn't land in a rigorous training course so much as a level of hell.

While training in the jungle we carried logs the size of short telephone poles. This was comparable to the standard abuse you see endured in a SEALs or Pararescue indoctrination program, except instead of carrying a pole down a road or along a beach, we marched over sketchy three-strand rope bridges spanning deep jungle chasms. This was the rain forest and steep canyons from King Kong's island. We packed those logs across the swinging rope bridge with the instructors yelling and hauling on the cables in an attempt to get us to lose our balance.

The instructors named the two logs Romeo and Juliet. They would yell at us in their broken English and heavy French accents, "Some of you want to make love with Juliet?" the commando said, as we're holding that impossible weight up over our heads. Then he says, "Or do some of you want to make love with Romeo, no?" This was all just to fuck with us. As I said, *Commando Brevet* training meant we would survive some severe shit. The language barriers made everything feel more brutal.

Speaking of shit . . .

One day we approached a series of sewage pipes. I sensed, and smelled, that something nasty was about to go down; we probably all did. But then again, we were all probably saying to ourselves the same thing: *No way—no way would they make us do that.* And then, on cue, as if he knew our thoughts, the instructor pointed and yelled, "Infiltrate!" The whole team had to climb up and into the smelliest sort of hell you can imagine: a pipe with a foul-looking liquid trickling out. Two hundred feet. Crawling. Pitch-black. The diameter barely a shoulder's width. Imagine crawling through an underground pipeline while not even knowing where the outlet is, or if it will ever end. I'd never been claustrophobic. But after I had to crawl half the length of a football field through a narrow pipe, and add human feces I'm mucking through and choking on?

There is a limit to the concept that what doesn't kill you will only make you stronger. To me, the sewage-pipe training exemplified that. We all got dysentery and stomach parasites during the course. I suspect I know where the illnesses originated.

The shit-pipe training was a part of close-quarters battle

training, or CQB. Since we couldn't enter a building through the toilet, they showed us how French commandos enter a two- or three-story house. No ladder? No problem. All you need is a pole, a thin pole at that. The instructors showed us how to grab a rail-thin log to run up, monkey style, against the side of any building you wanted to get into. Those who weren't successful getting up the pole went home with a broken leg or ankle.

The French commandos did not concern themselves with safety.

Their ropes course was ridiculously high above the ground, with no safety protocols. If you fell and survived, you were looking at your femur jutting out of your thigh. At one point in the course we stood on a metal platform at least sixty feet up, with a stack of used tires at the bottom to break our fall. A rope spanned the ninety-foot length. A bigger, heavy rope dangled vertically ten feet out. Another ten feet out from that, a net. The objective was to run, jump, swing out, and hit the net. Then let go of the rope and climb up and over the net. That was just the start of the course. From there you were jumping from tree to tree, ten feet out and ten feet down to another platform, and at any given point you were thirty to sixty feet above the bare ground, or above the tire pile if you were lucky.

At another spot they would have you do the commando crawl on a single strand of rope, across a span fifty feet off the jungle floor. You were instructed to go out in the middle, hang from the rope with your bare hands, do ten pull-ups, and then chicken-wing back up and keep going across.

The intensity and danger didn't ever let up. It felt as if there was no end in sight. Day in and day out they had us doing the impossible. I reached a point where I no longer questioned the insanity of the tasks they were asking us to accomplish. When they would point and yell at us to do something, we would shrug and say, "Okay, fuck it. Let's do this."

Our numbers dwindled. We began with twenty that day beneath the upside-down flag; soon, there weren't many of us left. But as far as I was concerned, only two things were going to keep me from completing the course: death or diarrhea. Or death by diarrhea. The dysentery I was suffering from became so bad that I was shitting clear water.

The final mission for the course, a sniper mission, required a marathonlike infiltration on a remote island where big-league surfers go to ride heavy waves. We inserted from a huge transport ship in these shitty little versions of an Avon-type rubber raiding craft. We floated in between monster waves. Thirty- or forty-foot seas. Epic waves. We're on the backside of this mountain of a swell. Similar to Waimea-style shit in Hawaii, so I'm thinking: *These waves are going to kill us.*

We survived the beach landing, and started the thirty-mile jungle infiltration up and over this mountain. I didn't know it at the time, but I had rhabdomyolysis, and the loss of fluids due to the dysentery was literally killing me. My kidneys were shutting down. I would fall to the ground; curl up into ball, cramped up; and then I'd shit myself while I was lying there. Then, after a few minutes, I'd struggle to my feet and keep going.

This happened four or five times during that marathon distance hike up and over King Kong's island. It was a lush and dense rain forest and rugged terrain. We reached the objective to find jeeps sitting on moving flatbed railroad cars. We set up our sniper positions and took them out. With that we were done.

Only a few of us graduated. We took certificates home, while others left empty-handed, some with compound-fractured legs. We all left with parasites. I basically destroyed the lining of my intestine. I lost ten or fifteen pounds that I would never gain back.

Those French commandos were hard fuckers. They were passionate about doing their job despite the circumstances. They would scream at us in broken French, "We're not going to give it to you!" Thanks to our inability to speak French, we had to follow intuition and read body language to inhabit that space. It is difficult to articulate being exposed to such a grueling, surreal, and dangerous test of endurance and spirit.

There was the historical aspect of the French Foreign Legion, and undergoing the training of a French commando. Who we were, where we were, what we were doing, and the men we were training with said it all. For a young Marine, this was integral to the person I would become, both as a warrior and a human being.

When I returned to Oahu, in the middle of the night on a Saturday, after two or three months in that course, I came back to my Marine barracks and found my bunkroom taped off. No one was around, so I ducked in anyway. Dried blood splatter covered the walls and floor. Obviously something horrible had happened in my room. It looked like someone had been murdered.

Later I would learn my roommate had attempted suicide. Turns out his girl left him. Possibly wacked out on LSD, he slit his wrists. I was an E3 in the Marine Corps, I'd just returned from this epic experience with the French commandos in French Polynesia, and that was my late-night homecoming. I was beyond exhausted and I had nowhere else to go. Welcome to the bizarre world of the grunt barracks.

I don't care to remember the smells of my room that first night back, but I do remember how my roommate's bullshit meant a drug test for the infantry company. A good number of the guys got popped for LSD and other illicit substances.

The only substances in my blood system were the bugs I'd picked up in the South Pacific, plus a tapeworm in my belly.

That was in 1994. With *Commando Brevet* training behind me, I was ready to marry Jen and apply for Recon indoctrination for a slot on Alpha Company 3rd Reconnaissance. When I returned home to marry her I noticed something different.

It was weird: When I came back from the Marine Corps, something notable had changed inside me. I'd lost my skill at instantly sizing the right wrench. My world view had changed, and oddly this had also affected my perceptions of standard nut and bolt diameters. For what might need a half-inch wrench, I would guess nine-sixteenths smaller. My perceptions were now larger than the size needed. Things seemed smaller when I returned home: my house, my neighborhood. My dad had become more emotional. He'd be the one there to meet when I landed at the airport. He'd give the biggest smile and turn his cheek away from me to hide his proud tears.

7

SNAKE KILLING DAYS

It is a mistake for parents to thoughtlessly make their children dread lightning, or to have them not go into dark places, or to tell them frightening things in order to stop them from crying.

—YAMAMOTO TSUNETOMO, *HAGAKURE*

I grew up catching these enormous crawdads, and all sorts of snakes, out in the creeks and lakes near where we lived. We went after the big-ass water moccasins. We would kill them, or catch them live, and sell or trade them to the kids around where we lived who were more squeamish, or not brave enough to catch one themselves.

We played BB gun wars out there, too, almost as if I were training for something I couldn't define. With the BB guns, we had a strict two-pump rule. Next thing you knew, guys would be doing multiple pumps. Someone would always get an entrance without an exit wound from a BB gun shot. Free from any adult supervision, and not afraid of anything, we would do crazy stuff like make pipe bombs or homemade grenades.

Joey's dad lived in a gated community next to a lake, so we would go down there. If we weren't snake hunting, we would play tag under and through the active boat docks. Boats would be taxiing and driving by, props whirring, while we swam underneath.

That was my childhood: basically unsupervised.

The combat dive operations that would come later, and approaching piers and harbors at night were never spooky or worrisome. I'd been training and inoculating myself against fear for as long as I can remember. It was only a slightly more serious game of tag.

Snakes played a role in that training.

We were always on the lookout for snakes. My friends and I would bike or walk for hours just to get to our hidden spots that hosted dens of water moccasins. We would swim into these giant creeks and ponds with sticks in search of a nest. The water was often over-our-head deep, and leech infested. Once we found a water moccasin nest, we'd begin beating it with the ends of our sticks. It didn't take too many whacks until they all come streaming out after you, and you'd swim like hell to the shore, twenty feet away, where friends would be waiting with big rocks. The snakes would be there, hot on your trail, coming to bite your ass, but as soon as you swam up, the snakes right on you, your buddies were there smash them with rocks.

One time, as if we were acting out a scene from the movie

Predator, I reached the shore just in time, turned around to look, and my buddy smashed a huge rock down right between my legs. The water moccasin was just a foot or so from my crotch when he smashed it. A big sucker.

Back then, there was something enchanting about playing with serpents, the more deadly the better. What we were doing was chilling. To fuck with an angry, poisonous snake brings you alive at a DNA level.

To catch water moccasins alive, we would get a stick, pin the snake down, and then grab it behind the head. At the time I thought this was cool, death at my fingers, while the snake's body wound itself around my arm.

My snake-killing days didn't end the way you'd expect.

One summer day at the lake, I killed a monster.

That day I rode my lake bike, a beater, designed specifically for water jumps. By then I had really high-end bikes that I'd built myself. I am still extremely proud of those builds and the efforts taken to acquire them. We rode off-ramps on the end of docks to practice aerials. I'd been riding the bike I built for lake stunt jumping. We'd spent the day at the lake, jumping, and then we saw the snake.

In my kid's mind the snake was ten feet long. Now, as an adult, I'm not totally convinced it was any shorter than that.

After I killed this snake, the mother of all snakes, I decided it would go home with me. I had to show my dad. I took off for home, hands holding both the snake and the handlebars. The snake was so long that its head and tail dragged on the pavement. I'll never forget the soft sandpaper sound, trailing behind and at my side the whole time, of the asphalt against the snake's skin as I rode.

I pedaled my ass off on the thirty-minute ride home. My dad was in the garage, rocking Steppenwolf, and turning wrenches on his bike. I hefted the giant snake up in the air to show him, waiting for some sign of approval or pride. Instead, he just looked at me and said, "What the fuck you going to do with that?"

In his defense, he was right.

It was a good question. One that hadn't occurred to my young mind.

I went and threw the dead water moccasin in the trash can. Remember, this was Texas in the summer, and that means hot. The time between trash service? Once a month, back in those days. The giant snake began to reek. Smells I wouldn't know again until I'd been to war. The stench became unbearable. With the days of rotting-snake odor came a slithering guilt. I should have skinned it out, tacked it to a board or something, but I was only ten or eleven. I knew I should have done something, but I didn't know taxidermy. In retrospect, I think if someone had shown me how, then I would have eaten that son of a bitch.

I suppose that snake, as huge as it was, might have actually been a little under ten feet. But that giant snake, like so much in my childhood, brought with it a lesson about life that I wouldn't forget.

My dad's lesson with the snake wasn't much different from how he taught me to swim. Big Roger was a competitive swimmer and champion diver in high school, but he never showed pride. He wouldn't allow himself to feel pride. But he would *almost* get emotional when he was intoxicated, reminiscing about his childhood and diving and swimming. One of the last conversations I had with my father was when he was relating his suffering to me through our shared love for swimming. Dying of lung cancer, he referred back to the water, to that feeling of being a kid trying to swim the length of the pool underwater. It's emotional for me to share, but he said, "I feel like I'm swimming and I'm drowning."

The day he taught me how to swim I remember vividly. We were at Twin Points Park, at one of the lakes our family would go to. Steely Dan or Tom Petty blaring on the radio. BBQ. Beer. Suntan oil. Every time we'd go to the lake, my dad would buy me something cool. Aquaman goggles and fins, an old truck tube. He never failed to surprise me with a treat for the water. We were always rolling with Big Mike and the crew, and this was like early '80s, late '70s, the time of aviator sunglasses. My dad was jacked. Solid muscle. All those guys were muscled. They blew off a fair bit of steam at the lake, and this was a fun lake. Plenty of action. And a really cool location. Sometimes there would be so many people swimming that you could taste the suntan oil in the water. People with motor homes, tailgating and camping and enjoying summer. Out past a certain point sat this flotilla with a huge floating dive platform. The floats were covered in green, smelly moss. I couldn't swim, but my dad, strong and powerful, would swim out with me on his back.

He said, "Grab on to my neck. I'll swim you out. Hold my beer." He started for the platform, me with one arm around his neck, the other holding his Coors high. Beer and weed emanated from him, and I was gripping on to him for dear life, but I could just sense his power as he swam beneath me.

And then on the way to the platform, he went under. Down we went. At a certain point I let go. I could see, above me, the green algae on the bottom and edges of the platform. I swam for the light and found it and grabbed on and climbed up on top, and that was me learning to swim.

I still held the beer. When I reached the platform, I set the can on the deck. It was filled with lake water, but I wasn't about to let his Coors go. He surfaced behind me, then climbed to the very top of that huge platform and did a perfect flip with a splashless dive. He climbed once again on the platform where I was watching him. Dad guzzled that waterlogged Coors with a smile on his face.

The lessons from my father were unending. All building upon themselves. They would become ingrained memories and life lessons to cherish. Later, I would see the connection with learning how to swim and something bigger: When you're holding something important, you never let it go.

I carried other things for my dad, too—some of them no doubt illegal. Packages of money. A lot of coin. Even then, I was always cautious of how I would hold it. I think about that now—something of grave importance, and I would hold it accordingly. Whether I was going to buy cigarettes for my dad at the convenience store, or whatever, I would always feel the weight of what I was carrying. And the mindfulness of my task. For whatever reason, I was mindful of the significance placed upon the tasks my father assigned me.

I've thought forever about this notion of holding something, and about placing other people or things above you. Whether I was a kid riding my little banana-seat Sears &

Roebuck bike to get my dad a six-pack of beer, or carrying a package of ten grand in drug money. Or later when I was a Marine, ordered to deliver a stupid form from my boss to some other asshole. Or hauling mutilated corpses of fellow Americans to Conex boxes before they could be transported home. Whatever it is, I am only an agent of something bigger. The task is always more important than me.

8

THE SPIRIT WORLD

It is spiritless to think that you cannot attain to that
which you have seen and heard the masters attain.
The masters are men. You are also a man.

—YAMAMOTO TSUNETOMO, *HAGAKURE*

The selection process for Reconnaissance consisted of one day.
At the time I entered, Reconnaissance Marines of the mid-
1990s were deeply respected throughout Special Operations.
They were considered by many to be the most metaphysical,
pipe-hitting, Shaolin monks of the ranks. The *Hawaii Marine*
paper on March 2, 1995, had a photo of me on selection day,
passed out on the beach. I was supposed to be on a weeklong
honeymoon, partying and making love to Jennifer in New
Orleans. Instead, I found myself making the paper, collapsed
on the beach, not far from Pyramid Rock, with black-marker
"#4" written across my forehead.

Inside a torii gate was a giant pit, and in the pit they had a boulder taken from Vietnam. This was where you could expect to be hazed to near death. You'd be so thoroughly exhausted that when you left you could only manage to crawl up out of the hole. Everyone called the pit "the spirit world."

"Enter the spirit world!" the instructor would say.

"Enter the spirit world, aye aye, Sergeant!" we would echo.

After you entered hell you were instructed to jack your feet up on the rock and immediately do twenty-five four-count push-ups. Then an extra for airborne, scuba, Recon, Ranger, and the Recon platoon; and then one for every Reconnaissance Marine within eyesight. And the Reconnaissance Marines would often hide and reappear, forcing us to begin again.

In the spirit world you encountered a brutality designed to see if your mind is stronger than your body. You could spend hours in the spirit world, but time was irrelevant. When done we would rake the sand, as if it were the most pristine botanical garden in existence.

Eight guys started that morning, and I woke up to learn they took myself and two other dudes. I was on my way to becoming a Reconnaissance Marine.

Recon indoctrination is a nine-month test. They call this time in a Recon Marine's career "RIP," the notorious Reconnaissance indoctrination period. It's a loose time where they are hazing the shit out of you with the sole intention of making you quit. To break your will. Yes, that goal is juvenile, but it is also essential. If you make it past RIP, then you go to the basic Reconnaissance courses to get your military occupational specialty (MOS) designation as a Reconnaissance Marine.

Instead of failing or dying in RIP, something was awakened within me. I owe that to one guy. At the time, all I really remember was getting my ass handed to me each day. There was one instructor I really looked up to. His name was David, but everyone called him Chilly. They called him that for one reason: he was the coolest motherfucker on Planet Earth, a ridiculously relaxed guy doing a very complex, cool job. He wasn't egotistical, and even when he hazed us, I sensed a purpose and intention behind his actions. That approach really attracted me. I fell head over heels with his style of teaching and discipline. I can't explain it any better than that.

One day, Chilly handed me this tattered book and said two words: "Read this."

It wasn't like you questioned anything that came from Chilly's mouth. I was busy and stressed and getting slaughtered every day in RIP, so I didn't have time for pleasure reading. But there also wasn't any way in hell I was going to say, "Thanks, Chilly. I'll get to it."

No. When Chilly says "Jump," you're jumping with all you have.

I read it cover to cover that night. The book that Chilly had passed into my hands, into my being, was Dan Millman's *Way of the Peaceful Warrior*. You could say, tongue in cheek, that this is the self-help bullshit that sits in the Spiritual section of Barnes & Noble. Its cover said *A Book That Changes Lives*. It was a metaphysical self-help book, a young gymnast's true story. The work was profound, reflecting all I had thought, all my trials and tribulations to that point. I felt synergistically involved with the character in the story, and with the message that Chilly was trying to tell me in insisting that I read the book. I believed then, and still do today, whatever vector you're on, once you've read Millman's book, you'll be deflected one way or the other.

After reading Dan Millman, I got into metaphysical spirituality, trying to understand what it was, and connecting it to efforts of human endurance or strength. I guess I would call it performance-based spirituality.

I realized Chilly must have been seeing more in me than I saw in myself. I was blown away that he would think so much of me. Chilly's belief in me, and the message in the book, opened a world I'd only touched upon as a young boy, me then staring at the poster board over my bed and wishing away the pain in my knee. I began to understand the real practicality of meditation, and immersed myself in it.

These guys were doing such brutal stuff to us that I knew there was something magical about the hidden gems in that book, and the other writings Chilly had us read. I figured if I mastered what I read, then I would master myself a little better, and in the process the whole RIP period would become easier.

Meditation's proof is in the pudding when it comes to the power of the mind. If you tell yourself *I can't do a hundred push-ups,* obviously, when you attempt those push-ups, you'll fail. But if you tell yourself you can, then you'll be able. This was very apparent to me at young age, but I wanted to go deeper than that. It wasn't a question of, Does it work or not? It was more a question of, What are the limitations of where it works and where it doesn't? To me it was the same as being able to stare at a ten-millimeter nut head and to know the size intuitively. This was the beginning of me being very critical even of my own metaphysical limitations. I wanted to discover what of my capabilities came from nature or nurture, when my fortitude faced my natural limits. One of the most profound conclusions I took from these experiences was that to lead men, you must be confident of such strengths and limits. When that exists, they will kill themselves following you.

During Reconnaissance selection course, all of the instructors routinely competed in local races, thus we had to compete to represent Recon as well. We were also in Hawaii, where there was a race or two every weekend. On the Kaneohe base, there was a biathlon where all the instructors from the selection courses would participate and whip everyone's ass, but I won that biathlon for the whole base. Chilly said, "Good job, man." I'd beaten him and a bunch of other guys who were my role models. We had been running at least seventy miles a week, back then, and I would go on to do that for a decade. Fast-paced and intense runs; by sheer will, I had turned myself into a machine. I'd tackle the selection process during the week; then, what I was doing to myself on the weekends was crazy. Most weekends were spent riding my triathlon bike, doing laps around the island, eight hours at a pop. I was probably sitting at 2 percent or less body fat, and around 198 pounds. My resting heart rate was forty beats per minute. I taught myself to regulate my heart: I could lie on a table and take deep breaths, doing transcendental meditation, to mentally drop my heart rate from sixty to thirty beats. I was into riding the razor's edge of both my physiology and my mental ability.

Still, Chilly and the other instructors pushed me further.

In reconnaissance training, during a weeklong patrol the instructors will allow minimal sleep. People will say, "I've gone a week without sleeping!" But that is bullshit. When you really go that long without slumber, your very existence becomes spiritual. You start hallucinating; your mind begins to slip; everything gets strange. Weird and insidious things happen when you go without sleep, but a lot of the mental realization is about understanding that the night doesn't last forever. You can go without food, without water, without air, and you can go without all these things so very central to our existence, but you have to be able to see beyond them, to see beyond the now. I realized this during my reconnaissance patrolling phase. We hadn't slept in days. They were gassing us, and doing horrible things. The whole time was relentless. They were making us endure a vision quest of sorts. We were so distraught with hunger, thirst, and weariness. And then one of my buddies sat on a hornet's nest. The results, any other time, would have been horrifying, but instead what happened was amazing. They swarmed us, a buzzing, stinging blur of pain and adrenaline. We all got destroyed by these hornets, yet I felt completely alive and euphoric. Moments before the swarm I was apathetic, yet after the stinging and buzzing, I felt completely rejuvenated and alive.

That moment with the hornets was a reminder of how life is mostly mental, and how much we live in our heads. This concept transfers directly to what I would learn later is related to the samurai belief that "the worth of a human being is based on his desperation." I truly feel that desperation and courage are the same thing. That isn't coming from me. I'm stealing that from a World War I novel called *The Middle Parts of For-*

tune. Courage and desperation are one and the same. They are inseparable. When you run to save a child trapped beneath a wrecked car, you find strength in that situation in sheer desperation, not out of being courageous. You just do it. It's not *you* being *you*, it's *you* taking action out of desperation. Then later we digest that as courage, but it's really desperation. Sure, your connectedness to mankind or the people you are with play a part; so too does sacrifice, but it's the desperation of the whole that matters.

A life lived without ever tasting the tears that come with desperation is a life that also will never know courage.

I drank those tears of desperation in RIP, and survived. You're trained and selected for your physical and mental durability, and your ability to act without orders. So surviving any "indoctrination" is really based on your character and your self-resilience. The attrition rate for such courses is high. It's such a tight brotherhood within such a very small subculture for those to actually say, "I am truly a Reconnaissance Marine" (or a SEAL, or a Ranger, or a pararescueman, or a combat controller, or whatever Special Operations unit you want to throw in there).

There is an enormous weight to the realization that you are suddenly representing the best of that combat arm of that service. You come to understand that you and your teammates are Achilles, not the old broken men telling you what to do. You are that Greek mythological character that you're trying to live up to. You have a duty in that role.

I had possessed only one goal: Become a Reconnaissance Marine.

Once had I achieved that goal, I was no longer one of the

grunts, and therein lies the rub. The role of the grunt is the toughest job in the military. That moment you become an operator within Special Operations, you're saved from an oppressed reality because now, instead of being shit on and sent into the worst scenarios imaginable, you're going to get the best training in the world; you're going to get the best equipment in the world; you're going to be around the most motivated and capable men on Planet Earth. And when the day is done? You're probably going to survive the meat grinder. But the odds aren't so good when you're an infantryman and you're a number, you're that kid who came from the trailer parks and the country farms. This is your one shot at a better life in the trenches, and it's as good as it gets. Infantry is the toughest job in the military. When you're in the infantry you're around the very heart and soul of America. These kids are the children who know poverty, hardship, and struggle. These are the kids who are capable of doing more with less. They've done it their whole life.

In some ways, in achieving my goal to become a Reconnaissance Marine, I was leaving behind all I knew, heading into uncharted territory.

9

TURNING WRENCHES

*The Way of the Samurai is one of immediacy, and it
is best to dash in headlong.*

—YAMAMOTO TSUNETOMO, *HAGAKURE*

I'd served my time—survived infantry, endured French Foreign Legion training, and lived through some harrowing times
in reconnaissance—all that to become a fucking lifeguard in
Hawaii. At that point, I really thought I was done with the military. Jen and I decided we were going to try to make Texas
work. We lived with her parents for some time, then moved
into a crappy apartment by the local junior college. I tried to
find meaningful employment. Easier said than done. Once out
of the Marines, I went to a career counselor at the downtown
VA to help me transition to my next career. I sat across the desk
from her, watching as she scanned my résumé. She asked me,
"What are your goals in life, Roger?"

Never being one to be uncertain, I replied as best I could:
"I want to master myself physically, mentally, and spiritually."

She cocked her head to the side, "Don't you think that is a bit of a tall order?" she asked.

"I feel that's what I've been doing my entire life and I intend on continuing to do so," I said.

She didn't know what to do with me, and in her defense, I didn't know what to do with myself. I applied to be a cop in Dallas. I went through the academy and began working the streets of Fort Worth. I hated the job more than anything I'd ever done. I'd stumbled upon a subtle and powerful reminder that I was not following the right path.

I quit after a month.

After I bailed on working for the Fort Worth–area sheriff's office, I took a job as a personal trainer at a local gym. That didn't last long. I thought: *Fuck it. I want to do something fun. Something I enjoy.* Triathlons became my thing right after I left the Marines, and since bikes and cycling had always brought me pleasure, I starting wondering if that wasn't something I should consider. While working at a bike shop, I figured, I could at least purchase discounted parts. Bike building felt meditative and enjoyable. So I tucked my tail between my legs and went to this shop in town, right down the road from our apartment in Bedford. This guy named Scott interviewed me. He studied my résumé and said, "Wow! You were like *really* in the military!"

"What do you mean?" I asked.

"There are people who were *in* the military," he said, "but not like in the *military* military!"

I laughed.

He said he had a spot for me on the team. They were building and growing and working to establish their own corporate vibe. They had a couple of shops and dealt with quite a bit of overhead and bike service; a big shop. I started building bikes.

The shop I landed in was a bit more roughneck, down in south Fort Worth, and a guy named Craig Chalmers and his wife at the time managed it. The south Fort Worth location was kind of on its own, a satellite shop. Craig managed and ran the storefront. I could instantly feel that Craig was a cool guy, someone I could spend time with. When you look up to someone, it is because they possess something intangible you wish in yourself.

I knew it was going to be worth my time to work there. That was all that I wanted. Up to that point, all the jobs I had been trying to do in other places—even if I went through the police academy, or getting certified to help people lift weights in a gym—had left a bad taste in my mouth every time I punched the clock. But when I met Craig, I felt like I was home. I didn't care if I was getting minimum wage. I was going to have a good time and be around good people. That was all that mattered to me. Period.

Exercise is *my* time. There is nothing that I allow to get in the way of that. I biked to work from our shitty apartment in Fort Worth, from Haltom City to south Fort Worth, thirty miles one way. I rode in that sweltering Texas heat every day. Fast. I've never known slow. There were days over 110 degrees, yet I ripped through those congested roads. Rich, soft yuppies in their cars with the air-conditioning on full blast, their hair blowing from the force of the fans, honking and shaking their weak, soft hands at me.

I'll sacrifice sleep for a good workout. There is no way I'm not going to exercise. Craig and I began to ride and work out together. Texas is not a good place for exercise. You either go to a gym for fitness or you don't really exercise. We both recognized that we didn't want to be a part of gym fitness; we just wanted to get outside.

I worked there for a while, but I didn't always get to work with Craig. I was a grunt worker for maintenance and building new bikes, but that was okay when Craig was around. Things weren't so great when he was off; I had to deal with the real owner when he was around. He was a tool bag. Everything was all about the bottom line; it wasn't about mojo. He was the antithesis of why I enjoyed working at the shop.

The move to the bike shop after four years of hard service in the military was a complete culture shock. The people I found myself surrounded by weren't the same. I realized I'd neglected to appreciate the quality of human beings I'd worked with while I was in the Marines. I didn't notice that until I'd quit. This is especially true of those men in Reconnaissance. There is a hidden power that comes with living at risk. Constantly embracing risk attracts virtue, in a way.

The men in Reconnaissance have to be vetted to get there, and then they work harder than anyone you've met to belong there. Such people always try to improve themselves, and not in like some bullshit Atkins diet way; these are men constantly striving to improve themselves so they will not get someone else killed. Instead of saying "I need to lose a little weight," these are the guys that say, "I need to be able to run thirty miles because I don't want to let my buddy next to me down if he gets shot." These men function out of virtue. All of those subtleties I took for granted because I'd spent my young adult life immersed in that culture.

But I felt that same way around Craig. I felt that kinship with him. Sure, people mostly avoid working toward virtue; however, if you see a guy on the side of the road who needs help, you stop to help him. If there is something you need to improve in your life, *don't talk about it, fucking do it.* That was what I identified in Craig. In that way, he was a savior to me. The three or four days a week I got to work with him were enough. After about a year of working together, we began spending time together outside the job. Craig quickly became a soft-spoken mentor. Working retail sucks; you need someone. We were there for each other.

Craig introduced me to his friend Oliver Peck, one of his best friends growing up in high school. We'd go eat lunch and ride around in his hot rods.

One day Craig said, "Let's go visit Oliver and get a tattoo." Oliver learned to tattoo on Craig. Oliver crafted a full-body suit of tattoos on Craig in his basement while he was mastering the craft, all without proper equipment. Oliver later opened Elm Street Tattoo and is now an icon in the tattooing scene. The Elm Street Music & Tattoo Festival would later become something Oliver hosts, and he's now a judge on the television show *Ink Master*.

I got tattooed on my arm at Elm Street. Oliver tattooed the

Recon jack on me, a heavy piece to get tattooed on a Marine. I explain it to guys by saying that getting the Recon jack is like having a checking account. We all understand and have checking accounts, and you know you can't take out more than you put in. When you've put in enough of yourself, once you've been through the meat grinder a bit, then you have earned the Recon jack. Essentially, once you've given more than it gave you, only then do you deserve to get that tattoo. The Recon jack is the jack of all trades, master of none. There is a parachute, scuba diver, boat paddle, and a knife crossed through a cracked skull. The Recon jack is the iconic symbol for Marine Reconnaissance.

I'd survived a fair share of surreal experiences by that point. Getting that tattoo struck a powerful chord in me, and sharing that experience with Craig and his dear friend Oliver carried deep meaning for me, but I wouldn't fully understand just how much until much later in life.

Somewhere along the line, Jennifer called me at work. Craig was so in tune to me that as soon as I hung up the phone, he looked at me and said, "Jen's pregnant?"

"How the hell did you know?"

He smiled and clapped me on the back. "You're fucked, Roger," he said. Craig was humorous in a genuine way. Good humor comes from knowing pain.

A couple of weeks after we found out Jennifer was pregnant, Craig and I went to Pancho's for lunch. I grew up on Pancho's; it's an all-you-can-eat buffet where you raise this small Mexican flag when you want the waitress to deliver more food.

Pancho's is a staple of Dallas–Fort Worth fare for kids who grew up like me. Craig and I sat there drinking Cherry Cokes that hot afternoon. He broke some serious news to me: "You have a kid coming, Roger. You need to go back to the Marine Corps."

"Why?"

He replied, in his soft-spoken Texas twang, "You have a look in your eye whenever you talk about those experiences, Rog. You just need to do it."

Craig was right.

"All right, man," I said.

Craig's advice laid the groundwork for my reenlistment in the Marines, but we still had time to share.

The shop I worked at with Craig sat right by the super-structure of a freeway bridge: huge pillars the size of a two-car garage. One day during work, a dump truck traveling sixty or seventy miles an hour lost its brakes. Its driver was swerving in and out of the lanes, trying his best to avoid cars. He sailed over the expressway, with no way to stop, and T-boned one of those giant concrete pilings, wrapping the whole rig around it. The impact sounded like an artillery round exploding. From inside the shop we heard this enormous *boom!*

All the energy from the twisted steel was dispersed. This big truck, filled to the brim with dirt and gravel, threw rocks and dirt hundreds of feet.

When the truck hit, a coworker and I went running out to the crash site, less than a hundred yards from the store. A crowd of people stood there, slack-jawed, staring at the pile of smoldering metal and concrete. We pushed through them and ran toward the wreck to help. Smoke poured out from all around the engine compartment. There wasn't much time before the truck would be engulfed in flames. I reached the driver first, a small, slender, older black man. The door was busted open. The steering wheel had penetrated down into his chest. I grabbed hold of him. My coworker helped me pull him out, away from the smoking truck, toward the gravel.

As he was lying there, in retrograde amnesia, he repeated the same thing over and over: "Don't tell my boss. Don't tell my boss. Don't tell my boss." With that, the whites of the old man's eyes started to turn red, and he died right there on the hot Texas pavement in front of us.

I didn't know it then, but this would set the stage for me to learn about the reality of traumatic rescue and grief. Robert Frost captures this well in "Out, Out" when he writes, "And that ended it. No more to build on there. And they, since they were not the one dead, turned to their affairs." A simple stepping-stone of compartmentalization that I'd learned from combat: life goes on for the living.

There was a police satellite station, the cops on bikes, adjacent to our building. By the time the police made it there the driver was already dead. We'd left the store unattended, so we stood up and headed back inside to finish the day turning wrenches, a heaviness weighing on the entire shop until we closed.

10

TEA LEAVES AND CHICKEN BONES

Courage is gritting one's teeth; it is simply doing that and pushing ahead, paying no attention to the circumstances.

—YAMAMOTO TSUNETOMO, *HAGAKURE*

In Tokyo, as a grunt, long before I knew anything about samurai or warrior culture beyond my upbringing with my dad and his friends, I had this strange moment of insight. A buddy and I went to check out this famous castle in Tokyo from the Edo period. I had no idea what the Edo period was. We were doing the quick tourist walk-through, right before closing time, and then reached this cordoned-off, "do not enter" area.

Naturally, being two young Marines, we entered and quickly became lost in a complex garden maze. At some point, thirty minutes to an hour in, my friend said, "Dude, we're lost." Then, in typical young Marine fashion, we started plowing through the maze walls, comprising burly bushes. I mean we were smashing through them. We weren't hurting the bushes, but it was a physical feat in itself to get through the walls of foliage. All we were just trying to do was get the fuck out of the maze. By this time, the castle had closed; it was six or seven at night, the sun setting, and we were lost in that damn maze. And this is a sizeable labyrinth, at that.

Then we started hearing the sounds of men screaming and loud hitting, whacking, and popping. Some sort of controlled violence taking place somewhere. Of course we headed toward the sounds, finally busting through the brush and tumbling into this open area beside this intricate ceremonial mat, a beautiful wooden platform, and all kinds of decorum, and here in front of us were these two men fighting in full samurai garb. The warriors were imperial guards for the palace. You wouldn't have known they were battling with wooden samurai swords. The fight was intense. These men were getting after it, as if their lives were on the line. This stuck with me, and unbeknown to me, I would be introduced to samurai culture when I devoted myself to reconnaissance work.

I found myself back in Hawaii as an RIP instructor. I'd been through nine months of RIP, BRC, and dive school myself, and now I was tasked to be a teacher of what we called "ropers." These were students new to the amphibious reconnaissance environment. During this tenure, they learn the recon doctrines, the concepts and techniques of ground and amphibious missions.

I saw my job as turning those I worked with into insightful and hard men. I was expected to haze the fuck out of these guys. I knew the world intimately, so I wondered, *How do I use my position and insights to add value to these guys?* Not like, *How do I oppress them or use them*, but *How do I use my position as their instructor to enlighten them directly in some sort of bodhisattva style, where they would embrace qualities like self-sacrifice and morality?* Together we would look for a way to get closer to our humanity. Jim Jones–style shit.

Jen and I lived in this five-hundred-square-foot apartment over a used-car lot in Honolulu. No air-conditioning. We didn't even have a car. At night in our crappy little apartment, I obsessed over training these guys.

An explanation of the physical training will come later, but I would challenge them intellectually just as I would test their endurance. One thing I taught them was how to use tidal charts. This was before readily available GPS, back when we had these giant books that revealed the moon's position and how lunar phases would affect the tides and currents at a specific latitude and longitude in the ocean at a specific time and place. Kind of like a *Farmer's Almanac* of tides and currents, all tied to astronomy.

Teaching someone how to use tidal current tables wasn't easy, and I had to explain to them why such knowledge was important. As I prepped for this class, I had the same feeling as when I was in charge of a training patrol as a young Marine in Okinawa, in the Northern Training Area. We were in the jungle, living in tents, covered in red clay mud. We might as well have been in the jungle of Vietnam. The forest had giant spiders, banana spiders, as big as your hand. I was in the infantry, a young Marine leading a mock combat patrol through the jungle. I was learning to coordinate fire-support plans and radio-frequency overlays and dictate a patrol order. I was in charge and I took it as seriously as I could. Life-and-death serious. When I was attempting to coordinate fire-support plans and overlay machine-gun fire positions, all the platoon commanders I went to reacted with a certain level of respect that fed the monkey. I felt as if they had asked me to lead, and I could sense their reaction to my resolve. That feeling of their belief in me was heavy, propelling me. Not in the sense of inflating my ego, but in the sense of connecting with that responsibility, which would hold true throughout my reconnaissance career, and then solidify when the combat was everything but "mock."

I took the responsibility very seriously when someone's training was in my hands. It was irrelevant what I was teaching or having you perform; I'm teaching about what I'm turned on to, and what you should be trying to figure out: a deeper sense of why you want to do this, and why the things I am teaching are important. There *are* severe consequences to getting tidal currents wrong, but I was using that as a medium for self-development. From there, my work as an instructor blossomed.

Planning around the tidal ebbs and flows help you decide when and where you insert and at what location you will make your landing. Your team needs you to be spot-on within five hundred yards of where you're going to land. You must become an expert in understanding the tides. You live and love by the ebb, flow, and slack. Imagine landing on a shallow beach at low tide. You're screwed. Now you have to carry all your shit across a mile of open beach. At high tide on that same beach, you're exposed to the enemy for only a few hundred feet. When there are fewer steps across a beach, there are fewer footprints or drag marks—showing that you were there. You have to plan everything just right. All amphibious assaults are planned at high tide. That's why we stormed Normandy when we did: an epic high tide at a specific moment let us get over more obstacles and hit the beach. Arrive on the right tide, at the right moment, and you're disembarking from the craft closer to the machine-gun nests. That means less open distance to travel, so you increase survivability or stealth. All amphibious landings, reconnaissance or all-out assaults, are based on the tides.

Beyond all of this, I wanted to create an understanding for them, a way of directly interacting with the powers of nature. To be aware and sensitive to the forces at play. Use the knowledge as a way to connect to the world around you. Knowledge is useless without wisdom. Enable them; allow them to ask the questions, how and why should we use the tools. In the military people love to get wrapped around the axel. It's important to remember the techniques and always transcend the tools.

I am using the story of the tidal vectors to make a point, I took a different approach to training the guys. There are countless books and stories written of the hardship of special operations training; however, my perspective is likely a bit different. I engaged it all with a different level of intimacy. I wanted to get at the heart of the training and brutality. To use training as a point of self-discovery and development. I'd endured hardships my entire life. Pain and suffering were dear friends. During my own training I was aware of what was happening and why, and I would be thinking deeply about how the instructors would interact with the students. I also studied the reactions, and attitudes of those men around me. At some point in this process I envisioned how I would begin to train teams under my care. I saw flaws in the process and imagined the ways I would instruct men with the hope they would feel the same way I felt about Chilly and the others, the Recon instructor who opened my eyes into the mystic nature of it all.

Once I entered the Recon instructor phase of my career, I discovered a job that I felt a deep calling to and which would change the trajectory of my life.

As a Recon instructor, I reached the height of my mojo. I found myself in charge of selecting and training candidates for reconnaissance, and I developed numerous pre-scuba programs. I had the power to select and train you as I saw fit. Sure tap-dance and sell the plan to the commander; however, where the rubber meets the road comes plenty of gray area. With the help of some amazing men we developed and carried out multiple programs hardening the steel within the Reconnaissance community.

I became the Yoda of training the California Recon guys. My superiors had given me enormous latitude to do this. They trusted me with the keys to the candy shop, so I was deadly serious about my job. I really enjoyed training men and I knew how to do it, but only because I had looked so deeply within myself and the situations around me to really understand what it took. So much of that autonomy was given to me as an instructor, a young instructor. When our colonel had given me the green light to grant the MOS to the marines we trained, he added, "If you ever want to travel anywhere or do anything for your own training, you let me know." I took him up on the offer, going to meet with one of the commanders from 1st Force Reconnaissance Company during the Vietnam era to talk with him about how he trained his guys. This crusty bastard was one of the famed "Frozen Chosin." He was a lance corporal and one of the only guys to survive from his platoon in Korea during the brutal and cold battles along the Chosin Reservoir in Korea, and afterward was battlefield commissioned; a notable Marine. He shared with me pictures of himself as a young Marine, an E3, with Chesty Puller, the Marine who is essentially considered the St. Christopher of the Corps.

One of the first sub-ops ever done in reconnaissance was done by this guy. I would have sworn after meeting him that he was the original inspiration for Colonel Kurtz in *Apocalypse Now*; that was *this* guy. I had a series of long and sincere conversations with him about what it takes to train men for war. Specifically, we spoke in detail about Special Operations and guerrilla warfare.

The hairs stood up on the back of my neck when he finally said, "Look, Roger. We can talk about a lot of things, but the main thing is to make them suffer, help them identify with their suffering and if you can, have them overcome it. That's the magic."

I took his advice to heart and began doing strange things to these strangely gifted people under my wing, in essence, to make them even more gifted. I spent time teaching them how to control their body temperature in cold water, forcing them to become extremely hypothermic, and then willing themselves back out. I did not train them in a harsh and horrible POW style, but instead helped them understand that the limitations they faced were of their mind, not their body.

It's a pretty simple recipe. Basically you can't take someone and say, "If you don't break the four-minute mile, I'm sending you back to the grunts." They won't be able to do it. You can't give them a task they think is impossible. Instead, you hand them something subtler and more insidious. For example, I knew when they were hypothermic to the point that they were hallucinating, because I had them "sleeping" in the surf zone in the water near San Diego. I was standing over them and they were lying with linked arms in the sand and surf. I'd say, "If somebody quits, right now, you can all stand by the fire." I'd have a big crackling fire a hundred feet away, a raging bonfire with the promise of warmth and comfort. I'd drink a steaming cup of coffee and stare at them. It is always very important to never lose your temper and always be in control. Never raise your voice. Yelling at your men means you've lost control. If you lose control, you're not really there. So I was always very calm. "If one person quits," I'd say, "you can all go stand by the fire." And what I'm saying is, *Do you want to be stronger than the next guy, or are you strong together?* This is such a psychological mind meld with people right there. If you haven't experienced something like that, you can't fully understand it. It's a pretty horrible thing to be involved in. Some guys will almost martyr themselves for the team. Say you do have a guy who martyrs himself. Then you all get to go stand by the fire, but it is almost worse to go warm up. Because a few minutes later, I'm going to make you go lie back in the water after you get warm. It's really better to just not even think about it. You need them to become inoculated to the precepts of the mind, and that has to be taught directly, and at the same time has to be learned indirectly. To be practical, the method must be subtle, rooted in psychology, and for the warrior experiencing it: profound.

The mind must not have limits when it comes to war. If someone says, "I can only do twenty-five yards underwater." Well, then, what happens when you have to do an underwater swim in combat and you're subsurface, and the enemy does a depth charge or shoots a straight round into the water and hits your buddy in the lungs, or your diving rig gets damaged or floods? You might have to hold your breath for two minutes to get your buddy's rig in your mouth. There is not a time associated with what it might take to survive, so you have to teach strength of mind. There can be no limit, then, to temperatures or to measurements of distance or time, hunger or fear. Warfare is immeasurable. I knew this, and I knew I needed these men to understand this. I needed to force them into staying in that state of mind where anything was possible. Your mind is your castle. That is it. That was the secret.

They needed to think: *If there is a firefight happening out there, I will go bring everyone back.* Again, I love the gray area but what we're talking about is resolve. There is something very intangible and profound to saying, *I can do that, and really mean it. Because now I'm going to hold the thought in my mind and make it happen.* The process is similar to when you find your child has walked out on the ice and broken through. You're going to go get him out of the ice. You're not going to think: *I'm not going to go die trying to get him out.* No. Instead you think one thought: *I'm going to go get him out of the ice.* That is the strength of mind.

I've joked for years about how fickle our minds can be. Part of being in the military is dealing with an onslaught of physical-fitness tests. Go run a six-minute mile for three miles. Eighteen minutes or less for three miles. Some people will say, "I can't do that." But if I lower the time to seventeen minutes, the same exact percentage will pass, as if it were just eighteen minutes. It's all in the head. The same thing goes for pull-ups. If you have to do twenty pull-ups to get the prize, then that is the point where men will fail; it doesn't matter if I change it to thirty pull-ups. The same guys who were capable of twenty are going to do thirty pull-ups. It's a yardstick that is completely irrelevant and relative. But some guys will make those numbers unachievable, too relative, and limit themselves: "Oh, I can only do eighteen," they'll say. But once they break that barrier in their minds, everything changes.

I was working one particular class really hard when Rudy Reyes showed up. He was a young guy at the time. I was hazing the shit out of the team. At this point, I had never heard anything about the *Hagakure* or anything related to samurai culture, other than that odd encounter with the imperial guards fighting at the Edo Castle. The methods I employed with students were all my own boiled-down understanding of reality, metaphysics, and all these different bits and pieces of historical military lore and indigenous warrior training I'd found in books. The focus always dealt with the limits of our mind and our body.

When I met Rudy I was the senior Reconnaissance instructor in California. If you thought you had what it took to be a Recon Marine, you probably came through me. On the day I met Rudy and his team, they were standing outside, in the hot sun, in dress uniform. I opened with, "You know we are all coming from different backgrounds here, and I am the gatekeeper for you on this. Hopefully we are going to learn a lot from each other. Start with a thousand eight-count bodybuilders together, and I'm going to watch, and if say it a second time, it's going to be two thousand."

Instantly someone took charge, so they started in. But they were in their alphas which is a dress uniform. A dress uniform is not designed for any sort of physical activity. An eight-count bodybuilder is where you go from standing to a squat, to a plank, then a push-up, then kick your feet apart and back, return to the squat and then stand. Eight moves. The average person will struggle to do 30. These guys had just been told to do 1000.

Instantly, in their first few minutes, pushed beyond the framing of the mind.

Their patent leather Corfam shoes would begin to fall apart after about a hundred or so, and the back of their jackets would rip out. I knew all this was going to happen within the first couple hundred. Another hundred on the asphalt and their socks would be wet with blood, bloody footprints covering the ground. I waited for someone to start moaning. Then I said, very softly, and again, never yelling, "please learn to appreciate silence. Everyone, stop. Find a rock and place it in your mouth. Now continue."

I would say this very calmly, just watching. Often, in times and situations like this, the resolve of people will be brought out right there in that moment. Seeing that transformation is palpable. During those moments of insensitivity, and in the face of the impossible, Rudy would shine. He had a warrior's heart.

One evening I headed out for a run, after a long day of putting Rudy and his teammates through one test after another. As I ran past a picnic table, I noticed Rudy. There he was standing on the park picnic table, wearing a blindfold. I wasn't sure what was going on. All of the sudden he jumped, executing a perfectly timed backflip off the picnic table.

"Reyes," I said, stopping to watch him, "what the hell are you doing?"

His answer was simple and curt: "I'm experiencing weightlessness, Sergeant."

That's the level that Rudy operated at. Cirque de Soleil–, Bruce Lee–level shit, and not in a nerdy bullshit way, but in a very practical manner. I enjoyed this about him. I saw in him something very real, a kindred spirit. We really clicked. Even as his instructor, I enjoyed and appreciated his energy. But at the time I certainly didn't make things any easier on him or his friends.

Rudy understood the importance of what I was doing with them. We saw eye to eye, and became dear friends once he completed training.

I'd later learn that Rudy grew up on his own taking care of his brothers. He was the oldest of the siblings. Eventually an eclectic fatherly man took him under his wing. The guy was a devoted practitioner of Chinese kung fu and qigong. His name was Sit. I had the pleasure of meeting the man while visiting Rudy after a deployment in Kansas City. Rudy had told Sit about me, and had in turn told me quite a bit about Sit. We both had a deep respect for each other because we'd both had helped shape Rudy. Sit was the real deal; he gave Rudy structure, disciple, and the insights of qigong. Qigong is a form of martial arts that coordinates body mechanics, breathing, meditation, and energy into a way of living. For Rudy, qigong was his religion. Rudy, as he began learning qigong at an early age, had also mastered kung fu. They would always train outside, which is important to qigong. Between qigong and kung fu, Rudy was Cirque du Soleil capable. I would often see him doing a handstand on a pull-up bar. He would touch his nose to the bar, and extend back to a full one-hand stand. This would be alone at night by the barracks with no one around. Rudy was a special creature.

When I'd finished training Rudy's class, the men would go to additional schools and eventually be placed in different platoons. The two of us began to spend downtime together. He wasn't a skilled swimmer, but he was a superb athlete, so we would refine these skills all the time. We did the Escape from Alcatraz Triathlon, and would regularly endure intense physical activities together. One of these activities was free diving. Free diving is where you dive down into the ocean, with no gear, holding your breath, and attempting to descend as deep as possible. The two of us would go to La Jolla Cove and swim into the kelp beds and follow the buoy chains down to see if we could go down to a hundred feet on a single breath, We dove at night because of our work schedules. It wasn't planned but added considerable ambiance.

The teacher became the student when Rudy began to teach me qigong. At some point Rudy innocently asked me, "Roger, have you ever heard of the *Hagakure*?"

"No," I said.

"I'll give you my copy." Later he handed me this dog-eared book that had been read to tatters.

And that book, the *Hagakure*, is a warrior's guide of samurai wisdom collected by Yamamoto Tsunetomo in the early 1700s. The book blew my hair back. As soon as I started reading this thing I thought to myself, *Fuck, man, my whole life I've lived by these tenets and attributes without even knowing they were a thing.* When something exists without ever having an explanation it is real as bone. The book was a powerful affirmation.

Nowhere else are written those intangibles about living. To read something that resonates from centuries ago, you know that it is bedrock. If my religion was Special Operations, I had found the bible.

The book confirmed that I was onto something. The samurai approach to life mirrored what I was already doing, whether that connection came from my upbringing or overcoming the injuries, weakness, and self-doubt or to seeking a sense of truth in elite military units. The connection wasn't contrived.

I found methods and a philosophical approach to develop the ideas I utilized. I discovered new ways of pushing the limitations of the mind. For example, let's say it was winter, snowing and cold, and I told you to put on some warm clothing, gloves, a hat, and shoes, and go run for an hour outside. If it's freezing cold out, a person's inclination is to say, "Fuck you, it's cold out!" Yet you can easily run in cold weather. However, if I say, in those same cold conditions, "lets swim across the river," I've upped that ante where you will need to cross a line. The limitations you have set in your mind. A lot of that line has to do with your level of desperation. How comfortable you are with yourself. To live up to your potential you cannot be comfortable. Remove the desire to be comfortable and the line will disappear.

Books, a couple of colored rocks, and chicken bones would help me erase the lines in their minds.

I had read a book on tea leaf reading where the author explained, in no-bullshit terms, what reading chicken bones, tea leaves, or palm reading is and how it can be used to influence people. If you're reading someone's palm, it's more important to know what the person is seeking from you than what you're going to say to them. Not to manipulate them in a negative or insidious way, but to understand the moment for what it is. Tea leaf reading is about the power of perception, or perceiving what people seek from you. I connected with that idea.

Then I read Paulo Coelho's *The Alchemist*, a simple parable about a young shepherd with a dream, and all that he has to give up in life to follow his dream. It's proverbial, and was profound. You could read it in a night and then lie there until morning thinking, *Holy shit! I've been blind and my life is meaningless.*

In *The Alchemist*, the young boy meets an old man. However you want to look at the man, the man explains metaphysics or alchemy as understanding the soul of the world. The personified being has these two stones. One called Urim and the other is Thummim. White and black. I would use those.

In divination, there are chicken bones. For my own use, I would shake the bones and depending upon which bones come closer or farther from the white or black, I could make an intellectual, processed thought about different outcomes for things. This allows your conscious to meld with the subconscious in a way you wouldn't normally put things together. The chicken bones became a tool for me.

I would throw the chicken bones all the time as an instructor. In the Gypsy way I could use the bones to manipulate you if you were asking for something. Most often, I employed the bones as a tool to look into my own intuition. That's all the chicken bones are, a tool. I would use this approach with these young Marines and it would blow their fucking minds.

A scenario with the bones might look like this:

A Marine, mustering up a great deal of courage, would approach me and ask, "Sergeant Sparks, Captain America requesting permission to speak."

"Speak." (And you always talk in the third person; again, that is selflessness in the face of adversity, and I personified adversity to them. He's asking to talk to me.)

"Sergeant Sparks, we're requesting that we wear wet suits for the morning swim. The air temperature is in the 40's, water temperature is in the 50's."

And I would nod my head in thought, and reply, "Let's see what the chicken bones say."

His face would say: *Oh, fuck*.

Then I would take out the small pouch that held the special goods. I'd roll out a small suede mat, and I'd throw Urim and Thummim, the white and black rocks, down. The white rocks I'd picked up on a deployment in Bali. My Urim substitute was a piece of white reef coral, and the black was real Thummim, discovered in Egypt. Next came the bones. Leg bones from a chicken, dried and painted. I'd throw the bones, and depending upon the colors, whatever one came closer to white or black, that forced me to look at things in a way that I wouldn't before. In this case, I could ask myself, Why is he asking this of me, and what can we both learn from the question? Affirmative would be white. Black would be negative.

The bones weren't all that I carried in the pouch. I had gathered other things that I considered sacred. One of my Reconnaissance buddies, Lanny LaPlante, gave me a little piece of felt that he thought was sacred, so I carried that in the bag with all the other stuff. If on a special beach somewhere, like Iwo Jima, I would pick up a little sand and throw it in my little medicine bag. I've created a ceremony to make it sacred. And it was very sacred to me. In the position that I held, I had dramatic authority over people's comfort and their future. The Marines felt the power because I was projecting a great deal of power on what the stones and bones would reveal. In a way it pulled me out of the transaction and allowed the larger issues to take center stage. The contents were a muse that give insight to our reality.

So whatever color bone fell closest to black and white, I would look at the question and the circumstance and think about what the men thought they needed. Then I would think about their welfare and what I wanted the outcome of this situation to be. I might say something along the lines of, "I appreciate you asking me. You guys can wear wet suits." Then I would say, "Navigator, come here." Everyone had different team positions. I'd give him a new order: "The insert for this point is here." I'd point at the map, and I'd have changed the location by five miles. "You can wear the wet suits," I'd say, "but you're going to run to the insert." Now that they had to run five miles in their wet suits, and halfway through their run to reach the insertion point, I'd ask, "Are you guys hot? Do you want to take your suits off?"

"Yes, sergeant!" they would shout.

"Then take them off. You've got two minutes." Removing a wet suit is hard to do once you've been sweating in it. Then, when the time was up and they weren't all out of their suits, it was punishment time. I'd say, "Go get wet and sandy and flail around in the surf and like a dying fish."

They took off running, half-dressed in these awful, clammy wet suits, toward the beach. Flopped down in the surf and rolled in the sand. Then came the next order: "Now put your suits back on, and let's go."

Now they were wet, coated in sand, and running inside a sandpaper suit.

I was inoculating them to the sensitivities and feelings of misery. How they interacted with desires and comfort. How the reality is that combat doesn't give a shit how miserable you might be. *Are you still resolved?* We are not here to seek comfort. Growth hurts, you're welcome.

Now, as they were enduring this horrible situation, they weren't thinking about whether they can make it or not. Instead they were thinking about the lesson and saying to themselves, *Shit. We shouldn't have asked for that.*

You're asking or admitting weakness and then I'm going to exploit it, but I'm going to exploit it in a way that helps you grow, so you'll remember down the road. You'll be doing some operational mission, and you might be wet and sandy, but it won't ever be as bad as it was when I trained you. You're going to be okay. I've completely inoculated you to misery. It is my gift.

I would use the bones and stones in a similar capacity all the time.

I was always peeling the onion with the guys. An old story I recalled spoke about the Apache spirit runners. Apache boys learned early that running went hand in hand with becoming a warrior. The young boys would fill their mouths with water and go for a long run, all throughout the day, in the scorching summer heat of what is now New Mexico, and when they got back, they would spit out the water. Only the ones who spat out the water could be trusted and trained. Those who swallowed or spit it out during the run couldn't be trained, because they didn't have discipline. Holding the water in the mouth forced deep rhythmic breathing through the nose, and kept the young future warriors from panting and drying out their mouths and throats. Carrying the water in the mouth also required deep focus.

I really liked that particular approach to training, so I

used it religiously. If guys spat the water out or swallowed it, then I would have them fill their mouths with gravel. Not fine, clean gravel; I'm talking the dirt on the side of the road. I'd point and say, "Fill your mouth with that gravel. You have no discipline. Those around you will suffer because of your lack of character. If you fall out of the run, I'm going to condition everyone while you watch. You're going to keep your boots on, and your team will finish the run barefoot."

We would run seventy-plus miles a week. We'd go on a ten-mile run with the water in our mouths. I really got behind the water in the mouth, especially after I read John Douillard's *Body, Mind, and Sport*. That book was about principles of human performance. If you breathe through your nose when you exercise, you generally will not go beyond 50 percent of your max threshold for your heart rate, no matter. When I read that there was no benefit from training endurance that went past 50 percent of the maximum heart rate, I thought, *those Apaches had it all figured out*. That was when I really fell in love with the rocks and water. The idea that the Apache could run sixty miles a day like that only added to the allure for both myself and my men.

The Apache could do those runs through some harsh terrain barefoot, and that knowledge, coupled with what I knew about the Vietnam War, had me doing the same. I was really into mixing it up. The Vietnam vets I spoke with were really big on this when it came to training, due to what too many of our troops endured during the war. The first thing Vietcong were going to do if they caught you was to have you take your boots off. They knew American feet would be not tough. If you did try to run away barefoot, they were going to catch you quickly. One of the things that resonated from the Vietnam-era instructors was that they periodically make their guys go barefoot. They were Vietnam-era Reconnaissance, the Rangers, or the Long Range Recon Patrol; they would do everything without socks or insoles in their boots to toughen their feet up.

I constantly incorporated odd approaches into my warrior training, too; strange things, like studying mimes. Marcel Marceau, the French mime of the late 1940s, was famous for these really weird performances. In one of Marceau's routines he went from standing to lying down in an hour, but you couldn't see him move. That was the entire act. As soon as I read that, I said to myself, "I'm doing this to my guys when I train them to patrol."

Patrolling correctly requires discipline and patience.

Stalking requires having your body pressed down into the earth and crawling where the creatures live; in a word, it's horrible. Crawl over an ant colony and have them destroy you; then crawl for another four hours and act as if you weren't eaten alive. An encounter with an ant hill is minor, but stalking requires a certain level of life-and-death discipline and patience. Patience is the most difficult thing to teach.

I would give them all the rules. "Listen," I would say, "You're going to go from standing up to laying down. If I see you move, if I see you physically move, you're going to owe me a thousand eight-count bodybuilders, with one shoe on and one shoe in your mouth." I would sit out there for an hour or so watching them, and at some point I might abruptly leave. When I returned and they still weren't on the ground, I would ask, "Why didn't you just lie down when I left? If you ain't cheating, you ain't trying. Life as well as combat is not fair. If you're going to cheat, don't get caught." This Marceau method again forced them to go beyond themselves, which is essential, especially when you're asking guys to do the things they will be asked to do in reconnaissance: Suffer and be patient.

While I did horrible stuff to my guys all the time, I always took what we were doing mortally serious. I wasn't asking them to do anything that I had personally not done or couldn't do. I was in extreme physical condition at the time. I would run them all into the dirt, but I would do that *with them* myself every day. Granted, I was training them on top of that, but they knew it was coming from a place of concern and responsibility. I was representing the reality of the job to them.

I remember a moment when, as a young Recon student, we were going through a patrol phase. Our instructors had been putting us through our paces continuously. We had been in the field about a week. The area we were training in was overrun with poison oak. We were covered in the oil from being exposed and our skin was broken and oozing. We would be harassed with flash bangs and tear gas to keep us on our toes when we were not stealthy enough. We were deeply weary and exhausted to the point of delirium. I remember witnessing a teammate on a security halt take a knee mumbling and attempting to stick his ID card into a tree. He thought he was buying a can of soda. Now that's exhausted. Next time you're tired think about that Coke machine tree. I hope it gives you a laugh.

This was the same week I sat on that underground hornet's nest, awakening the tiger below. Those fuckers tore our ass up. The experience was emotional to say the least. We were swollen and throbbing from the vicious assault of stings. Above all of that, I felt something very peculiar. I felt elated and powerful. I am sure the adrenaline had everything to do with that, and to me the memory has always represented the power of our minds and our perspective. We have far more in us than we could ever imagine.

The body is secondary to the mind. Hop on a pull-up bar and do as many as you can. Did you stop because that's all you had? Did you physically collapse or did you tell yourself to stop?

That was all I was doing with those guys, teaching them to establish within themselves a framework that would make them unstoppable.

I would tell them, "Just because you haven't slept in a few days, or eaten a meal? That doesn't change anything. You are much more capable than you know." In some cases I'd challenge them with swims, runs, and calisthenics until they were delirious, and with a short break I would have them take the physical fitness test that would establish the basis for their promotions as well as their career in Reconnaissance.

And you know what? They would pass the test with flying colors.

We develop what is demanded of us.

Success has nothing to do with how someone appears. I think it is quite the contrary. Success is directly tied to desire and desperation. The extreme of desire is desperation. Early bushido culture knew all about this. They believed a man's worth in combat was equal to his desperation. Being fit is nothing more than intelligence and discipline, but there is so much more. To change and grow you have to be uncomfortable with yourself. If you look into someone's eyes, you can see it. Are they too comfortable and unwilling to change? Most people are. Discomfort and pain are generally the price of growth. It's the human condition. This is not some new age bullshit, it's all very simple and quite practical. Once you eat, sleep, and breathe this stuff, the world blossoms before your eyes. Anything can be accomplished.

What I was doing to those guys wasn't about being healthy or fit. Training for combat you have to be unforgiving. You have to harden your resolve by testing it. The samurai called it *suigyo*, a purification, and they said you should do that once a month for your entire life. Do something that has nothing to do with benefiting you physically, think of the guy that works out regularly, drinks his protein shakes and shaves his arms. He may be fit but he's too comfortable with himself. You must test your resolve to improve it. Go on a hike nonstop for twenty-four hours, lie in an ice bath, go run barefoot until your feet bleed. Get outside of your comforts and limitations, that's suigyo. Understanding our limitations by exceeding them has great importance. Whatever training you're going through, whether military or struggling with a chemistry class, it's all the same.

Simply put, beware of comfort.

When I recall all those men, I am overwhelmed with emotion. They went on to do some amazing things. After 9/11, Rudy's platoon took part in the invasion of Iraq. His platoon headed that up, and that's what they based the HBO series *Generation Kill* on. I trained the men who inspired that show. However, I personally dislike how the film industry displays wars and warfighters as sensationalized entertainment. Closing the gap between warfighters and civilians is desperately important for both sides, but there has to be more than just entertainment. Again I have a deep affinity for those men I trained. Many are still in the Marine Corps filling leadership roles within MARSOC and Reconnaissance. I have run into many throughout my life and it is always a warm reunion. We are a reflection of each other. I have photos of them lying in the surf zone, probably thinking about the black and white stones in my medicine pouch. Most Americans have no idea what hardships are paid to play the games of war. Those guys endured more suffering and grief than people would care to understand. They took it on the chin and are better for it. But that's the way it has always been. Such sacrifice has always reminded me of the saying, "They sleep well in their beds only because rough men stand ready in the night to visit violence on those that would do them harm."

11

BREAKING BACK

It is better to have some unhappiness while one is still young, for if a person does not experience some bitterness, his disposition will not settle down. A person who becomes fatigued when unhappy is useless.

—YAMAMOTO TSUNETOMO, *HAGAKURE*

I had this love-hate relationship with the Marine Corps. I hated some of the bullshit of life in the Corps, but loved Reconnaissance. Every time I would reach the end of my four-year enlistment I would feel the need to get out and attempt to do something else. 9/11 only amplified that sentiment. Something intangible had been reached within my experiences in combat that followed and the way our talents as Reconnaissance Marines were being used. Many stories of war are not worth telling, mostly because of the way they are told or, even more so, how they are interpreted. Like Kurt Vonnegut says in *Slaughterhouse-Five*, "War will look just wonderful, so we'll have a lot more of them."

It was time for me to move on.

I felt like I needed to leave the Marine Corps in order to grow. Military service, especially Special Operations, hurts families because of the time away, not to mention how the experiences of war and training begin to collect in your psyche and are not shared with your loved ones. It becomes invasive and consuming, so the more surreal and difficult your experiences, the less you're sharing with the ones you love. You are forced into isolation. Because of this our marriage was suffering. Family mattered enough for me to leave behind my identity as a Marine for Jennifer, the love of my life, my high school sweetheart, and the bedrock of my personality and who I am. We had our son, Orion, at the time. I was willing to definitely change everything in my life to salvage my relationship with him, too.

But because the regular work world didn't make sense, ultimately I missed the brotherhood. I don't mean in a bullshit, clichéd kind of way, or some way that you feel watching a stupid fucking movie. I missed the very deep dedication to shared purpose beyond yourself, the connection that happens only when you find yourself in the midst of true mortal risk. You would never physically or mentally let down one of your teammates, to the point to where you were capable of digesting and dealing with whatever horror is thrown at you. This is where we grow, where the rubber meets the road. The drive to develop myself physically, mentally, and spiritually had kept drawing me back into the military. Each time I got out, the reality of strip malls and consumerism and petty bullshit had me coming back. Even though I had some issues with the political and bureaucratic quagmire of the military, that muse of something more called, and it would always have me returning.

Times were hard for my family, and I needed to make adjustments.

Again, hard is relative, and for a determined human being, hard only means adversity. The world makes way for a determined human being; you shape reality around you with determination. That was how I felt about my situation.

When I left the Marine Corps for the second time, they had me write a résumé. I'd done some pretty colorful things in the service, but it isn't like a résumé translates true experience. How exactly do I say that I've got a completion certificate for the French Foreign Legion commando program, or these other brutal experiences? I didn't give a shit about putting medals or awards on paper, or anything like that. But I wanted to express how my life's focus had been to cultivate those things within me, to nurture and develop my strength mentally, physically, and spiritually, and that my military service had been a rich environment to do so.

I took my new shiny résumé and applied for a job at a high school pool. When I gave it to the staff member who ran the aquatics program, he stood there reading that thing and then said, "Yeah, you got the job, man." But he also added, "So you were like really in the military?"

When I'd heard that before, I'd just smiled. Now a realization struck me, and I nodded my head. I guess he was right: I hadn't really left. Subconsciously, perhaps, I chose that job so I could train for a future military career I hadn't yet settled on. I used that job to stay in the water. And did I swim. I probably averaged over five thousand yards a day, the base mileage of an Olympic swimmer. The pool became my place of meditation.

In a very direct way I had wound up choosing civilian jobs that would keep me in an environment to develop myself physically, mentally, and spiritually, so I would be able to strengthen the relationship with myself and my family. I needed to find balance in my life. After some deep soul-searching, I had the conversation with Jennifer. "I'm going to go back in the military," I said. "I think I will go into pararescue. I'm done with the Marine Reconnaissance thing. I don't want my life to be about the same thing; I want to grow in other capacities."

The details did not matter. I wanted the brotherhood and the environment back. The more different or newer the flavor, the better. I needed to be around others with the same resolve.

I visited an Air Force recruiter. I knew that the Air Force had a brilliant Special Operations program: combat controllers (CCTs) and pararescuemen (PJs). The majority of people in the military don't really know or understand what a CCT or PJ is, but in Special Operations, the roles are widely known about and respected. When people think of the Special Operations, they generally think of Green Berets, Rangers, or Navy SEALs. Whatever media feeds people, that's what they know. Obviously with my long look behind the wizard's curtain, I knew very intimately what I was getting into. But I didn't care about the details. I wanted the environment and the medium back. Pararescue seemed like a place where I could use what

I'd learned in a way I felt was more virtuous, and I'd always been interested in medicine. So the combat rescue role of being a PJ intrigued me, but really, I was waiting for whichever bullshit recruiter called me first. When the phone rang, the voice on the other end of the line introduced himself and invited me into his office to chat.

When I arrived I got right to the point and gave him a copy of my DD-214, which is basically a direct record of a military career. This was not that silly résumé I turned in for the swimming coach job, and not the bullshit of what someone might allude to or misrepresent about his service record. This was a direct copy of the events that had occurred with my military career. The Air Force recruiter was a soft man behind a big desk. After some small talk he perused my DD-214, looked up at me, and said, "Wow, man!" I'll be the first to admit that the majority of the Air Force is paramilitary and does not operate as a completely militarized force built around combat like the Marine Corps or the Army. I mean this in the no-nonsense, discipline that comes with understanding ground combat. So this guy, despite being in the Air Force, really had no idea what pararescue was. Honestly, I do not think he understood the details printed on my DD-214. The dude had no concept of what I was into or trying to do.

After a while, he looks at me and asked, "Why do you want to do all the hard jobs?" His tone revealed he wasn't trying to be funny.

I replied, "Are you fucking kidding me? Listen, I know what needs to happen. You need to get on the phone and contact a PJ or CCT recruiter who will proctor the PAST test. Make the call; I work at a pool. They can test me there."

I gave him my contact info and left.

After some wrangling they found a local PJ, who was supposed to come to administer the test. He never showed up, so they sent another recruiter from a different office. I did all that this guy instructed me to do. Swimming, push-ups, running, etc. At the end, the guy acted pretty giddy, as if he'd get some sort of recruitment bonus or something. He wanted to chat. "Jesus," he said, "you're the first person I've seen pass this damn test!" To be honest, the test was a joke. I felt isolated, and wondered if I was heading in the right direction.

What I wanted to say after all the drama of finding someone to test me was, "Can you please stop talking, man, and just sign the paperwork."

Within a month I was going through their indoctrination, or indoc, the pararescue selection program at Lackland Air Force Base. I felt at home once again.

Even with my experiences within Reconnaissance, after years of creating, dictating, and implementing policy within that subculture, the cadre at indoc impressed me with what they could get away with. Again, the Air Force is really more of a paramilitary organization; however, within the select group of people in pararescue and combat control, something is different. It is almost as if because the rest of the Air Force are such leaf-eaters that they don't understand combat or warrior culture, so the response of the higher-ups seems to be, *Just do you what need to do.* And what they do is select the right people for an impossible job. Picking the right guys for the job requires looking between the lines, and finding the gray area. There's something more behind being able to do the push-ups, the pull-ups and whatever, swim times, run times, who gives a shit . . . passing tests on medicine or dive physics; put whatever test or course you want in that capacity, but you're looking for people who can fix things that are unfixable, and who are willing to sacrifice their own mortality, their humanity. That is something that doesn't have a number.

The instructors impressed me with their candor and crowd control. Most of time, I felt as if I'd landed in a kind of retribution for the things that I'd done to students of mine as a Reconnaissance instructor.

Training people through injustice was a primary technique they would use. Let's see how this person reacts whenever he's hurting and we single him out and make him hurt more. Let's see how the team reacts to him, and what's the team dynamic to that treatment? Did they stick up for him? Did they shelter him? Because you can judge character that way. I felt like I had a PhD in what these guys were doing to us. It was interesting to see it continually from both sides.

So while others might write of the trials and tribulations of indoc, I was deeply enjoying the experience. I enjoyed, at a visceral level, being on the receiving end of the suffering. I was literally a fish to water to the things that they were doing to us, and I enjoyed the suffering. Whether they were trying to drown us in the pool or had us carrying the logs around the base, I loved it.

The instructors placed me in a leadership capacity shortly into the course, and I thrived in the training. As the team leader for the PJs at indoc, I felt compelled to get as many of the guys through as I could. Pararescue indoc at that time had one of the highest attrition rates of all the Special Operations courses, which was a 90 percent fail rate. The physical and mental punishment was often too much. Guys would suddenly get out of the pool and quit. They would blow the horn, the signal that they'd caved in, and I would jump out of the pool, grab them, and throw them back in. The instructors would laugh, but my tactics worked. Indoc was a good time; I was having a blast. I was wrestling with some monkeys but this was an escape from all that. I'd rather do push-ups, laugh at everything. Don't get me wrong, we all have our days, but it felt like a welcomed homecoming.

All indoc classes are famous for some form of a departing prank. Together we planned an epic mission. What came next is history, the only evidence is a few heralded photos. The mission required that we steal a trailer and a few vehicles. We needed to get the infamous log, and boats used to crush the souls of wannabe pararescuers and combat controllers for decades, to the target, snap a few photos with all of us in place for two minutes, and then have every trace of it immediately vanish. I trained all the men like we were partaking in a real mission, complete with briefs, terrain models, and rehearsals. Hushed voices in the barracks, and I was pointing at guys. "You're here. You're here. We'll all be wearing aloha shirts; if a security guard walks around this way, sip on your Big Gulp, and that is the signal for us to hold back."

The end result of our efforts: the entire indoc team holding the PJ log and two rubber Zodiac boats directly in front of the Alamo. More important to me than the epic prank, my team graduated twenty-one from indoc, which at the time was the highest number of any class to graduate. We started with over 120 men. On graduation day I received the Commandant's Award, and enjoyed the team's efforts.

My introduction to pararescue wouldn't be all roses and sunshine, though. After indoc, students enter the "pipeline," a series of courses of dive, jump, and survival schools. Coming from my previous military background, I had already completed the majority of these. All that remained of my official pararescue training was paramedic and then pararescue school. Some of the training would get ridiculous, even malignant. I wouldn't have to crawl through a pipe full of shit like I did in the French commando course, but there would be plenty of shit to deal with.

Rudy said it best when I chatted with him while going back through training: "You're going to handle it physically, whatever, but that's a spiritual trip." What he was saying was that to go from being the guy who was kicking people in the face, to now getting kicked in the face, was part of a spiritual transformation. He was right. Many of the instructors at Kirtland really got off on degrading us as students. What we found ourselves in was a bizarre version of the Stanford Prison Experiment. They were purposefully working to humiliate and degrade us.

In some cases, especially in the paramedic course, they did way out-of-line shit. That's coming from me. The treatment was caustic and completely unregulated. It demeaned us and stripped us of our humanity. It caused us to hate them—listen, you don't want to take guys at this stage in training and beat them down into submissive zombies. As soon as you break men down to where they are malleable to authority, they become worthless. They really ground us down. For us to pass and become PJs, we had to really become less of ourselves. The harassment throughout the paramedic course became malignant. Hell, do whatever you want, and at indoc they certainly did. But this is years into training. At this point in training we were way past the bubblegum stuff.

I'm fine with you as an instructor getting in my head and attempting to instill some metaphysical lessons in me. If you're wise enough to apply those techniques have at it. But I don't think these guys were capable of teaching anything of value. What they were doing to our team was completely out of line. We had all graduated indoc, as well as the entire Special Operations pipeline. We were doing our best to walk the line of the Nationally Registered Paramedic exams and deal with ass clowns as instructors. The men in charge of us were goons, wasting our time, energy, and our desire to even be there. To lead highly selected men you have to do so with virtue and charisma. The cadre in charge of us had neither. If the rest of the career field was anything like this, none of us wanted anything to do with it. They had absolute power over us and abused every ounce. Things continually escalated. Often during a "mentoring" session of harassment, the instructors would talk shit to us. Real out-of-line stuff. Once they did that, we had no choice to engage in the banter with them. We would tell them matter-of-factly what we thought of them. They would hold it against us of course but we didn't care.

There was this one guy in our group, Mark Van Weezen-donk, who would later became a lieutenant colonel and the commander of the pararescue schoolhouse, and what he said sums it up. While the "instructors" would be counseling us in the mud pit behind the school, they would childishly taunt us. "What's wrong, don't you like me? Do you all want to kick my ass?" Van Weezendonk, this massively muscled human being, a brute who looked like he could rip a bumper or tire off a car, replied, "No, I don't want to kick your ass. I was just thinking how far I could throw your head . . . after I pulled it off. Pulling it off isn't the question. What I do question is how far I could throw your skull." This was at two in the morning, wearing only our underwear, in the back of a parking lot, covered in mud, barefoot, and doing eight counts while being sprayed with water.

"Are you threatening me?" the instructor asked.

To say we had a bad relationship with the instructors is a dramatic understatement. They had nothing to offer.

We got through that bullshit for each other. It bonded us intimately as friends. We believed in each other more than our idea of what the career field of pararescue could give us. The guys looked to me for help because I possessed a sense of direction they needed to navigate the quagmire we found ourselves in. Something the instructors themselves didn't have. This all became a very personal battle of us versus them, but they held all the cards. We didn't want to be a part of what they were selling anymore.

We went on to complete another six months of Pararescue school, and endured more of the same bullshit. When we graduated we didn't have a party or anything. We just left, a lame and anticlimactic conclusion seemed fitting. At some point my teammates gave me a plaque that had a quote from Theodore Roosevelt and a personal inscription that read:

SSGT ROGER "BIG FROG" SPARKS
Warrior / Poet

Thank you for inspiring me to press on when times were tough. Thank you for giving me someone to look up to when I could barely keep my head up at all. Thank you for taking me to the next level and teaching me how to truly be a warrior at heart. You will always be my leader, my teammate, and most of all, my friend.

Those are the things to value. All those I graduated with are dear friends of mine to this day, guys like Tommy Boy, Lopaka, and Sweet Tooth. Those guys are real pipe hitters. Most of them went to the tactical top of the heap, or they became instructors themselves at the schoolhouse, and made it light-years better for others. They were giving their pain purpose. They had extremely bright careers as PJs, many of them still shouldering very influential positions. Perhaps it is true that the hotter the fire the harder the steel, but the hazing wasn't an intentional fire. What got us through was the hatred against the clowns. Us versus them. "Fuck those guys," I would say, "They are not our reality."

I am sure the experience we had with the Pararescue instructors at Kirtland destroyed much of my trust and loyalty for any leadership or authority for the rest of my career. I would always project the ignorance and lack of character of those instructors onto my future supervisor, boss, or instructors. I am sure I was hard to manage, but in all I hope I gave more than I received.

After I graduated I was sent to my first Pararescue team, the 23rd Special Tactics Squadron at Hurlburt Field, FL. My introduction to the unit didn't go over so well. I landed in a unit that had a real close-knit college fraternity feel. They hadn't received new guys in years, so they were ready to give the FNGs (the fucking new guys) plenty of shit. When I checked in to the unit on the first day there were my two buddies, Geno and Cheney, pushing a Humvee around the parking lot. I could tell what I was in for with this assignment.

I went right to my new team leader. He said, "Your buddies are outside, why don't you go join them?"

"Fuck no," I said, "If you want to fight, let's fight, right now. I'm not going to do that shit anymore."

He was instantly caught off guard, "Whoa . . . No, I didn't mean it like that."

"Yes," I said, "Yes, you did. You don't know what we've gone through to get here. I sold who I am to stand here with this stupid fuckin' hat."

From there I was sent to Advance Skills Training, the finish school for guys assigned to a Special Tactics unit. PJs and CCT's often get passed out to units. SEALs, Reconnaissance Marines, and Rangers use our services frequently. We get tasked with serving the needs of those units, so we have to learn to integrate and work well with them.

The instructors once again were trying to be tough guys with us, but I was over the act. You have to appreciate the headspace. At that point I was pretty much over it all. I was ready to scrap for my crumbs. In the course I was in they train combat controllers and pararescuemen together. You train together to go into a Special Tactics Squadron. So right away we're getting hazed, enduring what we'd gone through in pararescue training. If you didn't wear the right socks for PT they would want to shit on us and treat us like we hadn't earned the right to be there. We were going through this silly shit and we'd graduated as fully qualified PJs and we're integrating with combat controllers and these young guys haven't ever done air operations and we're regressing to be put in with them.

One day they had us climbing a rope ladder up into a helicopter and fast-roping out the other side while we hovered. An instructor was at the front of the helicopters, controlling the aircraft. I could hear him over my headset: "Hold hover. Move back five. Five." We had twenty students climbing rope ladders as the helicopters hovered close together. There were three helicopters and the instructor was controlling them all. (It's somber to run through my memory of this, because half the guys that I went through that course with are now dead from combat fatalities or aircraft crashes.) The instructor was yelling and screaming away and one of guys said, "Sparks, what is he saying?"

I yelled, "I think he wants you to change your socks!" I was just joking, not really thinking anyone would hear or notice. All of the sudden, I got tackled. *Boom!* I was down on the ground, underneath the helicopter, and I was getting pounded.

The instructor unloaded on me, and we're both wearing full combat equipment beneath a hovering helicopter. Obviously I'd upset this guy's ego enough, so he was having his way with me, having caught me completely off guard. We hustled and tussled and the guys pulled us apart.

Later that day we stood on the carpet of the commander. For all I knew, my career was over. At some point we have to own our mistakes. Some of it was on me. Before we left the office we were seeing eye to eye and they had my respect. These guys were different than the clowns at Kirtland. I felt good about it.

A week or so later I would be severely injured during an intense training scenario. There were destroyed buildings with simulated patients inside pinned under rubble. It was dynamic and very real training.

This was a cumulative exercise with all the bells and whistles. That night we had to access these pigs that were in the buildings, the pigs were our simulated patients. The pigs were beasts, some were two-hundred-pounders.

We had helo and Spooky gunship support. Once we located the correct building we had to clear the "patients" from the rubble. We used lift bags and extrication equipment to get the pigs out and treat them. An observer watches and sometimes videos the scene for later evaluation. Later as you watch the tape, they ask you, "Why did you make this decision; this; and this?" The pigs have critical injuries and you treat them up to a full surgical team handoff. Nothing is wasted. The anatomy of a pig is exactly like the inside of a human being. The airway. The organs. If you were to rip a pig apart and study the guts? The pig's is nearly the same as your own.

That night we had to extricate several rather large pigs. Big and fat, with pig shit and blood everywhere. The building was complete rubble. Rubbled buildings create extremely complex problems to solve. We had to move massive obstacles off the pigs to get to them. Florida. Humid summer heat. Two in the morning. After we had completed training for the night something felt out of place, like I had pulled a deep muscle in my lower back.

We had a reverse sleep schedule, so we woke up at noon the next day and headed out for PT. I noticed I started getting really bad foot drop. Then, all of a sudden, it felt as if something in my body switched off. I couldn't move my legs. I crumpled, falling in on myself, and collapsed to the asphalt like I'd been shot in the guts.

My buddy said, "Come on, stop fucking around, Roger. Get up!" He took one look at my face and realized this was something bad. "Oh, fuck, dude," he said. He dragged me to the side of the road and waved down a passing truck.

Whenever you damage your spinal cord you cannot will your body to move. You can't will your lower limbs to do anything because there's no signal. I knew something in my body had been seriously damaged. Something was stopping the signals from my brain telling my lower body to function.

Later that day I would learn that I had crushed and lacerated my spinal cord with disc fragments. In other words, I had partially severed my spine. The reality of this crashed over me in a devastating wave of grief, disbelief, and fear. The horror that overtook me that I had lost control of my lower limbs is beyond explanation. I would require surgery on my spine to remove the fragments that were inhibiting the signals within my back. These weren't herniated discs—they were fragmented.

Right away they wanted to put me on a heavy medication regimen. But I'd always resisted narcotics or pharmaceutical drugs of any kind. I don't know if this was from my upbringing as a kid, constantly being around drugs. Whatever the case, I wasn't into what they wanted to give me.

Because of referral management, insurance stuff, and my location, I waited three months to have surgery. I spent three months unable to truly walk. I couldn't bathe myself. I couldn't toilet myself. I couldn't help take care of our newborn son, Ozric. In terms of low points, this sat at the top of the shit heap of life events.

Being so utterly helpless at such a juncture in my life was completely humbling. I'd dealt with traumatic injuries as a young boy—the knee tumor, the fractured patella, and two knee surgeries—but I would recover from those. Constantly getting kicked in the balls, and recovering from physical damage, had in some way become a way of life for me. Plus, with my career choices, suffering was just a part of the job. But initially this was a bit different; in those three months of waiting, I hit the troughs of life's ups and downs.

At some point we get past ourselves and the pain that we inhabit creates our identity. I definitely passed through the tough phase with the help of friends and family, but some people don't; they don't survive that. Once again the level of pain, guilt, and shame forced me to realize I had to rise up again and defy what the doctors would tell me. I was a manifestation of the environment that had raised me, but I would define myself on my own terms.

I prepared myself mentally for the surgery and began making the needed mental preparations for my recovery as well. But the horror of what was coming the day after I got home from my spinal surgery would make everything I'd faced in my life pale in comparison.

12

SAVING OZ

There is a way of bringing up the child of a samurai.
—YAMAMOTO TSUNETOMO, *HAGAKURE*

My mom and dad came to Hurlburt Field to help Jennifer and Orion, my older son, watch the new baby and move us into a house on base. The house had nothing besides piles of boxes. My dad drove me to surgery while Jennifer, my mom, and Orion unpacked our stuff. Later, still affected by the drugs and trying to recover from the surgery, I sprawled out on a futon my dad and Jennifer had built for me to rest on while they unpacked the rest of the house. I was asleep and immobile, downstairs, and had been home no more than two hours from the hospital when I woke up to yelling and screaming. I was still wheelchair-bound and half-delirious from the anesthesia. I didn't know what the hell was happening. My dad came running into the room carrying our four-month-old. "Something's wrong, Rog!" he said.

He thrusts my baby boy into my arms. I didn't know this at the time, but my father went to go wake Oz from a nap and found him unresponsive. Oz's skin appeared pale blue. He wasn't breathing. I jumped up and leaned against the wall, standing on one leg and holding my baby boy tight against my chest. He wasn't breathing. I felt his neck. No pulse. Oz was small even for a four-month-old.

I had woken to a nightmarish scenario.

I began CPR by compressing his chest with my fingers, while holding him in my opposite forearm and hand.

We didn't have a phone connected in the new house yet, so Jennifer tore off for help, pulling the screen door off its hinges. This was before cell phones, so to go find a phone to call 911, she sprinted door to door to the neighbors we hadn't even met yet to call for an ambulance.

I continued working on Oz, pleading to him, talking to him, my tears running down my face and dripping onto his pale body.

After five or ten minutes he started having what are called agonal respirations. This is an abnormal gasping pattern of breathing, a brain reflex. This was better than nothing, but he really wasn't breathing or getting the oxygen he needed. I continued doing rescue breaths for twenty minutes, sweating and crying, and begging him to hold on until the paramedics came.

My older son, seven years old, Orion, stood in shock eight or ten feet away in the doorway, staring at Oz and me the whole time.

As a PJ, I was a fully credentialed paramedic. So I knew

that even when an ambulance would show up, someone with less medical knowledge than I had would likely step through the door. Often the people driving ambulances are EMTs, which is a vastly different level of medical expertise, and certainly not as advanced as a that of a paramedic. When the ambulance arrived I could tell these two weren't the best Florida had to offer. There was one paramedic, and the other guy a basic EMT. I was really hesitant to pass my son off to anyone, but I had no options; I couldn't walk. I handed him over. . . .

For me that was a helpless feeling, one I'll never forget. When the paramedic noticed that I couldn't walk we had a very awkward moment together. But I had little choice; I knew that in the process of trying to revive Oz that I'd probably damaged my back again. When the two guys had come into the room, they sort of stood there looking at me. I was this tall guy, leaning against the wall and giving chest compressions to my son. I could tell they were wondering why the hell I wasn't running my boy over to them.

I don't know what they thought of me. As a PJ, I had vast medical knowledge, and the Marine instructor in me took over. I lined out what they needed to do. After they left, I collapsed on the floor, emotional and shaking from pain and grief.

"Let's get you to the hospital," my dad said, adding, "Where is the hospital?"

"I don't know," I muttered, still wacked out from the surgery medication, starting to feel the physical pain from my efforts, and barely able to mentally process the emotions of what had suddenly happened to our lives.

The event occurred eight hours after surgery. I'd been instructed to be bedridden for weeks, yet instead I'm in the car with my dad, racing back to the hospital.

Jennifer had ridden in the ambulance with Oz to the emergency room. When we showed up I barged my way in, right as they were attempting to do an intraosseous infusion, basically a bone IV, because they couldn't get a normal IV in him. I screamed at them. They didn't know who I was, in terms of my medical skills, added to which I was in a wheelchair.

When you're in a wheelchair, you're very self-conscious of the fact that you're in a wheelchair.

I could tell they were thinking, *What the fuck kind of circus is this*? But I had to physically fight my way in to halt the procedure. "Stop doing that!" I said. "Don't fucking do that." And I was in the wheelchair shoving myself forward, and I was screaming at them, "Stop! I'm his father and you don't have consent to do that!" He wasn't dying of trauma so they didn't need to get an IV. I knew that when you do a procedure like that in a kid, you could stunt their bone development if you hit a growth plate. The intraosseous infusion (IVO) goes straight into the bone marrow and is supposed to be done only in life-and-death situations. In pararescue, we'll do an IVO on guys who are blown in half, but you don't do it to a kid who is breathing postresuscitation. But these medical professionals were freaking out, as if we'd entered a satiric skit of what happens in a country-bumpkin emergency room. I continued with my demands: "Your protocol is to get an IV, but not to stunt my son's growth. You don't have my consent. Stop!"

They seemed to think they were running a code still, but I pointed out that Oz was breathing. Once you have a patient breathing, as a paramedic, or in any emergency medicine, you administer blow-by oxygen. You don't even want your patient on 100 percent oxygen because that reduces the drive to breathe. They were freaking out, and I was really emotional, so they acquiesced. My wife was beside herself. Orion was hanging out: at seven, the perpetual silent observer. Outside I could hear a helo approaching, a neonatal helicopter arriving to fly my boy the hell out of the hillbilly ER.

The real medical professionals arrived, picked Oz and Jennifer up, and delivered them to Pensacola, the same place where I'd had surgery that day.

My dad took me home. I ate, still reeling from the whole junk show.

When I finally arrived to find Oz, he was sleeping, with IVs and tubes and wires running everywhere. They were trying to figure out what had happened. I told them it was positional asphyxia, that he'd rolled over while sleeping and couldn't breathe. But they had to do their full-court medical press to confirm that.

I spent the next week at the neonatal ICU, sleeping on the floor. I couldn't walk. We were so concerned about Oz that I couldn't focus on my own recovery.

After a week of being there, I went down to my neurosurgeon. "I think I fucked some shit up," I said.

"What happened?" he asked.

After I told him the story he got me an MRI that day. It turns out I had torn a bunch of deep sutures in my back while resuscitating Oz. I would endure a horrible recovery. The surgeon said he wasn't going back in for a minimum of three months. I waited another three months, but life at that point was all about Oz anyway.

A few years later, Oz would be diagnosed with cerebral palsy, which is basically a very loose term that means neurological lack of development. Neuroscience is voodoo medicine at best. They don't know the cause or the extent of the damage, but it can be anything. A person can be catatonic, have tremors, be unable to speak, or they have a limb that they can't use. Cerebral palsy is a neurological deficit that's caused by something that's not quite explainable. So as my son wasn't meeting some of his childhood milestones, he received the label of cerebral palsy.

At the same time we were dealing with all this, I was trying to recover from this severe and humbling injury of being paralyzed. I was using a walker and shuffling my feet, and unless you've never had to ride the little cart to go shopping at Walmart, you might not know what rock bottom is.

After my back surgery I went to my unit. I was on what we call "DNIF," duty not including flying. This was that first pararescue unit where I'd been assigned, the one they tried to get me to push Humvees around the parking lot. I was now pushing my walker. I'm usually tall and lean, but after the injury I was bone skinny. I looked like a giant version of Stephen Hawking. No muscle tone. The guys there were calling me all these names like "Auschwitz." They didn't even know about the stuff that had happened to my family and to Oz. The uncertainty to myself and my family was overwhelming.

No one knew to ask. This was my team. All they wanted to know was, "Are you ever getting off of DNIF?" "When the fuck are you coming back, Sparks?" I didn't even give them an answer, other than "Fuck you guys."

Emotionally, I found myself in a bad place. I had dear friends to help me out, but that was a dark time in my life for me and my wife, for my family. I used a walker for about six weeks, and did Pilates and yoga with every shred of my energy for about a year to get to where I could start to run again. At the end of two years I was running pretty well, and swimming pretty well, but I was not where I was before the injury. Before my paralysis, I ran five-minute miles, but this setback knocked me down. The only thing that I felt brought me back would be yoga and Pilates and the sheer determination to overcome the injury.

I also took a bit of the doctor's advice and accepted a little help from the pharmaceutical realm. I attribute what came next to the return to a positive shift in my mind-set, and to the Solu-Medrol the doc gave me, doses of a potent steroid anti-inflammatory which works specifically within the neural system to reduce inflammation. I did Pilates and yoga five or six times a day. Most of my waking hours I spent doing Pilates. That was what saved me. Not the weird Pilates with the devices, just the mat program.

On one of the last appointments with my neurosurgeon, he asked, "How are you doing?"

I responded by listing my routine of swimming and jogging, Pilates and yoga. "The one thing is that I've got to run on my toes, though," I said, "because I can't really control my right foot still. I've got a severe foot drop. But at least I can run on my toes, so I'm kind of figuring this thing out, Doc."

"So what is the strategy from here, Roger?"

"Well," I said, "I'm going to try to get back on status as soon as possible."

He looked at me, his face somewhat perplexed. "What is status? You don't plan on continuing your job as a Special Forces medic, are you, as a PJ?"

"Yeah," I replied, "that's what I'm doing."

He looked at me with deep concern. "What's wrong with you? Are you out of your mind?" His voice had that same tone as the doctor from my adolescence, the one who told me I'd never run again. "You know," he continued, "if you ever get injured again, you're not going to recover from this. Don't you realize this is probably going to happen again, and when it does, you aren't going to recover? You'll be in a chair the rest of your life. You're a weird success case, right now. I'd stick with that."

I shook my head. No way. I said, "This is what's happening, Doc."

Within two years of being paralyzed, I passed the PJ PT test again, and I was back on status. I attribute my recovery to many things: a little magic, resolve, and not allowing judgment to get in the way.

The guy who was with me in the street when I was paralyzed the first time introduced me to an old good friend, a charming and charismatic, honky-tonk kind of guy who grew up out in the sticks. He loved playing blues. They called him

June Bug. My friend knew I needed something to help me get through recovery and he knew I wanted to play guitar, so he brought me to June Bug. This man taught me how to play slide guitar in a four-hour period. June Bug knew magic when it came to slide and fingerpicking blues. He said, "Listen, man. Don't ever learn to read sheet music, and don't read them tabs or anything. Just try to make your music sound like a train."

"What do you mean?" I asked.

"Think about them old uneducated poor souls working them chain gangs and stuff, and those old suppressed brothers playing the Delta blues. You think you're as smart as them?" he asked me.

I nodded.

Then, "just think about it. Freedom to them was riding them trains. So all their songs have this backbone, this subconscious rhythm of a train. Think only about being on a train and play. That is the blues, man. That's the Delta blues, right there."

With that advice, I hopped on the train and escaped the confines of my wheelchair, using the three or four different chords he taught me. You have to be ready to hear advice like that, and I was. The words June Bug shared that day resonated right to the core of my being.

The magic ingredients of life are right there. Whether you are learning to play a guitar or walk again. You have to be open to the advice of the world, and then to have the grit to follow that advice. This is the magic ingredient. Think about it, then do it. Who cares if you fail, or fall, so long as you do try, and try again. If you see where you want to go, and do the things you need to get there? That is the magic.

If I've ever learned anything in life, it's this: Don't let the judgment of others get in your way.

13

THE ALASKA FACTOR

The wisdom and courage that come from compassion are real wisdom and courage. When one punishes or strives with the heart of compassion, what he does will be limitless in strength and correctness.

—YAMAMOTO TSUNETOMO, *HAGAKURE*

My recovery is very personal because it was tough, and I was desperate. I was never trying to be Superman or anything. Recovering my mobility and getting back in the saddle was all I knew how to do, so the healing kind of took care of itself. There are rigorous qualifications you have to maintain as a pararescueman. You have to be able to run three miles in around twenty minutes, and you have to be able to do a ridiculous amount of swimming, pull-ups, push-ups, and sit-ups in a short time. I basically trained myself to get back to that level of fitness, and surpass the simple standards, which allowed me to be able to return to my status as a PJ, but I was by no means physically right to do that job anymore. For all intents and purposes, my back was still really fucked up. When I carried heavy things my legs would go numb; and when I sat for long periods of time, I would lose the ability to feel my legs or wiggle my toes. Sure I passed the standards, but now I'm doing HALO drops with an absurd amount of weaponry and equipment, extrication tools to cut people out of burning wreckage, and all sorts of heavy shit. Training was difficult because I knew that everything still wasn't right with my back.

But again, the military was all I knew, so I continued to train myself to be able to do the job. I give much of the credit to Pilates; if you're injured, I really suggest you give that a shot, because that is the elixir of life, it's not any bullshit. If there was a fountain of youth to be found in my life, Pilates was it. Those are the things that really brought me back. But recovery was not a simple process. It would take five years of dedicated effort to get closer to my old self.

Florida had tried to kill me, so I couldn't wait to ditch Hurlburt Field and try somewhere new. The hallmark of being one of the elite within pararescue, in my opinion, means going to Alaska. The Alaska PJs, the 212th, are cut from a special cloth. Basically they do all of the same combat stuff within Special Operations when they deploy, but they handle the highest rate of civilian rescue in the world. As a pararescueman I was attracted to that opportunity, so when a spot opened, I applied for it. Honestly, I was also pretty scared they wouldn't take me because of my injuries.

I dialed the 212th. It turned out I knew the guy who answered. Once I told him I was interested he said, "We'll take you, Roger!" I didn't even check out. I took leave and drove the 4,480 miles straight to Alaska. I shared the trip with my father, and that in and of itself was a special time for both of us.

When I arrived, I strolled into the old 212th Section, an old building in Spenard, a seedy part of Anchorage at the time, complete with pimps and drugged-out hookers, and announced my presence, "I'm here. Roger Sparks."

The guy at the desk looked down at my paperwork and said, "We can't take you in, Roger! You're still haven't completely checked out of active duty." For a while it seemed I'd gotten myself into a bit of a pickle. But Skip Kula, the chief at the time, looked into my situation and took care of it for me. The Alaska team can really make stuff happen.

I'd found my new home. Alaska wasn't only a beautiful place to live, it would provide me with a lifetime of surreal experiences. It wasn't uncommon for us to rescue people once a week, sometimes more. With remote and hard-to-reach places, and people living in places of extreme weather and far from medical assistance, it's hard to really describe the scope of what an Alaskan PJ does. For perspective, when we head off on a search, rescue, or recovery, it's similar to someone getting in a helo and taking off from Dallas, Texas, to execute a rescue in Montana. These are huge distances, with aerial refueling of the helo from a C-130, endless hours in the helo, and those on the ground awaiting help in truly desperate circumstances. Without us, they would most likely die. As an Alaskan PJ, in each situation you face you're taking all the skills you have to salvage human life. Not only were we doing that with Special

Operations units and combatants in Afghanistan and around the world, we're executing those risky civilian rescues weekly, year in and year out in Alaska.

I'd landed in a coveted position, in Valhalla for para-rescue. Everybody in the business knows about the Alaska 212th. At the absolute apex of my career, at the height of my capability, I would get to serve in that capacity. I'd successfully moved from being an instrument of destruction to focus on protecting and saving lives.

The first rescue of my Alaskan PJ career brought to bear the impact my new job would have on me, and helped me better understand my new role saving lives and my new home. A church group had hiked thirty miles out in the middle of nowhere. The pastor leading the group had arranged for a pilot to buzz the hikers and surprise them with an airdrop of a bunch of warm Kentucky Fried Chicken or something. The pilot was a member of the congregation, and inside he had the pastor's son, as well as another passenger. In the middle of attempting to drop the chicken, the pilot miscalculated and crashed the plane right into the mountain in front of them. The impact killed the pilot and the other adult passenger instantly. But the son, trapped inside, was still alive, with what appeared to be a mortal injury. This wreckage sat on a narrow finger ridge far above the hikers. In desperation they raced up the mountain to reach the small Cessna, and placed the call for help.

We arrived with our Pave Hawk. Normally we have two PJs inside, but on this day we had four, because from the sounds of the call we knew the situation was bad.

We hoisted in from the ridge above. The crashed plane sat in a precarious position, right on the edge of a precipice, with a steep cliff below. The aircraft threatened to come off the mountain, so we had to secure the wreckage before we could even access those inside. The pastor had climbed up into the aircraft and sat holding his son in his arms, rocking him, his face red, his cheeks covered with tears.

Since I was the junior guy, they sent me in as the medic. I climbed into the wreckage. Inside I discovered a grisly crash scene. The pilot and the passenger in front were dead. The yoke of the plane had smashed into the pilot's chest. The plane smelled of blood, bile, and aviation fuel.

The boy's eyes were swollen shut, and his guts were hanging out of his ass. He was all ripped up, coughing out black gelatinous globs. When people are involved in trauma they will swallow a lot of blood. The stomach congeals the blood and turns it into something that looks like coffee grounds.

This poor father, grief-stricken and in a state of utter despair, looked right at me. He was stroking his son's bloody hair. Then he spoke to his boy, saying, "I told you the PJs were coming, buddy." Then he looked right at me again and said, "Please. Don't let my boy die."

The kid was probably sixteen. He handed him right to me, so I started doing my assessment and started treating him. The intensity and weight of what my position was in that moment, and the weight of what I was representing to that father, that I was this mercy, love, and grace, that I was supposed to work a miracle for him, that he was asking me to do the impossible right then and there, and this was my new job deeply hit home.

What I represented to him at that moment overwhelmed me. The responsibility was empowering, but also horrifying.

Aviators in Alaska know who the PJs are. In my hometown back in Texas no one would know what a PJ was. But there I was on the side of a mountain, thousands of miles and light-years away from the world I grew up in, and this father holding his dying son knew more about me than anyone.

Save his boy? How was I supposed to do that when I knew full well what would most likely happen on the helicopter flight to the hospital, despite anything I could do? Pre–hospital treatment, short of stopping bleeding and providing blood products, is about all that can be done in the field. I can place a surgical airway into someone's throat, but other than that, those are the three solid tools I have at my disposal.

I did all I could for the kid, and emotionally I knew how that father felt. I knew that awful, sinking, powerless feeling of sending your boy away with strangers and knowing you might not see him alive again. The one difference might have been that this man seemed to have complete faith in me, a PJ. As gently as possible, I extracted the boy from the wreckage. One of my teammates helped me place him on a litter, and we hoisted him up and into the helo. We raced him back to Providence Hospital in Anchorage, managing to keep him stable during the flight. I couldn't get the look of the father's eyes out of my head. I kept hearing him pleading with me over and over, "Don't let my boy die. Don't let my boy die."

I never followed up on the boy's condition after we processed him at the hospital and flew back to base. I pushed thoughts of him from my mind.

Paying the price to represent so much hope for the father at that moment overwhelmed me. That was a powerful beginning to my work in Alaska, and I thought about it as a metaphor for my new career field. I'd lived on the cliff edge of life and death my entire military career, always going toward danger, and too often for destructive purposes. But now I would be making rescues and recoveries on the edge of Alaskan precipices, in often the most beautiful wilderness landscapes you can imagine, and I would be heading into harm's way for others. Yet risks, rewards, and emotional toll accumulate like snowflakes on a growing glacier.

A year or so later my world would come full circle. Commonly new guys on the team draw the short straws. This time I was "voluntold" to put in some face time with the public by sitting with one of our Pave Hawks during the Fourth of July weekend, hanging out at Anchorage's Park Strip and mingling with the kids and their parents. I was sitting there, basically twiddling my thumbs, showing off the helo to little wide-eyed children. I looked out among the sea of faces as two men slowly approached me: the father and his son from the plane wreck.

I'd had men die at my hands, and had seen many teammates die, and watched that old truck driver die in my arms, but other than Oz—being faced with the mortality of a human being's existence dependent on me—this was the second person whose life was in my hands.

And there the boy stood, smiling. On crutches, but alive. The boy and his father thanked me. That moment hit home in a strange and powerful way.

Craig, my former boss from the bike shop, and I had stayed connected throughout our time apart. When I moved to Alaska I invited him to come north. One of the beautiful things about Alaska is sharing it with people you care about. Craig was able-bodied enough and of the right mind. It was just perfect for me to share some hair-raising adventures with him.

It's with Craig that I learned how quickly a day of Alaskan fun might quickly escalate into a situation where the services of the 212th could come in handy.

I'd gotten Craig into pack rafting. These are small, lightweight, single-person rafts for white water. I was really into the excitement and the feel of being on the water. I lived right by Eagle River and had access to some great rapids. The very first time I took Craig on the river, he was hooked.

"What do you think?" I asked as we made our way up the bank.

He responded in his classic Texas drawl: "*Holy shit*, Rog." He loved it. Craig was in his element in Alaska. Craig was at that perfect moment in his life where he synced with the beauty of everything going on around him. I loved how much he appreciated and admired where we lived. Together we became very enamored with the beauty of Alaska. We did more and more pack rafting together, and began to get into some gnarly stuff, by anybody's standards. We began to take our rafting a step further. We're actually lucky we're not dead. Much of what we were attempting could have killed us. If you're doing the local Campground Rapids, if you know what you're doing, it's not a big deal, but we were learning on the bad stuff, and learning the "Alaska factor" together. The Alaska factor is when the danger level of what you're attempting is, well, Alaskan size.

As a PJ, I could experience the Alaska factor stuff with fellow PJs, but to do this stuff with Craig made the time really special. I could go on adventures with the PJs I worked with, but it wasn't the same. I'm not exactly sure why; the two of us sparked something different. Perhaps it was personal versus professional, the mentor role versus being with a dear friend, where I'm learning and sharing alongside him.

One of our most intense Alaska factor moments came when we hiked Crow Pass together, a twenty-six-mile hike and raft combo, which in and of itself isn't a big deal when skilled and prepared, but there were a couple of things against us. They always say there are three things that are going to kill you, not one. We had our three things lined up quite nicely. One, we got a late start, so dark was falling when we hit the river. Two, the entire week leading up to the time we did the hike had been torrential downpour. Three, the evening temperature sat right at the freezing point. Horrible, wet cold. That's what kills people.

By this point Craig and I were competent pack rafters, but we were really pushing the audacity envelope. We had never surveyed the river. One of the biggest dangers of rafting Alaskan rivers are the trees extending out from the banks. These are called sweepers. The rivers in Alaska are geologically new, so when you're rafting, you're constantly getting dumped into these sweepers. Even the most competent pack rafters, or at least the ones who want to survive, will survey the river to determine the situation ahead.

When we reached the river, with evening dark falling fast, we took one look at it and I said, "Fuck it, let's do it." We worked quick to get the boats built. We were going to cannonball-run it. We were thinking we had nothing to lose. The water was too high to ford to get to the trail on the other side of the river. We faced a walk back in the dark, or a freezing night with no tent or sleeping bags. Moments earlier we had walked by a bear. The sun had just set. We needed to get home.

The river was, in one word, huge. Whatever the water volume at the head of Eagle River is normally was doubled that night. The rapids thundered. You couldn't hear yourself scream.

I tried to hatch a plan before we launched. I didn't like the looks of things. I yelled to Craig, "Watch close! If you see me get out, then get out with me! I'm going to give it a hundred yards, we're going to go up around this bend, and if I don't like it, we're getting out on the other side."

That's all it took. In seconds, we were fucked.

We would always travel alpine style, light and fast. I was wearing shorts and a raincoat. Ideally, I would be wearing a dry suit, a life jacket, and a helmet. This was glacier-cooled water, hovering a few degrees above freezing. I've had a friend cross the river at the point we put our rafts in, and the water was so cold that his brand-new hiking sandals delaminated, so the soles came off. This water is so cold that it feels more like a burn when it hits your skin. It will instantly reduce your body core temperature to dangerously hypothermic levels.

So we entered this frigid raging water by our own wits, because that is how you learn, right? I went first, and Craig was right behind me, and immediately I realized that the standing waves were so big we'd gotten lost in the height of the rollers. I couldn't see anything ahead, not the sweepers or the boulders ahead of us. The very moment I dropped into the river, I shot down into the first huge trough and drenched the boat. I was paddling like crazy, instantly worried about Craig, and I was thinking, *FUCK! We need to get out right now! This is bad!*

I paddled out of the hole. This was where the situation got crazy. The water was so big, and we were both dealing with so much of the torrent, that Craig couldn't really track me. At about the moment I pulled my boat out, the valley went dark. We didn't have visual aids like chem lights or strobe lights. And this dense blanket of ice fog began dropping down on us, so I couldn't see more than five or ten yards down the river.

Standing on the riverbank, I saw Craig whipping past. He was going fast. He was chasing a ghost. My ghost. I screamed at the top of my lungs, "Craig!!!!" He couldn't hear, and he was twenty feet away and disappearing into the darkness.

I threw my raft into the river, dove into it, and started paddling as fast as I could toward him. Twenty or thirty feet down, the river curved to the left, and I hit a giant boulder. Hard. I flipped. I was underwater, pinned within a hydraulic, which is like being thrown into one of those front-facing Laundromat washers, if they came in a size that could fit a sedan. I was frantic, but not frantic about myself. I was frenzied with the thought of getting to my buddy before the same thing happened to him and I couldn't find him. I was so jacked with adrenaline that I couldn't even feel the cold. I was pinned underwater, in a horrible situation, but all I could think about was Craig. I fought myself out and swam to shore. I looked around. *Where the fuck did my boat go?* I had no survival equipment, no boat, nothing. There was a firearm in my raft pack, too. I needed everything in there, but now I had nothing. *Fuck it.*

Desperation took hold. Something like a gear clicked in my brain. Nothing mattered but the task at hand. In the *Hagakure* there is a passage about how you can get your head cut off, but you can still do two actions after that occurs. That is how focused you have to be in situations like this. They'll cut your head off but you'll sheath your sword before you fall over. You'll do two things after your head is rolling away. That is how focused you are in moments of life and death, because this is what you're doing and what you know; you have to get scuffed up and beat up to be that way.

I did the unthinkable. I dove back into the water and found myself pinned in the same hydraulic. I swept my arms around, searching for my boat. Despite the numbing cold, I could feel something smooth. I could differentiate between the rock and the raft. I was underwater, feeling for the rock and the boat. I grabbed the rubber and planted my feet on the rock, and with every ounce of strength left in me, I wrenched it and *boom!* Out came the raft. I stayed clinging to it, and it popped to the surface. At first I was upside down underneath. I was floating downstream, my body getting hit by rocks. Then I flipped it over and jumped inside.

I had no paddle, and the pack that was secured on my

boat was gone. *Fuck.* I lay facedown in my boat and hit a series of big rapids. Using my long arms to paddle, I half rafted, half swam until I hit a strainer—a big tree leaning down into the water—and grabbed the log, jumping up on it to get out of the river.

I was standing there shivering with an empty raft, alone.

A horrible, sinking feeling fell over me. I couldn't even think about what I'd just dealt with because I knew Craig was likely dead. I ran up and down the river, through dense alders and brush. When I hit slower sections of the water I would lie in my boat and swim, trying to close distance, but then I worried that he would be trying to come back for me.

I stopped in this one section where the river rolled around to the right. Despite the dark, I had a decent view. I could only hope he was probably holed up. I got out of the water, tossed my raft and searched the immediate area. I hoped liked hell we were just missing each other. I didn't have a light. I didn't have anything.

That night was cold, too. Really cold. All I could do was wait for enough light, but I knew that when the light started to break, the air would get a little colder at first. I had to keep moving, so I did calisthenics to keep warm. As soon as the light came up enough, I ran up and down the river searching for him and searching for his boat. Then, when the sense of loss and desperation became too much, I got back in my boat, flying down the river toward the rapids near the Eagle River Yurt, a structure people can hike to and camp at. The river conditions were still gnarly. I was lying on my stomach in the boat and swimming in that freezing water, in a state of utter despair. I got to this spot where the trail was and sprinted the final few miles back to the Nature Center. I jumped on the pay phone and called Jennifer collect. I'm sure she sensed the desperation in my voice: "Come get me. I need coffee. A change of clothes, and some food," I said, adding, "I think Craig might be dead."

Jennifer hauled ass up the valley. She picked me up. I was emotional and deeply exhausted. Blaming myself for my friend's death. We drove back to our house. I was shell-shocked. We arrived back at our home and got a plan together. "Fuck it," I said, "I'm going back to get Craig's body. I've got to go find him."

I packed up some gear and headed back.

I'd been gone for a few moments when Jennifer's phone rang. Distraught herself, she picked it up. "Jennifer," the trembling voice on the other line said, "It's Craig; we ran into some trouble on the river, and I think Roger might be dead."

"Hold your thunder, Craig," Jennifer said. "Roger will be there in a little bit. He's driving that way right now."

I pulled into the parking lot at the trailhead, and there stood Craig. We shared an intense hug of friendship renewed, and in a way resurrected. Neither of us thought we'd see each other alive again. We took a photo to commemorate the moment, though we'd never need the photo to remind us of how lucky we'd been.

Later, Craig would share his story. He'd wisely gotten out of his boat right away and then searched the banks for me, with no luck. He'd struggled to keep warm that night, certain he'd freeze to death, even going so far as to take out his camera and record a good-bye video to his family. When morning came he hiked his way out, probably on the trail around the same time as I raced on down the river.

A few days passed and we headed back to the river in search of my pack and pistol. We found the pack a few miles downriver caught up in a sweeper downstream from where I'd gotten stuck under the hydraulic.

In my career as a PJ here, I would see more than my share of people who weren't as lucky as Craig and me that night on Eagle River.

14

A WOLF'S RESOLVE

When something out of the ordinary happens, it is ridiculous to say that it is a mystery or a portent of something to come. Eclipses of the sun and moon, comets, clouds that flutter like flags, snow in the fifth month, lightning in the twelfth month, and so on, are all things that occur every fifty or one hundred years. They occur according to the evolution of Yin and Yang. The fact that the sun rises in the east and sets in the west would be a mystery, too.

—YAMAMOTO TSUNETOMO, *HAGAKURE*

We received a call of a plane crash in the Brooks Range. The Brooks Range is a long way from Anchorage, where we were based. This is that helicopter ride from Texas to Montana I told you about. We hear: plane crash, six people isolated. That's all it takes for us to get airborne and headed north. Sometimes the reports we get are fragmented, and since the reports are often erroneous, we always plan for the worst-case scenario.

Sometimes "worst case" simply refers to worst use of government resources.

This time we flew out with four PJs. We spotted a short, primitive runway on a small open clearing in the mountains. A Cessna sat in a crumpled wreck there, balled up on landing in an attempt to pick up hunters. When we landed the helo, we had to set down uncomfortably close to the wreck, because there wasn't space to land anywhere else. Leaking fuel from the wreckage had spilled all over the ground. Luckily there was no fire.

A bunch of sheep hunters stood there staring at us. We were in a helicopter, so we didn't need the runway, but these guys seemed incompetent, and insensitive to the situation. They appeared only concerned about their trophy kills and getting out. Their pilot sat upside down, dead in the aircraft. The plane sat flipped over and lying on the runway, shuddering from the winds whipped up by our rotors. Planes don't weigh much for their size. They needed to move it off the runway for another plane to come in and help get their asses out of the wilderness, and they hadn't even done that, the dead body of the pilot was still in the aircraft.

I yelled orders at the hunters. The helicopter was refueling with a C-130 above us while I got the hunters to help us flip the plane over. I began to remove the pilot, and forced those guys to help me. They were just completely detached from what had taken place. They acted as if they didn't know what to do. We had to explain to them that if they wanted us to help them, they needed to leave their trophy kills to get into our aircraft, and we would drop them in the nearest village or with the authorities. When we take control of people, whether they are injured or uninjured, or need care or deny medical care, we have to hand them over to the Alaska State Troopers. That is just the responsible thing to do, because now we're involved legally.

The hunters refused. Essentially they said, "No, we'll just stay with our trophies. We'll just stay here. We'll call in another aircraft."

"Are you fucking kidding me?" I said. I was just amazed at how detached they were at what had taken place. They acted like they didn't even give a shit that a man had died coming to get them. That we had flown for hours to pick them up. All they appeared concerned about was not giving up their trophies. *Really?* That blew me away. I was pissed. They denied service from us, but I made them carry the pilot to our helicopter. With our gear and the body, the quarters in the helo would be cramped anyway.

I had some time to let the anger toward those hunters stew during the next six hours on the flight home, all the while leaning against the pilot's body.

One bizarre rescue came in August 2006, when the Alaskan fall rains were really starting up. A mudslide hit outside of Girdwood. The road running up to the Crow Pass trailhead, the one Craig and I had left from on our near-death rafting trip, had been wiped out by a big slab of mud, so all these tourists and hikers were trapped.

We hoisted dogs, luggage, and nearly fifty people from one side of the slide to the other. That was a bizarre rescue in the sense of how it felt routine. We were there for nearly six hours, with multiple midair refueling runs. Sometimes I would go with the aircraft; sometimes, when there were kids or elderly, I would stay on the ground with them to explain how the hoist up would work. The littlest kids took extra effort. I would stuff a child into an A3 kit bag, zip the little one in, and signal the helo for a hoist up. The dogs weren't to be left behind. I had never imagined my work as a PJ would include tucking a big golden retriever in a nylon zip bag, with only his head poking out, fighting like hell to get out and hoisting him up into the blue summer sky.

Refueling for that mission was classic Alaska factor. All happening in Turnagain Arm, a shallow fjord with steep mountains on each side. We were flying at two thousand feet, in a constant bank, with a pretty serious butt-pucker factor, poking the end of a long lance that sticks out from the front of the Pave Hawk into what looks like a balloon trailing out behind the back of a C-130. At several points while we refueled, small bush planes would fly alongside us with the passengers waving. We'd shake our heads, all thinking: *Get the hell out of here, man! You can't just fly a bush plane a hundred feet from a C-130 and a Pave Hawk refueling*!

That was one bizarre day of Alaskan rescue, but just one of countless experiences.

If we can't fly a helo in for a rescue, we can jump. After all, PJ means pararescue, and the *para* is for parachuting.

We train constantly, which means jumping all the time,

but jump missions don't happen that often. There has to be "definitive loss of life" if we don't interact. It's a risk threshold calculation. It takes the command approval to execute a jump mission, but our commander, Blake Gettys, trusted our judgment in the field. The C-130 has satellite communications onboard. When it came down to it, Gettys would discuss with the crew asking, "are people's lives in danger? Can you reasonably mitigate the dangers involved?" And if we said yes, then he'd say, "Then execute."

Then, once a teammate and I had landed and we made an assessment of the scene, the first person we called to relay the situation would be the commander of the rescue assets in Alaska, Gettys.

The jumps are notable because you have to have reason to believe you'll have loss of life if you don't interrupt what is taking place. Sometimes it makes more sense to jump than not jump. Usually it will take twice as long for the helicopter to reach the scene. Most of the time you should just wait. You ask yourself, *Are you making the situation better or worse by jumping in?* If you jump, then you're adding more men on the ground who have to be retrieved. Now you have a helo filled with PJs and equipment, and then it becomes like *Planes, Trains, and Automobiles* to recover all those resources. It's a risk matrix.

An example of how we would choose to jump or not happened one time when I was training a really dear friend and PJ, Leo Claunan. We received a Mayday call. A guy was having a heart attack on a clamming boat that was beached not far from where we were about to jump. This was a total bluebird day. Perfect for jumping. Ten-knot winds, with an elderly man having a heart attack on a boat. We were already rigged and ready to jump. I was now going to have the PJ I was training be the guy to do the jump. So his first rescue jumpmaster training procedure was going to be on a real mission. I was excited for him. We flew over the boat, and threw streamers to gauge the wind. We were ready to execute. The helo was en route and not far behind us. So it didn't make sense for us to jump, but at the same time, it did. The guy was having a heart attack. The natural instinct was to jump and get on him right away. The more suddenly you defibrillate and get certain drugs in the body, the better the threshold for recovery.

I have no doubt we would have landed five feet from the boat and run in there and taken care of everything, but it didn't happen that way. We could see the helo out in Cook Inlet below us, and they shut us down. *Damn.* I felt bad for Leo. But jumping and getting on the ground and placing hands on the patient would have taken 15–20 minutes. So to parachute in just didn't make sense.

For the 212th, situations like that happen all the time.

I've been through that scenario half a dozen times. In the open door of a C-130 ready to jump and at the last moment we're called off.

Brandon Stuemke and I did a very risky mission to Little Diomede. We made the 538-mile flight from Anchorage in the C-130. This was an infant-in-distress call. The baby suffered from breathing difficulty. It is fair to say that Little Diomede is an island in the middle of nowhere. The village has no landing strip, and if the ocean isn't frozen, the only way in is by helicopter. The situation sounded dire for the child, but would be equally risky for Stuemke and myself. We would be intentionally jumping into the water with all our gear, including pediatric gear to sustain him, until we could get a helo in to recover us and the child. We had approval before we even launched from Anchorage. Leadership said, "Jump authorized. Execute."

I was the team leader, with Stuemke at my side. We were ready. We were ready to do it and it was going to be sketchy. There are certain procedures you have to take with windy conditions. If it's blowing one way, you've got to do a crosswind pattern, and it would be as gnarly as it could be, technically. Add to this extreme cold. The ocean wasn't frozen, but it was as close to freezing as it could get. We'd initially planned to jump to their helo pad on the west side, where a road comes around the side of a very steep mountain. The helicopter pad was small, thirty by thirty feet, and elevated thirty or forty feet. Stuemke and I were certainly capable of landing on that helo pad in the most adverse of conditions. But with the high winds we were facing, plus or minus a second or two, it would have been catastrophic to land off the pad. Initially I thought, *Let's just go for the fucking pad*. But as the team leader, you have to consider bad possibilities and mitigate the risk. So I said, "No, fuck it, Stuemke; we're doing a water jump."

Off this little town on the edge of the world, Stuemke and I were going to jump into the water near where they had metal junk and debris. I figured we might get hurt jumping in there, but the risk was better than trying to hit the small helo pad in the winds.

We were in the aircraft, rigged and ready. We threw streamers, gauged the wind speeds, and readied to jump. Then in came a call from Nome. They said they had an Army Black Hawk that could deliver us in. We were seconds from jumping into the Bering Sea.

Then came the always deflating order: "Stand down."

We turned back and landed in Nome. Stuemke and I piled into the Black Hawk. There wasn't any crew. Just one pilot, Stuemke, and myself. We flew twenty to thirty feet over the ocean, the whole way there. Battered by these crazy winds, with rough seas beneath us.

We landed on the same helo pad to a little bit of a surprise.

The infant wasn't really in that much distress. But there waiting for us were three pregnant women with bags packed, all in their third trimester, and ready to get off the island to go have their babies at a warm hospital in a city.

We didn't even need to attempt that jump for what we found on the ground, but we didn't know that until we got there. The kid was having a hard time breathing, but a little oxygen and an albuterol treatment and the kid was fine. We loaded the three women with their bags and flew back to Nome.

Classic Alaska. It is what it is. We felt a bit duped after being so close to taking such a risky leap, but that would not be my last helicopter flight with pregnant women. One rescue would stand out, not for *who* we were saving, but *what* we were saving the expectant mother and her young child *from*.

This call came in as a pregnant woman in distress, and the situation had all the right elements for a modern-day horror movie. We were dispatched by helicopter to the northern Yukon Territory, close to the border. The location was close enough that the rescue coordination center was going to call in SAR Techs, the Canadian version of the PJs. Our unit often coordinates with Canada for missions along the Yukon border. This was one of those cases; the assessment was that we could get there quicker than they could.

A pregnant woman, a young child, and a grandmother were essentially being held hostage in their cabin. The men had gone on an extended hunting party, and the cabin was surrounded by a pack of aggressive wolves. The wolves were becoming increasingly brazen, beginning to attempt to get into the cabin. The two women were actively trying to fend off the wolves with 7.62 assault rifles, but despite the gunfire, the wolves continued to threaten them.

As soon as we were within range, we could see it was a "no bullshit" call. This pregnant woman had every right to be in distress. We could see the dozen or so members of the pack. Gray, white, black, and big. The wolves had packed a trail, in the deep snow, in rings around the cabin where they had continually circled.

The ambient temperature, without wind, sat at nearly sixty below. Right at the cutoff for safe flight in the HH-60. As he set us up to hoist in, the pilot said, "You guys have about thirty seconds, Roger!" He needed Doug, the other PJ, and me to get out fast because at those temperatures the cold air sinks. This is called a temperature inversion. At sixty below we're beyond the limit of the hydraulic systems of the helicopter, everything inside freezes up, and something can malfunction.

As soon as we touched the ground and unhooked, the helicopter took off. My eyelids froze open. I couldn't move my eyes. The whirly-whirl effect of 120 mph rotors at that temperature created a blizzard of wind chill beyond description. The chill on human flesh in those conditions is roughly 132 degrees below zero. Add to the ridiculous cold that we had landed in the worst possible place: a garbage heap. Doug and I were cutting up our legs from tin cans and sharp old chunks of discarded snow-machine parts. The helo hovered as low and close to the cabin as it could, offering us the only protection we had. Those wolves were circling in, trying to get us. They showed no fear. In the middle of winter deep in the Yukon these stoic animals have nothing to lose. *Desperation is the coldest of killers and they were at the point of risking their lives to eat.*

Unlike when we're deployed overseas, we were unarmed. We only had that big-ass helicopter for protection as we made our way to the cabin. The pilot flared the rotors in an attempt to scare the wolves away.

We post-holed our way through deep surface hoarfrost to the cabin. Inside we found the grandmother, expectant mom, and toddler. We introduced ourselves and quickly assessed that we didn't need to render any immediate aid there in the cabin. We needed to get out to the helicopter and out of there. I could see both the worry and relief on their faces. "Do you have your IDs and your wallets?" I asked.

They readied themselves to go, and we helped quickly close up the cabin. We put out the bear boards—boards with big nails facing outward—and secured everything. The wolves continued to circle. The helicopter seemed to be keeping them at bay for the time being.

I searched for the best way to safely carry the infant to the helo without freezing the poor critter. I glanced around the small log cabin and spotted a sleeping bag.

I told Doug to help the granny. I grabbed the kid and stuffed him in the bottom of the sleeping bag, which I lifted into the air and gave a twist, and then tied the top in a knot. With the kid slung over my back and crying, I picked up the woman, and we shuffled out through the snow to the pickup point.

We had carefully coordinated the timing and location the helo would land to minimize the cold inversion as well as our exposure from the pack. As we lifted away the wolves grouped together and stared up at our departure.

The wolves would have to find something or someone else to eat that night.

You get to see a lot of things by helicopter in remote Alaska that you just can't see otherwise. Sights even most Alaskans will never see. One of the weirdest things I saw occurred north of the Alaska Range. We were headed to Eielson Air Force Base in Fairbanks to spend a week on alert. Every once in a while in flight we'll see a pack of wolves. In my decade or so of para-rescue I've seen them only half a dozen times. Any Alaskans who spend time in the wilderness will tell you it is special to see a pack of wolves, perhaps with the rare exception of the people in the past story.

This particular time we flew over a full pack, two dozen or more. This pack was unbelievably coordinated. When they saw us they immediately started to take what I can only call evasive maneuvers, revealing a palpable hyperintelligence. Almost like a school of orca, they orchestrated their movements. You could tell communication was happening on the ground. They were barking to each other; some sort of intelligent vocabulary, you could plainly see, because they were reacting in ways that were strategic. The females and the pups cut off in a specific direction into the woods while the males raced off into the open, as if to lure us to them. And then, once they reached the open meadow, they ran in circles at first, then all simultaneously stopped. The helicopter banked, and we came into a low hover. The whole pack of adult males lined out in front of us. Then, in a flash, all the wolves took off except one.

A massive black wolf stood in front of us.

I don't know a lot about wolves, but of the ones that I've seen, this was the king. He was really long-legged, and tall. Gangly. Kind of like me. Strong and lean. Black, jet-black fur.

He stood there showing no fear. In a hover forty feet away we opened the door and started snapping photos. We'd all fallen into total Alaskan tourist mode. In our defense this was an extraordinary sight for even the saltiest of Alaskan sourdoughs.

The alpha stood his ground. Imagine a helicopter hovering forty feet above a creature that it completely outweighs and outsizes, with the supernatural abilities this helicopter has to the wolf, yet here was this wolf, ready to kill the helicopter. The wolf felt threatened but stood his ground, as if to say, *You're dying today.*

To witness the wolf's resolve, focus, and intent to take on the impossible was profound to me that day. He knew exactly what he was doing. I felt this deep respect for those creatures in that moment, not in the humorous honey-badger-will-kick-your-ass kind of way, but more like *Damn—don't let me out of the helicopter.* I suppose it is easy to get clichéd about a moment like this. But that creature was so intelligent in the way he communicated his intentions with his pack, risking all for his family and fellow warriors. In a sense: *Here are your orders. You go this way. You go that. Now split. I've got this.*

To be honest, 90 percent of a pararescueman's career is window gazing. Part of the job is sitting at the window of a loud rumbling Pave Hawk or a droning C-130 for hours on end, lost in thought, and looking out at terrain so beautiful a person could become numb to the landscape if he's not careful. I'd spend time imagining places I might return for adventure someday. When you're an avid ice-climber and you spy a straight vertical ice waterfall that is turquoise blue and rises up two thousand feet, you can't help but dream big. I could look down and know for certain that no one had climbed those falls. Right away I'd ask the pilot, "Can you get a way point where that icefall is? I'd love to come back out to spend some quality time."

Sights like monstrous icefalls or volcanic mountains jutting out from the ocean take your breath away. The view isn't always pleasant, though, and usually when the PJs are needed, that means the weather conditions are too treacherous for anyone else to respond. In those situations there is nothing to see out the window, or, if you're looking out the window, it's part desperation or concern about what you'll see. In times like that—zero visibility, whether it's snow, or rain, or fog—you're relying on the skills of some extremely gifted pilots, and on luck. Your life is no longer in your own hands. After a while you become inoculated to any concerns for your own well-being at that moment, because there is nothing you can do but hold on and interact with what the crew tells you. Sometimes you never get to the folks you're supposed to rescue, and you become the one who needs rescuing.

One of many examples of this came when we took a call for a sinking fishing boat off the Aleutian Islands in the Bering Sea. We flew directly into a typical Alaska storm, the sort of monster on the weather radar that would get a name anywhere else. One crew would burn their effective crew day flying the fourteen hours just to get the helo in position for the rescue. Myself and an additional PJ flew in a C-130 for the eleven hundred miles from Anchorage to Adak Island. Once we landed in Adak we would relieve the crew that flew it that massive distance. From there we take the helicopter out toward the site of last known location of the fishing vessel.

All the guys in my crew were very solid and Alaska seasoned. Rick was the pilot and one of our best, a legend within Alaska rescue. I've been in an aircraft where he's done things that were supernatural. I'd be asking myself: *What just happened?* He understands everything about the needed torque of the aircraft to get us to a specific altitude, and then, once he would get us there, he knew how to let the aircraft fall at a specific rate to lose torque to pick up rpm to keep the thing from crashing. He's working all his pilot mojo, yet on top of that remaining a classically cool human being. In Alaska everything is understated and Rick's personality is a testament to this point.

If you've seen an episode of *Deadliest Catch* you might have some idea of what we were flying into, in terms of Bering Sea weather. Subzero temperature, winds around 100 knots. Since it was night, I had my night-vision goggles on initially, but once we got over the water I couldn't tell whether they were on or not. I turned them on and still couldn't see. I took the batteries out to see if they were even working. We had no visibility, even with them on. In those moments, when I could get a glimpse of the water below, the seas were as big as I've ever seen. Waves the size of buildings, seemed to be reaching up toward us. What we were attempting was insane. But there we were, at the very least making an effort to recover the bodies.

We were preparing for what was most likely going to be a body recovery, not a rescue. No one lives for long in water like that. This meant fixing up what we call the lobster basket. Usually when you pick up the deceased in that temperature of water, they aren't in rigor yet, but their body is frozen, so you can't strap them into a normal rescue basket. What we rely on is basically a big net to capture the corpse, and get that into the aircraft. Working with a body, frozen stiff, is a dangerous struggle itself. You've got to toil to deal with a body frozen in an awkward position. So, as we were being battered by winds, I was there in the dark in the back of the helo, hunched over on my knees and struggling to organize the netting, night vision goggles, and rigging. Working in the back of a helicopter for someone my size is a pain in the ass in good conditions. In these conditions, on this night, it was a comedy of errors. The lobster net is part rigid material and part netting. I was getting it prepared while trying to see the lines in my night-vision goggles, and being tossed around. It's hard in the helo, because with white light or green light, when the visibility is so bad, your sight gets ruined. You know how it feels at night when you can see in the dark, using your own natural night vision, and then someone shines a bright-ass light in your eyes and you can't see anything? You're burning that chemical within the eye that allows you to see. So while I was struggling to minimize that effect, and fix the net to get it ready to retrieve the bodies, and I finally got that done and was really focused on the mission and thinking about making the leap into these forty-foot seas, and this was all happening full tilt, I looked outside and I could not the horizon. The illumination was zero.

We flew for thirty to forty minutes out over the water, but even the pilots couldn't see. We were going a hundred miles an hour, and I could barely make out these mountains of water moving around us.

"Fuck, man," I said. "That's a big-seas state from what I can see."

Bobby added, "Let's call it, Rick. They're dead men."

At this point, from incident call to us on the scene, it had been ten hours. Mortality was four hours in the water, at best. I asked Turk, "Can you recover us in this?"

He replied with a flat "No, man."

Rick called it. "I don't feel good about it, guys. We've got to turn it around. I can't see anything."

At that point Rick didn't need to say anything more. We turned the helo around and headed back toward the only bit of land we could see, Adak—rising up out of the ocean like a Jurassic Park volcano.

Finding a few living dinosaurs on Adak would almost make sense, because little else on that island does. This place is *Road Warrior*–apocalypse strange, complete with a brand-new high school, and government housing, all abandoned. Manned and thriving up until the end of the Cold War, Adak is now mostly a ghost town, with a runway that now functions like a beacon for distressed aircraft.

It was nearly twenty below, with 100-knot winds, and we almost crashed the helicopter just to land. We had to park the helo behind a big building to shut it down and shield it from the raging gusts. A half hour later, to add to the surreal setting, this weird Alaskan hillbilly pulled up in a minivan without doors. I looked inside and the vehicle is filled with bags of garbage. I'm in my dry suit, and wearing all my gear, and he said, "I'll take you to one of the houses."

I was overwhelmed after nearly dying. We'd just risked our lives, and now we were done for the day and stranded in one of the strangest ghost towns on earth.

We crawled into the back of the minivan, lying on garbage with our gear. The guy pulled up to some houses and said,

"Find yourself a place to stay. Just open a door and go in. They're all open."

What came next is hard to articulate to the normal person, if you don't have an understanding of Alaska's history of boom and bust cycles and those who decide to stay behind when a town shuts down. The people we would meet while we were stranded in Adak inhabit the place year-round. Some of them live in one house, fill it up with garbage over a year, and then move on to the next one. That's how a few of them normally live. Bizarre, in a normal remote Alaska way.

We went into these modern houses, and found homes left as if the owners might come back the next day. There were still amenities, like canned food in the cupboards. At the time, the homes had been abandoned for half a decade or longer. We were hungry and cold. I kept my dry suit on all night to stay warm, and decided to go exploring. I went around base housing in search of something to eat. I found some peanut butter and jelly and went back to the main house. Someone gave us a few tortillas. I whipped up this horrible meal for myself.

At some point, we began walking around and found a little surplus store. Inside we found this chain-smoking owner sitting on an Igloo cooler. He didn't really have any food in the store, but he had cat food. I was half tempted to buy some of that to eat. I had two twenties in my survival kit.

I gave a lady twenty dollars and she made me a grilled cheese. I distinctly tasted cigarette ashes in that sandwich. Some senses have a way of sticking and never leave you.

We would be stranded there for a few days. The horrible weather continued. Repairs were made to the helo; we started the long trip home. The plan was to hop islands, not only to navigate, but to stay under the radar, so that if the weather got too bad we could just set down, shut the aircraft down, pull out my survival bag, and all sleep in the back of the aircraft together with the heater running.

We'd gone through quite an ordeal coming from Adak, and were ready to get home. But that Alaska factor wasn't done with us yet. The weather went to shit again and the C-130 couldn't refuel us midair. We went critical on fuel.

When that happened, I was in the back of the aircraft trying to sleep. I could hear the tension in everyone's voice. In situations like that I just shut my brain off and sit back and sleep. The aircraft was getting buffeted by wind, was all over the place. My response: lean back and sleep. *Fuck it, man.*

Bobby, my senior at the time, said, "Roger. Plug in." So I plugged my headset in. And I heard them running the ditching checklist. I immediately unplugged again and got my survival gear out. I took the neck ring out of my dry suit to prepare for immersion, and calmly got my shit in order. I was at the door. Ready. If we're doing it, we're doing it. That's all there was to discuss.

These are very experienced men. When the pilot says, "Run the ditching checklist," you run the ditching checklist. What that means is that in the next five minutes, we would need to deploy the PJs (myself and Bobby) and then deploy the survival raft. Then the pilot would come around on another pass to drop off the gunners and the copilot. Then the pilot would land the helicopter in the ocean, and Bobby and I would swim to him and get him out of the aircraft.

That is the ditching checklist.

You don't ever want to hear the pilot tell you that you're running the ditching checklist over the Bering Sea, but there we were.

I plugged my headset back in and could hear Rick going through the Mayday call: "Mayday, Mayday, this is Jolly 23. Critical fuel. At the point of ditching. This is our lat and long . . ."

I unplugged and got ready to bail.

I was crouched there, with my hand ready to open the door. Those are still huge seas. I'm going to jump and hit the water. I'll inflate my flotation device, because in big water like that you can just get rolled and taken under, and I'm completely ready for what is happening. Then I saw everybody's face change. I plugged back in and heard the Coast Guard directing us.

Nail-biting the entire time, we fumed it to a small pad on the outskirts of Dutch Harbor. After landing we all gave a deep sigh. We eventually made our way to a Coast Guard cutter that had docked nearby. We entered the galley where the crew excitedly greeted us and made us a meal.

I was still wearing my dry suit, because that was all I had. I'm in a giant Winnie-the-Pooh slumber party outfit. I had no clothes other than my silkies. I didn't even have shoes, just a dry suit. The situation was ridiculous but welcomed.

The cutter anchored at Dutch Harbor.

Rob Carte was the flight engineer on the helo. He's a wiz with the aircraft. He knows every system of the HH-60. The systems within the Pave Hawk are often problematic. We had done something to the engine with the flight the night before, causing several small malfunctions. He had to fix the issues with little to go on—Leatherman and duct tape–style.

Once we were repaired and refueled we made the eight-hundred-mile leg home, hopping island to island across the Aleutians on the way back to the mainland. On the way we capped the failed mission with a final surreal and mind-blowing sight. I spotted something strange on a beach. After I pointed it out, Rick banked the helo, and we dropped in for a closer look.

What we saw was incredible. A giant whale carcass had washed up on the rocky shoreline. The whale itself, as huge as it was, wouldn't be anything too unusual for us to spot, but what caught our eyes was the crowd of creatures that had gathered on the leviathan's carcass.

If there were twenty bears, there were a hundred, and they were monster brown bears feeding off the whale's flesh. The bears were inside and on top, ripping giant pieces of blubber and meat away with their claws and teeth. We were witnessing a giant food orgy. We were tempted to land and check it out, but it didn't take a genius to make a risk assessment that there were far too many bears. I doubt these bears had ever seen a helicopter, and definitely never a human. We were hovering close by, and they paid us no mind; they were too consumed with their feeding frenzy. The smell of rotten whale permeated the helo's cabin. We'd seen and smelled enough. As we lifted away I could see some bears, deep inside the enormous body cavity, gorging themselves on whale blubber and intestines.

It's unlikely you will forget seeing or smelling something like that. You register those events to the recesses of your mind. The subconscious paints them in ways we may never understand.

15

ARCTIC JUMP WEARING SNEAKERS

What is called generosity is really compassion.
—YAMAMOTO TSUNETOMO, *HAGAKURE*

Winter. Cold as fuck. In the heart of winter's darkness. All you think about is the cold. At times you can't imagine that anything exists but snow and ice. You're so used to the cold that you forget that summer is a thing. And then, in the middle of one of those frigid black nights, you get a call that rips you from your warm bed with the news that you'll be headed into a place somewhere even colder and darker: the Arctic.

This call came from deep in the Brooks Range, the furthest-north mountain range in Alaska. A trapper's wife was sick and bleeding out. She was vomiting and pissing blood, for weeks. She hadn't kept any food down for some time. A big part of the stuff we learn, not only as paramedics but for basic survival, is the rule of three. You can live for three minutes without air, three days without water, and three weeks without food. Try to break the rule of three and, well, you don't really break the rule of three. When we were told the woman hadn't kept anything down for weeks we were astounded she was still alive, and worried she wouldn't be for much longer.

We grabbed our gear, throwing it all in one big shit pile into the back of the C-130, and flew the helicopter crew, including the helicopter PJs, with myself and my alert partner, to Eielson Air Force Base in Fairbanks. The helicopter crew had a helo there awaiting them. By this point in my career I felt experienced, even by these surreal standards. I was with my partner Brandon Stuemke again. Standard procedure is to have the most experienced PJs on the C-130, and the other bubbas on the Pave Hawk. We assume we will use the helicopter to get out, so we always try to execute the mission with the Pave Hawk, because the landing options for the C-130 are limited. We always have the jump capability, which we reserve for life-and-death situations when we can't get the helicopter in. Gearwise, we had everything we needed in our bags. We were outfitted by the best companies, Arc'teryx and Patagonia are just the tip of the iceberg. The very best cold-weather and inclement gear money can buy. Our gear and bags were all carefully organized and labeled for efficiency on nights like this, when we've got to pack up quick and get in the air.

We landed in Fairbanks. We might as well have landed on Pluto. The standing temperature hovered around forty-five below, and we were only going farther north, where everything is even colder and drier. The PJs assigned to the helo offloaded their personal gear from the C-130 with the engines running at two in the morning, and it was a big pile of fuck. This is called ERO, engine running offload, and they are a horrible and smelly scramble in good weather. In the freezing-ass cold weather we were facing, we worked even faster to get those guys and their gear out and shut the tail of the aircraft back up as quickly as possible.

We were going to take the C-130 and push farther north, 160 miles north of Fort Yukon, to do a weather recon and scout for a safe route for the helicopter.

With those guys off, and several hours of flight ahead of us, Brandon and I sat back to chill, watching a movie that he had downloaded, *The Girl with the Dragon Tattoo*. After a while I said, "I'm going to sleep, man. Wake me up when we get home." I was about to fall asleep again; this was a helo mission, and we were there to support the helo. I pulled a poncho liner over my head in the back of the bird, and dozed off. At the time I was in no way dressed for the Arctic. My apparel was closer to what you'd wear if you were going skiing in spring in Colorado: running shoes; light outdoor soft-shell pants; a light, real thin, puffy down top. Basic casual clothes. The same thing I might wear if I'm going to dinner in Anchorage in the winter. I don't think I even had a beanie on my head.

A few hours later, someone shook me from my slumber. I was in this stupor. I pulled the poncho liner off my head and the flight engineer said, "Roger! You guys are jumping in fifteen minutes. You're fucking jumping."

I was half-awake, and you can't really hear much of anything in the back of the tin can, so I was just reading his lips. "We're fucking jumping?" I asked.

He nodded.

Shit.

Instantly, I went from zero to a hundred. Just like that. There wasn't really any fear, anticipation, or anxiety; there was only focus on the task at hand—*Okay, we're fucking doing this. I need to find my gear.*

The most important bag of any PJ in Alaska is his clothing bag. This bag is literally your telephone booth that you're going to use to put your Superman costume on. I started looking around the plane, checking the spot where I had put it. Nothing. Scrambled all over. Nothing. *No way.* The one bag I needed most, and that's the one that was missing. *You've got to be fucking kidding me.* My helmet bag and my clothing bag were just gone.

What had happened was in that goat-fuck at Fairbanks, they had accidentally offloaded my bag. I had long since marked the bag ROGER SPARKS BIG FROG RTL TEAM LEADER— which pretty much meant *please don't fucking touch this gear*— but it was two in the morning, we were pulling an ERO, and you're literally holding your breath, tears running down your face while throwing bags off the plane. My bags were now back at Eielson.

At those temperatures shit breaks all the time. What had transpired during my beauty rest was that the helo broke down, and now we were on a jump mission. We had the direct order from the second-in-command of the wing, as the flight commander for the C-130. He said, "This warrants a jump, you guys are jumping."

He had the authority to pull the trigger, and he had our general, Blake Gettys, on the satellite phone. Gettys said,

"Sparks is on board and Greaser is the pilot; you guys fucking jump. Authority approved. You guys are jumping."

At the time I was acting as the PJ team leader, so if I thought we were okay to jump, then we were going to fucking jump. Stuemke and I had been through hell and back together. I was comfortable with him in any situation. So I told him, "You're the medic. I trust you. Bring what you fucking need. We're jumping static line square, two thousand feet. Get the chutes and prep the gear; I'm going to go talk to the pilot."

We didn't have much time, not more than fifteen minutes. I went up and chatted with Greaser, our pilot, and said, "Hey, I don't have any of my equipment here, but it's all good. I want you to confirm they have a warm, heated, and stocked cabin. I'm going to go back there and get geared up."

Stuemke is the opposite of who I am physically. We're very much similar mentally; and metaphysically, like the same spirit animal; but physically, I'm almost seven feet tall and he's five nothing. We joke all the time that a lot of the missions he and I did together are always the weird shit. And when I say weird shit, I mean weird shit, man. And this was weird shit. The weird-shit factor was now through the roof.

"We're going to do this!" I told Brandon. He knew I didn't have my helmet bag or my clothing bag. I didn't need to articulate anything further to him. The whole point of me bringing up our physical dimensions was that I can't borrow any of his extra shit. I can't even wear his helmet because my head is so much bigger than his.

So I was thinking like MacGyver, trying to figure out how to make it work. I put on a little headset and duct-taped it to my head. I found and put on a little hoodie thing, and a small pair of glasses. I didn't even have a pair of real goggles, yet I was about to make a winter jump wearing sneakers. The ground temperature was nearly sixty below. Who knows what the temperature was at two thousand feet, flying at 120 knots.

I was going to jump carrying my survival ruck, which is enough to sustain me and another PJ and two patients in the Arctic for two or three days. But I wasn't jumping with what I would normally jump, even on a hot summer day.

I pushed those thoughts away and focused on the task at hand.

We got ready and prepped. One of the copilots said, "Are we going to brief this thing or what?"

And Greaser, who enjoys my candor and my personality enough, threw it back in my face and said, "Sparks said, 'Two-thousand-foot static line square,' that's the fucking brief."

We were inbound and heading right to the target where we were going to release, so I opened the left paratroop door. Now imagine doing a spacewalk; this is comparable to that. We were 160 miles north of Fort Yukon, and 160 miles north of Fort Yukon; you might as well be on Neptune. You open that door and in seconds it goes from 50 degrees in that giant sausage tube to a hundred below. It was coal-miner's-ass cold and black. The only thing allowing you to see was your NVGs.

One thing you learn as a rescue jumpmaster is that you always taper the lights as you get closer and closer to the target. If you dim the lights at the right speed, you can get your night vision slowly. But it was dark even in that regard. The

lights had been higher than we wanted because we were trying to fiddle-fuck our gear. So when the door was opened, the
sound decibels went up a thousandfold, and the rumble of
those four engines turned to a roar with the wind shear, and
we couldn't hear or see anything. It would put people over the
edge with fear if you didn't know what was about to happen.
It's amazing what human beings can get used to. With the
door open, I stepped up to the edge. The parts of my skin exposed to the air burned. We do training jumps constantly,
usually as PJs; up here you jump three to four times a week,
and we only call the ball on training if it is forty below. This
was at least sixty below on the deck, and this was cold unlike
anything I'd ever felt in that situation.

The complexity of jumping as a pararescueman is infinite.
We don't have a ground party. We don't know all the circumstances that await us below. The only person waiting for us is
the person needing our help, and they're probably not trained
in Special Operations or HALO operations at night. So you
have nothing to go off of except instincts, training, and the
most important, the pilots and the crew.

I oriented myself to the outside and leaned out into that
150 mph wind, trying to get eyes on what was going on. I
had at least 120 pounds of gear strapped to my chest and
back. The pilot was talking to me, and there was a lot of shit
going on. I was multitasking like a thirteen-year-old girl with
three smartphones. I was leaning out there, and over my radio
I could hear the trapper. It was his wife who was in this horrible
medical state, and I could hear him talking, but his auditory
volume was much different than the aircrew's voice—helmet

fire is what we call it. While I was dealing with that I looked at Stuemke—looked him right in the eyes said, "Are you fucking good?" He nodded. He was good to go. He was just waiting on me. I looked out and didn't see a fucking thing.

Greaser, the pilot, our aircraft commander, said, "Thirty seconds, Roger. Thirty seconds!"

"Roger," I said, but I couldn't see shit. There was zero horizon. Zero illumination. Zero anything. I couldn't even see the difference between the night sky and the earth below. So I counted. One, one thousand. Two, one thousand. I counted thirty, and I still couldn't see anything, and reported to the crew to continue.

At thirty seconds I threw out what we call the "disco ball" into the blackness.

The disco ball is something that we drop over our intended target; depending on where it lands in reference to where you release it, the wind direction is revealed. As the jumpmaster, I was basing my parachute release point off what the disco ball would tell me. It's kind of Kentucky windage for parachuting, and it works a hundred percent of the time, all the time. These are the techniques we develop as PJs that no other Special Operations units even fathom or do.

We train all the time with the disco ball in crew integration; it's really a no-brainer. They are doing my job for me and know what I'm doing when I release it. So I had released the disco ball, the only disco ball in the aircraft, and I wanted them to start turning—the jargon we use is "streamers released clear left turn"—so I can watch it fall to earth. The disco ball has intermittently blinking red and green lights. It has a parachute attached to it that descends at the same rate as our parachutes. So we did that at two thousand feet above where I thought our target was.

The pilot came over the radio and said, "Roger, I'm sorry but we're still five minutes from the target." *Fuck!* our "wad" was just literally blown.

I kept my cool, because that was all that was left. "Those are the only streamers we have," I said. "What are the winds doing?"

He replied, "Ten knots, off the skins, we're into the wind all night, Roger." Aircraft have the ability to sense what the yaw of wind is doing in relationship to the over-the-ground speed. What he meant by that was that we were into the windline.

"Okay. I feel good about it," I said. Everything I have done of value in my career has been done outside of the rules. Real work of virtue is done outside the rules in the gray.

"Rog. We're two minutes out. The real two minutes," he replied.

As the jumpmaster, two minutes, one minute, and thirty seconds are significant time calls. Once we're already in the terminal area, I gave Brandon the two-minutes sign and I was looking. The crew, again, they were doing a really great job, keeping me apprised of the situation.

Greaser said, "All right—basically he's got a giant snow-machine headlamp on, and he's on the machine and in a snow clearing with a frozen pond and a hundred feet from his cabin. Right off the nose. Approximately five miles; we have him in sight right now."

At this point I was flying the aircraft. He was flying it, but he's my meat puppet. He was following my commands. "Continue," I said.

"Continue," he repeated.

"Bump right 5 degrees." Then he yawed the aircraft, 5 degrees rudder, and then turned it and came back out. What this does is allow me to look out the aircraft to see what we're jumping into. So I had him do this a couple of times, and as we got closer I said, "Five left. Five left." I brought him back over that target. I need to see it, right? You have to see things to control them. We got over the cabin, and I said, "All right, safety checks complete. Are we clear to drop?" This is basically like an authority directive for the crew. If we were to jump and die, it's my fault. If I were to jump into a maniacal death machine, it's on me. I'm calling the ball at that point.

"Clear to drop" was the response; they turned the green light on and I could jump at any point. So now I was using "beer math." Having jumped so much out here with these aircrews, I knew that with the SOV-3 parachute system, my forward drive was 10 to 20 knots depending how much I wing load, how much weight I had under the canopy itself, that if the winds are 10 knots, I want to go five seconds past the target to release, to put me in a perfect position to control the wind velocity for me to land right there at the guy's cabin.

It sounds like a lot. It's distance, speed, and time, like a current vector triangle, but you do it so much that you get really quick at the computations. This is good old-fashioned beer math. So the winds were 10 knots and I was at two thousand feet. I could cut them in half and have plenty of drive to get to my intended target. I had five seconds, one second for every knot of wind, divided by two is five; five seconds past the target I would release, and I'll land right there.

I looked Brandon in the eyes, then looked at his equipment again. Shit happens. Goggles could have fogged up, pack straps shift or loosen, or he could need to fix something on his or my gear—anything. I looked at him and he gave me the bedroom eyes, so I know we can go. He knows that when the giraffe stands up, it's time. He sensed my body language; I didn't even need to talk to him. I watched that snow-machine light underneath the aircraft, and right as it passed I started counting.

"One potato. Two potatoes. Three potatoes. Four potatoes."

I launched from the aircraft. At first it was all violence. I came out, my chute opened, and it was such a giant juxtaposition of senses. You go from that tension and sheer violent terror to complete solitude and quietness. Just like that. Snap of the fingers, within a second or two. I looked up and it was just stone cold quiet, minus the roar of the C-130. Brandon's chute opened. I looked out of the corner of my eye—we had almost collided. Imagine if we entangled and fell those two thousand feet. A devastating situation, right? We missed each other by twenty feet or so.

I had instructed the aircraft to punch out flares every thirty seconds, because it was hard to tell how tall the trees were. Thirty seconds before we jump and thirty seconds after continuing for five minutes or so. The flares turns everything to daylight. The problem you have with flares is that they create vision problems, due to their changing angles and descent rates. With the setting sun or rising sun, you can look at shadows—but you can't do that with flares. I was trying to judge how tall the trees beneath me were. I was having a tough time judging if they were thirty feet, or sixty feet, or ten feet. Up in the Arctic, trees do strange shit. They might be stubby, but they are old. Their rings are densely packed. They could be three hundred years old and eight inches in diameter. I was trying to judge all that shit as I was falling under a canopy, above the Arctic Circle, me and my buddy. I was trying to judge all this really quickly, ignoring how underdressed I was. How I was freezing. I could see where we wanted to land. I wanted to separate vertically from Brandon, so I spiraled down four or five times, to give us distance, so there were no chances of us running into each other again. I was losing altitude quickly. I watched where I was going. I sashayed a couple of times, flared, and landed five feet away from the trapper and his idling snow machine.

I was in running shoes. And light ski gloves. The lightest weight. My hands felt like lobster claws. I felt the sense of frost nip burning all over my body, but I'd landed right next to him. It was a stand-up landing. The parachute slowly collapsed over both of us.

"Whoa!" was what he said.

It's really weird to be standing there when someone comes in on a parachute like that in such a remote location. All you hear is the wind going through the risers—like the sound of an eagle flying right past you, say within ten feet or so. To do it gently is kind of fascinating, even to someone like myself with countless jumps under my belt. Let alone that here is this guy who has had little human contact for months, other than his wife, and I have landed right beside him and his first word was "Whoa."

That was all he said for a moment. But the silence didn't last long, before the words came pouring from this extremely friendly fellow.

One thing I've learned is that survivors have a tendency to start talking a mile a minute when you arrive. They have been waiting some time for you to reach them. And you're so burdened by the events, and the responsibility, for the situation taking place that at first you want to shut them down, shut them up. I think at the time I was a bit curt with him, when all he wanted was to welcome us and get us into his wife. I was also freezing my ass off.

Brandon landed ten to twenty seconds after me, five feet from us, and this only added to this guy's amazement. Like we had just dropped out of the sky from Neptune, right on him. He kept talking at me, and Brandon started talking to me. I pulled my hoodie off and instantly the cold hit. I could feel it killing me. At that temperature it sears the skin like a branding iron. The adrenaline starts to subside and you realize your body is quickly being gripped by a cold death.

I looked right at the guy and said, "You're going to have to give me ten minutes. I need a moment." I had to get on the radio, let them know we were good to go, and what our next move was. He was desperate to help and talk. But we had to coordinate with our aircraft. This can seem rude to the person who has been waiting for hours in a dire situation, but it is essential. He understood. I was feeling a large sense of responsibility of talking to the aircraft, talking to my team-mate, and just patting myself down to get our shit together. There's a lot of adrenaline during a situation like that and you must be able to recognize this and consciously change gears. Adding to that the temperatures are so cold that the nylon of a parachute quickly turns into the composition of a plastic trash bag. Basically my parachute was freezing itself as it fell to the ground. As we were policing our chutes up. I told Stuemke, "Leave the gear, take the med ruck up there, and I'll be right behind you."

I turned to the guy. "How far is your cabin?" I asked. "And is it warm?"

"Two hundred feet," he said, "and plenty warm."

"Okay. Take my buddy and I'll be there in a minute." I ferried all the equipment to the cabin. In that short time I could feel frostbite setting in everywhere. My hands and feet were losing feeling. If we didn't have that warm and heated cabin we would not have jumped. Such a decision would have been fatally ignorant. It was that cold.

Cabin doors in the very far north tend to be shorter than the average entrance. This old handmade doorway was barely four feet high. I'm a giraffe, so I had to get on all fours just to get through the door. I crawled in, pulled our gear in after me, and shut the door as quickly as I could to keep the cold at bay.

When I got in the cabin it only took one glance to tell his wife was in a really bad way. But this guy was such a gentle-man, and such a conversationalist, that he instantly made us feel welcome. We were trying to take in what was going on, and this guy wanted to chew the fat. We were concerned about his wife's situation, and it wasn't that her situation didn't worry him, but he had such respect for us that he knew she was in good hands. What was more apparent than her poor condition was his kindness and his thirst for conversation. He and his wife had a lovely relationship, but he was clearly excited to visit with us and watch us do our thing.

Most of the human race could learn something from that couple in how they had lived. Decades of happy and healthy life in a cabin less than five hundred square feet in size, year round, and living off the land. These were powerful and intelligent people choosing to live in those conditions. Only a handful have the skills to live like that in the Brooks Range. At the time, I had no idea the guy and his wife were Heimo Korth and his wife, Edna. I would later learn that they were two Alaskans famous for their stories of being some of the only people who live in the Arctic National Wildlife Refuge. Instead of delving into the couple's past and personal history, Stuemke and I focused on what we were doing: trying to save Edna. At one point, Heimo looked me over in the glow of his lantern, and said, "Oh, you're not dressed for the weather!" He had this comforting Minnesota-type, *Fargo*-sounding accent.

"I know!" I said. "That's why I asked you about the warm cabin."

Stuemke's job was to assess his wife and stabilize her, and my job was to provide him with what he needed and report back to the rescue coordination center. I did that with a satellite phone, while vectoring with the C-130. The plane orbited overhead for an hour or so. I called the general, talking to him through the RCC, and said, "We're good to go. We can sustain our patient medically for twenty-four to seventy-two hours. We'll report back every six hours."

And that's what we did. She was really bad off. She was what we call hemodynamically unstable: internally bleeding with an abnormal blood pressure. As pararescuemen we're excellent trauma specialists, but strictly medical patients always cause us extra caution. However, as long as we have a communication link, we possess a variety of highly skilled brains on tap, right at our fingertips. If I need to, I can get the best internal medicine doctors in the world on the satellite phone. I made the call. "I'm 162 miles north of the Arctic Circle, it's four in the morning, and we have a woman who has been bleeding profusely, GI bleed, vomiting blood, bloody diarrhea, last oral intake has been weeks."

Heimo had already pretty much diagnosed Edna's condition as a parasitic infection. He'd even taken water samples. "Oh, I'm pretty sure it is giardia," he said, "and I feel foolish that we were ill equipped and even had to call for your help. But we couldn't get a ski-equipped plane."

The weather had been too cold for too long, and that is when surface snow turns into this loose sugar. A plane on skis would have balled up on landing, and then we would have been called in anyway. He'd already tried clearing a spot for a plane to land, but he knew it was too dangerous. With his wife dying, we were the last resort.

Heimo couldn't contain his surprise at how efficient we were at our jobs.

The helo sat in the hangar in Fairbanks, broken. A part was required for maintenance, which meant that the C-130 needed to fly all the way back to Anchorage, get the item and mechanics, and fly back to Fairbanks. After the helicopter would be fixed, the old crew would have to be replaced with a new crew, which would then need to fly out to get us in order to transport Edna to Fairbanks Regional Hospital. We needed to keep her alive until then.

What good did we do dropping into their cabin in the middle of the night? We were able to comfort her. Get eyes and hands on her and get some fluids in her. We provided the medical help she required while waiting for a helo. Rotary wings solve all the world's problems. I'll just put that out there: Pave Hawks in Alaska solve the problems period. My partner and I and our parachutes were just the air-to-ground component to help the patient in need to get into the aircraft and to the hospital.

We didn't have the cure in our bags to treat her for giardia. Nor could we differentially diagnose that she actually had giardia. All we could do was treat her symptomatically until the helicopter arrived, and then get her into the helicopter and sustain her until we rolled her into the hospital. Could she have lived another twenty-four hours? Yes. As tough as she was, I think she could have. But we didn't know that at the time. She was semiconscious when we arrived. With her blood pressure so low and the continuous bleeding and vomiting, who knew what was going to happen?

We set her up with an IV to get fluids into her, we gave her some medicine to sedate her, and we gave her Phenergan for the vomiting.

I can't begin to explain how cold it was there. Cold and

surreal. Beyond the odd feeling of jumping into a location like that without injury and getting our patient stabilized, I was thankful to meet Heimo and Edna, these two legends among those who know the backcountry, for the way they have lived. We blundered into these iconic Alaskan figures in the middle of winter, doing our jobs.

He was smitten with us, enjoying our conversation. I could tell. He is a master conversationalist. He would not shut up, which turned out to be good. The man was entertaining, engaging, and genuine. To live as he lives strips down sincerity into his very being. I've always found it cool to be around people like Heimo who don't have the pretensions that modern society places on so many of us.

We were with them for over twenty-four hours. He told us stories of documentary crews who were trying to talk him into being on camera. When I got back home, I looked him up online and watched a video about him and his life. It's hard to really fathom what is normal to him. It's a powerful thought to try to absorb. The closest most of us will ever come to transition from a life in the wilderness to the lives most Americans live is probably what those of us who know war experience, when we return home to shopping malls, cereal aisles, and reality television.

I might not have had any winter gear, but I had food. I like to eat. I had a plethora of freeze-dried food in my bag. Edna, despite her condition, was in good spirits too. She knew she was getting out of there and that we were taking good care of her. We quickly learned about her; she's an amazing and beautiful Alaska Native woman. The two had met on St. Lawrence Island.

I said, "Dinner is on me. What do you two want?"

How self-sustained we were surprised Heimo. That is no-bility in backcountry Alaska, how self-sustaining you are, and he had lived his whole life surviving at his own hands.

"Well," I asked, "what do you want? Want to go to a Mexican restaurant? Italian? Brunch?"

Heimo asked, "Oh, you got Mexican food, eh?"

Edna started laughing. She told us her husband absolutely loved Tex-Mex. So I whipped him up one of those freeze-dried Mountain House meals. Whatever it was made his day. I knew the helo was en route and that I'd be home by day's end. So I pulled out all the freeze-dried food packs I had and said, "Take these and keep them."

"Oh, I can't do that!" he said.

I said, "Take them, Heimo. I can buy some more. Take them."

He was blown away by that small gesture. So as we prepared to leave, I gave him most of the contents of my survival ruck. I could tell this was a gift of life and death to him. In the wilderness, survival equipment has a different value. If he's out and his equipment has failed, it could be the end of his family. I left him with my Sven saw and some other sexy survival gear, literally the best equipment that money can buy, NASA production-level shit. Heimo was genuinely appreciative. I knew that I had made a new friend.

It took another five- or six-hour helo flight to get Edna to the hospital. I remember flying back in the helicopter with both Edna and Heimo, refueling every few hours. What makes us the only show in town is that we can aerially refuel the helicopters. We do that every four hours with the Pave Hawk, on a mission like that. To be flying for four hours, and all of a sudden see the C-130 twenty feet outside your window, can be a little bit of a surprise. I knew the refuel was happening, but Heimo had no idea what was about to go down. When I pointed and yelled to him, "Hey, there is a C-130 coming," he might as well been on the Space Shuttle watching a UFO dock. He lost his mind. Astonishment swept over his face. I could tell this was mesmerizing for him to witness. Edna saw it too, and I realized how much I appreciated that part of my job, sharing special moments like that with cool people.

We dropped them off and they hugged Brandon and I. Heimo was so squared away that he had brought his water samples. I'd completely forgotten. Sure enough, his diagnosis of giardia would be correct.

Heimo called me once a month for a year. Each time he would invite me to come visit and build a cabin with him. He doesn't have only one cabin; he has several. They rotate where they live based on where the caribou are that they follow for sustenance. Unfortunately, I always turned him down because the cost of an air charter to get out there for a trip like that would destroy my bank account. I'm pretty certain Heimo thought that I could hop in the C-130, fly over again, and parachute into his cabin with dinner in my pack.

16

BACK BREAKING 2.0

The man who cut him down, compelled by unavoid-
able circumstances and feeling that there was nothing
else to be done, also put his life on the line, and thus
there should be no evidence of cowardice.

—YAMAMOTO TSUNETOMO, *HAGAKURE*

I woke up in the back of the helo, spitting blood and bits of my teeth. I watched as my legs shook, they were acting beyond my control. *Strangely I had felt this way before.* My legs refused to move, and something was wrong with my arm.

Chris Robertson, Leo Claunan, and I had been all set to fast-rope into an Afghan minefield, where a coalition vehicle had become the victim of an IED. There were men trapped inside. I slid down the rope first, landing carefully on some tire tracks left in the dirt, because we knew there wouldn't be a mine where the vehicle had driven over. I set down, boots in the tire track, tucked my chin down to my chest, and shielded my face from the dust and debris of the rotors. I waited for Leo and Chris to drop down along the same tracks.

The next thing I knew, I came to in the back of the helo.

We all had extrication gear on our backs. Leo carried our Jaws of Life that firemen use for car wrecks. He would come out of the helo next, and did he ever make an exit. As he made his move to begin the fast-rope, his harness caught an eyelet inside the helicopter, flipping him upside down and causing him to invert and lose control.

That two-hundred-pound Hawaiian, in all his gear and those Jaws of Life, fell thirty feet and landed on top of my head and the back of my neck.

I don't remember much, and it's a much better story to hear from Leo. But in the video the other helo recorded, you see him slip and plummet toward the earth. The only thing that saved his life in the video is the guy who looks like he's in prayer on the ground below. I was the crush zone. Leo would have been dead as fuck. Or certainly he'd be much worse off, if I hadn't broken his fall. You don't survive a thirty-foot fall on your head. Leo's helmet hit my pack and the Jaws of Life hit my arm, badly injuring my triceps.

Classic Hawaiian Leo, all heart and love, was so concerned about me. We'd always been good friends, so he knew my history of being paralyzed in the past. Then he'd just reinjured me. He wasn't dead, but he'd crushed me and I was semi-lucid. He was devastated, and decently injured as well.

I awoke to a reoccurrence of similar symptoms from the first time I had been paralyzed. The feeling of not being able to control your feet is frightening. Seeing something move on your body, but not feeling it, is the oddest of sensations. You're making your feet move in your mind, but you can't control anything. My right foot refused commands. *Fuck, man.* That was a dreadful reality to face again. The difference was my attitude and what I knew.

After being processed through the Bagram emergency room, where diagnostics and drugs were handed out, decisions were made. I would do a heavy Solu-medrol protocol and physical therapy. I was pleased that this was an option. I would be on the injured list for about a month or so and remain in Afghanistan. Daily physical therapy and the magical doses of Solu-Medrol once again became my religion. Solu-Medrol is a powerful and amazing drug. There are many different anti-inflammatory medications, but this goes straight to the neurological and spinal trauma to shut down the inflammation. I'd been given yet another chance to continue my work.

I'd have good days and bad days, and though it may sound strange, I felt comfortable in the desperation of it all. The biggest effect would be that I couldn't regain the ability to ever heel strike while running. The barefoot running craze helped. I transitioned to running on my toes.

My foot drop persisted and so did I. Being injured while deployed with your team is an extremely motivating elixir for recovery. At some point we all play injured and you get back in the game.

And that was that.

17

WISE ENDURANCE

If one were to say what it is to do good, in a single word it would be to endure suffering. Not enduring is bad without exception.

—YAMAMOTO TSUNETOMO, *HAGAKURE*

As Alaska PJs we are annually tasked to support the Denali Park Rangers during the summer climbing season. I and another PJ would spend over thirty days on Denali, the mountain formerly known outside of Alaska as Mount McKinley. We are paired with experienced climbing rangers and other mountain professionals to enforce regulations on the mountain during the climbing season and be there to aid in rescues or recoveries. Meg Perdue is one of the most respected female alpinists in Alaska and definitely a heralded and experienced Denali climbing ranger. She is unbelievably strong, smart, and wise when it comes to being in mountains, the Shaolin monk of the Alpine.

We worked with the National Park Service and helped man the patrols. There are generally four patrols on the mountain at a time, due to acclimatization and the vast distance between each of the camps. Generally we follow the West Buttress route and enforce park regulations there. It's not like we're the just the fun police. Many people need rescue and some less fortunate die. We're there primarily for safety: to assist or rescue those in need, or those who have been abandoned by their team, or are doing things that are unsafe for others on the mountain. For instance, if there's a team that had fallen in a crevasse and you went by them, well, you lack the basic virtues of being human, and we're going to let you know you're an asshole with fines and heavy restrictions. Within the climbing community there are certain taboos. You break the taboos and we'll be there. Some people will do speed ascents, and if someone else falls into a crevasse, those in a rush might choose to go right past the climber in need. This happens. It shouldn't, but it does.

Our mission was to work closely with all the other patrols on the mountain, not only for regulations, but for sharing weather reports, and managing the crowds and all the people on the peak. Kind of like a papa bear on the mountain.

One of the tasks of patrol is to go clean up the messes at 14 Camp. This is the camp at fourteen thousand feet, and is kind of where the wheels come off the bus for a lot of climbers. Denali is a hazardous mountain. As with the other tallest peaks in the world, climbing this mountain is a rigorous and metaphysical experience. Metaphysical because of where you are at and the volatility of the mountain and the weather, but so many of those other mountains have porters and sherpas. Not so on Denali. You're carrying everything your damn self, and because of the far northern latitude, the air's thinner here.

People with climbing experience on other peaks around the world come to Alaska and take on Denali and they get their asses crushed. We see it all the time. Arrogant climbers get their teeth kicked down their throat by that mountain. Fatalities occur nearly every year here.

On the mountain, we had taken about twenty days to acclimatize up to 14 Camp. I was having a hard time, throwing up in my sleeping bag, suffering from acute mountain sickness. I was borderline HACE (high altitude cerebral edema, a condition where your brain swells) when we got the call that we were needed at 17 Camp, the high camp.

When we reached 17 Camp, we learned that a couple, a man and woman, had attempted to descend by rope down the Orient Express. The Orient Express is an infamous section of the mountain, receiving its name after the deaths of several Asian teams on this hard-packed and ridiculously steep and windswept slope. Teams often decide to take a shortcut and drop down, and at some point one of them trips, and some or all of a team will die. It's very steep, and if you stumble you'll be riding the Orient Express down the mountain. The name is macabre and clichéd, but that section of the mountain is nothing to joke about.

This part of the mountain is known for the heinousness; one, you're at altitude, and two, the steep ice conditions switch from wading through hip-deep snow to slipping on glare blue ice. The slope drops for thousands of feet at a 50-to-60-degree angle. Unforgiving. Sure, you can cut some time off your trip down, and it might appear pretty attractive at the moment, but the Orient Express is merciless on climbing teams.

This climbing pair were no exception. The woman had climbed below her partner, which is what you should always do: keep the lighter person beneath you. If she falls, he can arrest. The problem arose when the guy tripped and began slipping. He tumbled past, ripping her right her out of her boots and crampons. That is how much force is involved in a steep fall like that. The two of them cartwheeled down, roped together, several thousand feet.

We were tasked with going up and attempting to salvage them. The problem, other than that we'd be on the Orient Express ourselves, was that a monster of a low-pressure system threatened to descend on the mountain. In the mountains a system like that is deadly, but we chose to go up because one of the climbers could still be alive. We had tents set up previously from the group before us, so we knew we had a camp. When we reached 17 Camp we first prepared for the coming storm. Meg directed us to cut snow blocks and to start building snow walls. We built six-foot-high walls, four feet thick, by cutting giant snow blocks. We knew what was going to happen and that we didn't have much time. We were preparing for the worst. We shored up our camp, then set out to find the victims of the fall.

After considerable effort, we found them. The fall killed the woman, but the man was miraculously still hanging on to life.

We strapped them both into sleds, dragged them back to

our tents, and continued to prepare for the coming storm. We left her body outside the tent, brought him inside, and tried in vain to treat him. His condition was critical; he wasn't going to make it. He had shattered bones, hypothermia, and internal injuries. We placed him in a sleeping bag and comforted him as much as possible. There was little else we could do.

The man died within hours, in my sleeping bag.

The storm began to rage. Winds over a hundred miles an hour battered our tent for eight days. We were at seventeen thousand feet, with temperatures at sixty below. It wasn't long before we were the ones who needed rescue, but we knew there was no way anyone could get to us. The winds screamed in a deafening roar, an endless freight train racing over our heads hour upon hour.

The feeling of being there stuck so high on the mountain is like being stranded in a submarine a thousand feet below the surface. We weren't going anywhere, and no one was coming. To get down to 14 Camp on a knife ridge in hurricane winds and zero visibility meant certain death.

Each tick of the clock up at seventeen thousand feet put us all a little closer to death. Generally, above fourteen you are dying with every tick of the clock. To be up there for eight days in those conditions is dreadful. To overnight above nineteen or anywhere close to twenty is considered fatal. That was my first experience at high altitude. At Denali's latitude, seventeen thousand feet is pretty much closer to nineteen thousand feet anywhere else. You add a two-thousand-foot factor because the air is denser at the equator, and Alaska is a long way from the equator.

We had two bodies outside our tent, but things would end up getting more grisly. We soon were forced to rummage through the deceaseds' belongings and eat all of the food in their packs. All of the food we carried up the mountain had run out. Meg, even with all her experience and wisdom, could only shake her head. At one point she looked me in the eyes and said, "If your tent rips apart, dig for your life straight down." The only thing keeping this from happening was the fortress of snow blocks we had cut in preparation for the storm. The hurricane force of the winds were constantly eating away at the walls and we were constantly wondering if we did a proper job.

When she said this, I was laying on solid ice. We weren't digging down into anything if the winds ripped our tent off.

In a situation like this, at some point, a sense of horror fills you. You're in all your gear, in your sleeping bag, doing calisthenics to keep warm. You're doing push-ups or flutter kicks in your sleeping bag, you're playing memory and number games in your mind in an attempt to stay sane.

To relieve yourself in those conditions, literally in your tent, is an experience of extreme intensity.

We ran out of food, but we had fuel, which is always a climber's saving grace. That's the life-and-death stuff, because we could melt snow to stay hydrated. Remember the rule of three.

We were cooked. I use that word, but I'm trying to classically understate that in Alaskan terms. We were completely out of food for three days. You might be able to survive three weeks without food, but combine that with hypothermia, hypoxia, and exhaustion and you're living on the margin of survival. Most people will tire of camping after eight days, but try eight days in hurricane winds on North America's tallest peak at sixty below. It's hard for people to imagine anything so ridiculous. It's hard for me to put myself in that headspace, sitting here writing this.

I don't have a lot weight to lose, and I'm sure I lost significant weight, and a lot of that was probably muscle and brain. When you're hypoxic and on reduced calories you're frying your own banana. Altitude punishes people who are aerobically in shape because you work beyond what your body can supply. Someone who is a smoker, a soccer dad who doesn't give a shit, he's always breathing hard, but on the mountain, he's not going to work his body beyond what he can acclimatize to. They call it a hypoxic ventilatory response. But compare someone who is fit, with a resting heart rate at forty beats per minute. If you're the fit guy you'll say, *I'll take rope, and the extra gear, I'll take that weight, I'll route find whatever . . .* —and you're working beyond what your body can adjust to. You're working too hard and in the process not feeding your brain. I've spent my life working to be fit as possible, not to look good but to be able to perform. For those eight days at 17 Camp, I suffered dearly. Imagine feeling like you're having the worst wine hangover of your life all day long. You throw up in your bag or shit yourself and you just don't care. When you cannot think clearly and your breath is strained it doesn't have as much of an effect.

When the winds had died to fifty or sixty knots, we made our descent to 14 Camp. As we dropped down the ridge, my partner and I had a rope attached to each other. The wind was blowing so hard that the 30 feet of rope was held straight out in the air between us. We were each prepared to dive off the opposite side of the ridge if one of us slipped. Wearily, we all made the climb down to 14 Camp, to safety and to sustenance. Suffering is relative, back at 14 Camp we dined and enjoyed ourselves, wholeheartedly reflecting on what good, if any, we had accomplished.

We had attempted to do right by saving the man and his partner, but failed. Our one success up there on the mountain had been to endure the suffering.

Whenever I was training the young PJs, I would teach them about the principles of making things better or worse. I would tell them, "There's no right or wrong, just better or worse." In truly dynamic situations there is generally not a right or wrong, you simply have to base your decisions from what will make the situation better or worse. Apply that to what the samurai believed and you have something powerful to contemplate. Their mantra was "If you have to choose between suffering and not suffering, always suffer." When we suffer, I believe it cultivates a kind of magic. This magic is what benefits the people and world around us. It is a sure way to live a meaningful life. Life without struggle is meaningless.

18

BULLDOG BITE

I have no miracles, I make right-action, my miracle.

—ANONYMOUS SAMURAI

There is something to be learned from a rainstorm. When meeting with a sudden shower, you try not to get wet and run quickly along the road. But doing such things as passing under the eaves of houses, you still get wet. When you are resolved from the beginning, you will not be perplexed, though you still get the same soaking. This understanding extends to everything.

—YAMAMOTO TSUNETOMO, *HAGAKURE*

Pararescue in Alaska is busy. We usually field about a mission per week: from plane crashes and injured climbers, to lost hunters, and to distressed ships at sea. Deployments to war zones for our unit come and go, but previous deployments mostly meant getting tan while working out beside an idle helicopter, time away from family, and a break from rescuing Alaskans in trouble. In the fall of 2010, we packed up our rescue gear and our weapons and headed for Afghanistan. We'd be working in familiar terrain: wicked mountains, high elevations, and remote rural villages.

We were attached to the 83rd Expeditionary Rescue Squadron at Bagram; our job was to perform CSAR or combat search and rescue. I was deployed as the senior enlisted guy in charge of the pararescue team and we would be there for just under six months. Some people might have heard of the call sign Pedro. Well, that was us. For combat troops in Afghanistan no explanation is necessary about who or what Pedro is. Simply put, Pedro is a call sign designated when pararescuemen are paired with Air Force Pave Hawk crews with the purpose of fighting into and out of combat zones to save coalition lives. We were lucky enough to have a progressive commander and wonderful leader: Lieutenant Colonel David St. Onge. His nickname was Sweaty. He was an effective leader in that he took chances. He was willing to take calculated risks where most military officers don't have the balls. They are risk averse because if something bad happens, their career is over. This is especially true in the Air Force. St. Onge was willing to shake and bake it and send us out on the fringe, the business end of freedom, if you will, where we could do what we were meant to do. Our services are not valuable unless we're in the middle of the maelstrom. St. Onge was willing to hang it out there for us, saying, "We can do whatever alert you guys want and we can support dynamic ground missions at the same time. We can do that. Period." He was taking risks with us so we could actually do the collective good. There is a certain magic in trusting your men to execute their charge.

Pedro is always being pulled in multiple directions because the primary objective was and is always personnel recovery. Any plane crash, or any aircraft that gets rolled up, alive or dead, we'll fly in immediately and do everything we can to get the pilot and crew back. Secondary is casualty evacuation, or CASVAC. In war, with so much outsourcing, we also deal with our fair share of overweight military contractors with chest pain, which is kind of like hiring Mr. T to babysit your children. Fifty percent of the time when we deploy overseas, we reposition from the main bases to remote locations in support of high threat operations. That is exactly what we were doing in Operation Bulldog Bite.

Bulldog Bite comprised one of many missions, and our role fell under Two Charlie. Bulldog Bite, Two Charlie. They briefed the mission to us and, in all honesty, the plan sounded just somewhat benign as the rest of them had been.

The 101st Airborne was basically doing a company-size raid, infilling high on the eastern ridges, in the area of the Watapur Valley in eastern Afghanistan. Ridges in the area are over ten thousand feet. The valley floor is three thousand feet.

We were prepositioning ourselves to be at the edge of the battle space. Since we were five or ten minutes out, we could fly right in to the troops in contact, mitigate the tactical situation, and start pulling out casualties. We are unlike other military medical teams like Dustoff or medevac. Under normal circumstances, Dustoff or medevac will not fly in to support troops in direct enemy contact. We specifically train for and anticipate this.

The commander intended Operation Bulldog Bite to take place from November 12 to 14, but the operation would last until the eighteenth. Our mission, Pedro's mission, was to provide direct support to the 101st Airborne. We were the soul combat search and rescue platform; there were no other helicopters in the area other than Apaches and Kiowas. We were pretty much it if things went bad and the bubbas needed our help.

The 101st was basically staging out of Forward Operating Base (FOB) Blessing. Our forward aerial refueling point was at FOB Joyce. Just north of that was the field surgery team's location, at Asadabad. Right on the edge of the battle space. The plan was to infil high on the ridges and move to contact down to the bottom of the valley. Our guys were doing raids of known insurgent camps. These are high-mountain, high-elevation operations, in rugged and unforgiving terrain.

There had been a lack of coalition presence for the past two years, and the area was notorious as a hotbed for insurgents. They had complete freedom of movement and we wanted to change that.

For these operations, when pararescue normally goes in support of the missions, leadership generally tells us to anticipate 20 percent casualties. We weren't exactly lulled into complacency, but I don't think we took that number to heart. They had made a similar estimate for a previous operation and very little had happened, so we were hearing only numbers and percentages and not equating the math in the proper terms. Perhaps, had they given us the same figures in terms of lost limbs, bullets, and units of blood, we would have taken the calculations a bit more to heart.

Of note for us was the elevation. We prepared for extremely high terrain. With ridges at ten thousand feet, all the hoists we would conduct would be at seven thousand feet. Altitude affects the ability of that aircraft to get in and do the work. Because of the altitude, we would have to fly without the protective ballistic flooring. We would have to strip all sorts of essentials, including fuel and ammo, just to reach to the altitudes required to rescue these guys. We were going in as good as naked.

The topography there was as rugged as Alaska's. We flew with the .50 cals, loaded with armor-piercing, exploding, and incendiary munitions. The aircrews call this "shake and bake." In the floor of the valley sat small huts, the houses of the locals. Their homes remind me what I imagine Tucson looked like in the '50s. These are *qalats*, and .50 cal rounds or 40 mike-mike won't budge these huts. You can land helicopters on them without question, they are that solid. Routinely, as we flew missions in there, we would take fire while flying to the objective area. The enemy would just hang out at the side of the village, or step out from one of the huts and take potshots at us. Most of the time we were so critical with fuel and ammunition that we would not engage back. We had to save those for the terminal area where our skills were needed.

I was in Bagram with the other half of the team. The regimented guy I am, I required my guys to train every day. I sent them out shooting, practicing cutting through armored vehicles, or driving M-RAPs. You constantly cycle guys through training to keep their skills fresh, their minds sharp, and keep them from boredom and complacency.

This is where the story gets kind of weird. A dear friend of mine, a philanthropist and passionate outdoorsman and climber, by Alaskan standards, would be paying a visit. You don't get visitors when you're deployed, so naturally I was a bit excited. I first met him through climbing and his sponsorship and support of the local ice climbing competitions in Alaska. He was a prior Marine as well, so the two of us hit it off from the outset. At the time he was a CEO for a corporation that had been awarded a contract to develop a renewable energy plan for Afghanistan.

When the Learjet carrying him set down in Bagram, I stood waiting in the heat and dust to greet him. And this is where the story gets even stranger: his contracted security detail pulled up to meet him as he disembarked, and there was another old buddy, a fellow Marine from my Reconnaissance days. The two of us stood there staring at each other. One of us said, "What the fuck? What are you doing here?" Here was an old friend waiting to convoy my new friend to Kabul. I knew my Alaskan friend would be in good hands.

There is no drinking in Afghanistan. So naturally that night we went drinking. "Coca-Colas" at my friend's little compound. We spent the night sharing stories and getting caught up, and he told us about his various projects. People might not realize this, but throughout history, countries project war as a means for profit. If you don't see that, and you don't see that directly and very clearly, well you're just fucking blind or ignorant. A vast majority of the people on Bagram are not even military; they are contractors. And those contractors are there to develop infrastructure. My friend was the CEO of the corporation that manages and funds those contractors. And now you also have an army of people who work in security detachments to protect those contractors. In so many ways it's a dirty business.

My friend liked to be involved and really see what is going on at the ground level. The night after our Coca-Colas, he popped in and I gave him the grand tour of our digs, a beat-up building we called the Opium Den. I wanted to show him our PJ section, and hoped I could score him an off-the-books helo flight in an HH-60. I planned to organize this for him while all my guys were at the range with some Special Forces boys shooting all kinds of stuff, doing call-for-fire and weapons-sustainment training.

I was giving him the real private tour, everything from the helos to our weaponry, and all the sudden the phone rang. Not just any phone, the *bat phone*.

The bat phone is a secure line that my guys can use to reach me directly, whether it is our unit in Alaska or someone from the other half of the team reporting from the ensuing mission. I picked up the phone and heard one of my guys: "Hey Rog. Jimmy has been shot in the head."

Shot in the head.

He didn't say dead, so I asked, "Is he conscious?"

This was a secure line, so we can freely discuss the details at hand.

The response came as, "He's semiconscious. We've got him snowed over."

"Keep him snowed over."

"Roger, one of the helos is so shot up we're flying single ship right now." I don't want to get to into tactics or anything, but flying single ship is really hanging your ass out there. Beyond all that, I got this: "We need *you*. You need to come with a replacement and some helo parts." The message wasn't just about a shot-up helo or the need for parts and replacements. It was necessary for us to get to FOB Joyce as soon as possible, not only for my team but the mission of saving the guys on the ground still in the fight.

"I'll be there as soon as I can," I said. "We will notify you as we are departing."

I'm sure my friend could tell from the look on my face that his tour had reached its conclusion. We said a quick goodbye, and I radioed the men at the range to get back to the Opium Den immediately.

We don't react in a flash and race out and jump on the helos. I knew we needed to access and manage my teammate, Jimmy Settle. But even if we took off in a helicopter that exact moment and flew straight there, the trip would take three hours over some seriously hostile terrain. Plus, we had to first go find the parts to repair the shot-up HH-60. This is the part of war you don't hear about. More often than not, wars are waged in remote locations, away from well-stocked warehouses. The results make for expeditions that seem ill equipped and ridiculous at times. People have no concept of this. I needed to get to my team, but first I had to go hunt down helicopter parts.

I checked in with Matt Kirby, the commander at the time, saying, "Here is what is happening. Ted and I are going. We're bringing another helo. We're going with more mechanics and a complete new aircrew. We're going integrate with the team as soon as we can get there."

We had to hop in the HH-60 and fly across the flight line. Then Ted "Ski" Sierocinski, myself, and a mechanic ran into the Army supply building. I had my night-vision goggles on, we had all our shit on, and we practically broke into this supply-shop warehouse. No one was inside to help, so the three of us were dumping shit off the shelves in some sort of desperate scavenger hunt to find just the right pieces to fix the helo. I didn't know what the hell I was looking for. Our helicopter sat outside, blades whirling, waiting. I heard from across the warehouse, "Got 'em!" It was the mechanic. He had found what was needed.

We hauled the parts out. These were big-ass parts. Cumbersome and heavy. It's like we'd been asked to bring the engine block of a goddamn Chevy. We piled all the shit into the helo, *Beverly Hillbillies* style. The aircraft was loaded top to bottom in capacity, and we had a one-way ticket. We climbed into the helo, once again there was nowhere to sit. Unfortunately, we were used to this; however, it was funny to see the mechanics attempt to squeeze in and lie on top of the parts and fly for two hours to Jallalabad, where we refueled, took a piss, and then flew the rest of the way.

Around eleven at night we made our approach at FOB Joyce, random and sporadic tracers flying up to greet us. Welcome to the Alamo. We sat down, the mechanics immediately began turning wrenches on the damaged helo, and I checked in with my team. My guys met us as our rotors slowed and helped us with our equipment. They showed us to the space we would be occupying between missions. As we came into the lights I could immediately see a change in their eyes. It was a hollow, worn look of emotion and rage. It's a very peculiar thing, everybody wants to be the guy, until you're the guy.

The first thing I did was go to see Jimmy. He was bandaged up, a fragment of the bullet stitched over in his head. He'd caught it from ground fire. On their first mission in the area, and Jimmy's first combat mission as a deployed PJ, a round came up through the floor of the HH-60 and hit him in the forehead. He wasn't even in the terminal area. That's how hot the entire region was. Shot right through the floor. The PJ in the aircraft sitting with him was someone I'd seen plenty of action with: Brandon Stuemke. One minute they were headed in for a rescue and the next Jimmy was down, covered in blood, and their helo all shot to shit.

We'd taken very calculated risks for this operation. Essentially we had chosen to sacrifice our own safety in order to be capable if the mission went sour and the troops needed our assistance. With the ballistic flooring removed to enable flight at high altitudes, where the battles were anticipated, we'd opened ourselves up for injury and possibly death. Essentially we had to remove the protective material put in the aircraft so a devastating injury like Jimmy's wouldn't happen. What we didn't know when we stripped the aircrafts bare was the intensity of the gunfire we would be facing. To be fair, though, not all the damage would be bad: at one point our satcom antennae would get hit and actually perform better.

While the team waited our arrival, they executed single ship, with no gunship support. An HH-60 with two .50 cals flying into bad-guy territory, picking up casualties. Solo; this was extremely dangerous. Extensive damage to the second helo occurred in the nonstop rescue and recoveries. The mission was suddenly no longer trivial at all. We were getting shot at constantly, one of us nearly killed, and those things begin to settle over you like a cold wet blanket.

We gathered in one of the makeshift buildings. I looked around at the team. They had that look. Men in war get the ten-thousand-yard stare. You can't tell if they had just stepped away from a fistfight or were pepper-sprayed by a cop. You stare into their eyes and they have that faraway gaze. And when they get that look, you have to manage that space of humanity. Combat is unforgiving and it doesn't give a fuck. With Ted and I there we would be able to rotate two guys at a time.

Jimmy had been shot in the head and knocked unconscious. The bullet did not penetrate his skull, but the fragments were embedded. The only treatment at the time was to sew him up and snow him with Valium. Looking back, I knew Jimmy was hurt and stunned. I didn't blame him and no one could. Hours ago he had the round fragments sewn into his forehead and the missions were continuing to become more dangerous. Protocol and common sense would say to medevac him back to Bagram on the next available flight.

Once again I found myself in the gray area.

But risk and suffering are the ways of virtue.

I sat privately with Jimmy and said, "You're back in." I told him the team needed him, and the truth was we did, but there

"BUKA"—the men of the platoon we did everything to save. COP Blessing, Afghanistan 2010.   *Courtesy of the ERQS PJ team archives.*

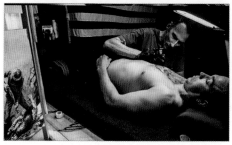

Taken from "Salvation," a photo exhibit of my tattoo work by Alaska-based photographer Joe Yelverton, Eagle River, Alaska, 2013. I urge readers to visit joeyelverton. com to read his piece "Anonymous Samurai."

Courtesy of Joe Yelverton.

A young Marine version of myself, mid to late 1990s.

Courtesy of the Marines.

"The Spirit World." Humble beginnings, Recon Indoc, Kaneohe Bay, Oahu, 1994. *Courtesy of the Marines.*

Absorbing the ominous grandeur of Alaska on the approach to the receding Eklutna Glacier, 2011.

Courtesy of the author.

Amphibious Reconnaissance Platoon, 3rd Marines, Kaneohe Bay, Hawaii, 1996, and a rare picture of David Cheairs and Jeff Atad somewhere in the Pacific, 1995.

Courtesy of the Marines.

Chris Robertson, Leo Claunan, and me prior to the fast-rope fiasco. Bagram, Afghanistan, 2008. *Courtesy of the ERQS PJ team archives.*

Fast-rope training in an old minefield. Afghanistan, 2008.

Courtesy of the ERQS PJ team archives.

Force Blue working with NOAA during restorative efforts post–Hurricane Irma, 2017.

Courtesy of Angelo Fiore.

French commando training, with no regards to safety… well, except for some old tires to break your fall. French Polynesia, 1995.

Courtesy of the author.

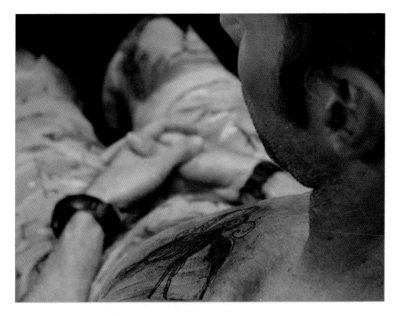

Freshly tattooed by Scott Campbell after our return from Bulldog Bite, late November 2010, Bagram, Afghanistan.　　*Courtesy of Casey Neistat.*

Getting "recovered" out of the ocean by a CH-46 via "Wet SPIE" and a bird's-eye view of fast-roping onto a submarine somewhere off the coast of Oahu 1995–96.　　*Courtesy of the author.*

Ground perspective of Operation Bulldog Bite 2-C. Photo taken shortly before the events of November 14, 2010, showing the steep and difficult terrain. *Courtesy of the ERQS PJ team archives.*

Hoist and litter training, Afghanistan, 2008.
Courtesy of the ERQS PJ team archives.

Indoc incident at the Alamo, San Antonio, Texas, 2001.

Courtesy of an innocent bystander.

Jennifer and me, downtown Anchorage, Alaska, 2009.

Courtesy of the author.

My family and friends at the Silver Star Ceremony Anchorage, Alaska, 2013. We deployed a few days after the ceremony. This would be the last time I would see and share time with my father.

Courtesy of the Air Force.

Me and the boys atop the Sunshine Buttress, Turnagain Arm, Alaska, 2018.

Courtesy of the Jennifer Sparks.

ROGER   20 DEC 12
MSGT/SPARKS —

HEARD ABOUT YOUR CONTINUED
HEROISM... THIS TIME IN ALASKA.

I'M PROUD TO SERVE
WITH YOU.   Martin E Dempsey
18TH CHAIRMAN JCS

Letter from General Martin Dempsey, the 18th chairman of the Joint Chiefs of Staff, December 2012, referring to Bulldog Bite and the jump mission into the Alaska National Wildlife Reserve to assist Heimo Korth and his wife, Edna.

Courtesy of the author.

Climbing in "Little Swiss," Alaska.

Courtesy of the author.

The sides of the mountain are steep, but the top is beautiful.

Courtesy of the author.

Life hanging by a thread with "Pedro." Pech Valley, Afghanistan, 2010.

Courtesy of the ERQS PJ team archives.

Meeting the Snow family and visiting Jesse's grave. Dayton, Ohio, 2012.

Courtesy of Jesse's father, John Snow.

My dad, "Big Rog" 1970s.
Courtesy of the author's family.

My dear friend Craig and I have shared many life-enriching experiences together. Seen here hours before a decision to test our fate. Crow Pass, Alaska, 2007.   *Courtesy of the author.*

My father's favorite things, and the home I grew up in. Fort Worth, Texas, 1970s.   *Courtesy of the author's family.*

My favorite picture of my sister, the toughest person I will ever know.

Courtesy of the author's family.

National Park Service Patrol. Denali, Alaska, 2007.

Courtesy of the author.

Packrafting remote Alaska with nothing but the absolute essentials, 2007.

Courtesy of Craig Chalmers.

PJ graduation photo. Albuquerque, New Mexico, 2003. If we are smiling it is because we're leaving.

Courtesy of the Air Force.

Post-dive bubble "Pinning Ceremony" with teammate and buddy Kent "Hambone" Odonell, Oahu, Hawaii, 1995. "Athletic cut" speedos were the rage in the 1990s, as shown here with my Recon buddies at some random triathlon on Oahu, 1995.

Courtesy of author's family.

Quality time with Jimmy Settle in Scott Campbell's studio. Los Angeles, California, 2017.

Courtesy of Joe Yelverton.

Reconnaissance Team "Jackal 2." Udari Range, Kuwait 1998.

Courtesy of the Marines.

Reloading and refueling at Asadabad, Afghanistan, November, 2010.

Courtesy of the ERQS PJ team archives.

Scenic views of the Pech and Watapur Valley, Afghanistan, 2010.

Courtesy of Brandon Stuemke.

Sharing what we can with Casey, Scott, and David. Bagram, Afghanistan, 2010.

Courtesy of David Kuhn.

Mom snapped a photo of some family time around the holidays, circa 1978 or 1979 Fort Worth, Texas.

Courtesy of the author's family.

The Alaska PJs involved in Bulldog Bite, FOB Joyce, Afghanistan, November, 2010.

Courtesy of the ERQS PJ team archives.

The entire CSAR team tasked with Bulldog Bite, FOB Joyce, Afghanistan, November 2010.

Courtesy of the ERQS PJ team archives.

These men fought and died with us on the hillside that night. The next time I saw them was looking into their eyes in the back of a magazine: *People,* December 2010.

Courtesy of the author.

Throwing them "chicken bones." Camp Pendleton, California, 1998.

Courtesy of the Marines.

are always larger aspects at play. Despite his injury he needed to climb back on the pale horse, and to face the tiger, for himself. Most never get a second chance in combat and I wanted Jimmy to have his. To be injured in combat and have to walk away from your team is something that you can never move past. This decision would save men's lives in the days to come.

In today's day and age when people get shot at they pull out their smartphones and take pictures. That's new, but timelessness eventually takes over. After a gunfight people will run their hands over bullet holes, or the congealing blood drying at different stages. Touching, gazing, and connecting to what happened. Attempting to capture and understand it. When this happens regularly and with continued intensity for a week you're no longer a voyeur to the peep show. You're the actor in your very own porno.

For the initiated there is a certain joy in sharing the experience of combat. In a way it could be the reckless abandon of our mortality. We all seek something visceral and real. In many ways like a moth to the flame. If you're seeking to find something intangible from this job, well, guess what? It's your lucky fucking day. Here's what you've been seeking.

What really fucks guys up is if they don't allow their experiences to change them. Some fight their emotions and refuse to face fear, grief, or horror. We have to grow from it and that takes courage, because in the end we'll be different. I think that grief is like the same force that causes a flower to bloom. Grief never goes away. To live with the grief you have to express it. It forever becomes a part of you. Wasn't it Sade who sang, "Tenderness comes from pain"?

It's our suffering that brings us to our humanity. Enduring all this makes us much more thoughtful. You cannot process these things while they're happening. In the heat of it there is a magical aspect to losing yourself and serving others.

That was how Bulldog Bite began for me.

The calls would continue to come about every three to four hours apart. We flew missions day and night. At times the objective area would be surreal. In my sleep-deprived stupor I would mistake Hellfire and artillery secondary fires as campfires. Wondering what crazy brazen lack of discipline on our bubbas' part. Hoisting down into these scenes on NVGs to haul mutilated remains and men half dead while being shot at. Ted and I performed a hoist where the pilot put the rear stabilizer into the cliff, damaging it badly. I didn't care about that but while still in the hover I told Ted to not disconnect from the hoist because it would be better to hoist him back up after he was shot. He agreed. Forty-eight hours into the operation we had hoisted thirty-eight casualties. These were not guys with stubbed toes. This was a guy missing his arm, dragging his dead buddy to you.

The aircrews we flew with were amazing. We felt a deep bond with them. None of these things could happen without complete trust in one another and our abilities. No matter what would take place we knew we were in it together.

In between missions we would try to maintain a sense of normalcy. Eat, sleep, clean your weapon, read, and work out. Working out to me has always been about taking control of my direction, and setting myself straight. Looking back on it now, it was clear how much I needed that in the difficult times between the desperate calls. We would just live with our gear on. If you were not wearing it, it was set next to you. We were covered in dry blood and feces. When men die they relax and release their remaining contents. We hoisted everyone. Everything becomes permeated in the smell of war. The scent of blood, cordite, sweat, and feces becomes a tangible memory.

A call came in while I was doing box jumps and calisthenics. My gear and weapon set next to the box, my radio was on full volume monitoring their frequencies. It was 4:11 p.m., the sun was hot and soon to be setting. The initial 9 line was two alphas and one hero.

My experience told me the two Cat A wounded were probably going to die within the next thirty minutes; and for one, the hero, his mortal life had passed. This all sounds extreme, and it is; however, for the surreal nature of what we had been doing that week it was somewhat practiced. We were looking at a hoist. Of note, the 9 line stated "armed escort required." Being Pedro, we didn't need an armed escort, it was built in, but we sure as hell wouldn't turn away from good help. That would be like turning down the chance to take an *Easy Rider* centerfold to your senior prom.

Our armed escorts were two Apaches and one Kiowa. This all happens quickly. In less than ten minutes we are all airborne. The initial plan was to just do a trail, with the understanding that if things got crazy, we would switch to a leader option. We utilize two helos for this, putting Jimmy Settle and Brandon Stuemke in the trail bird. The lead aircraft carried "Ski," myself, and our CRO, "Koa" Bailey. Although the situation was dire at the time, I felt confident about the information from the 9 line. As the lead element with two aircraft it's best to let your men do the work. You observe and control. We would apply this rule by allowing the trail bird to execute the hoist and patient treatment solo as we orbited, controlling the situation from above. If things changed for the worse en route we would switch and perform a leader option and put our ass on the line first in order to suss out the situation as we were solving it.

We launched very quickly and discussed the details on the way. We flew up the valley for what should be a short flight. Our objective was less than ten miles away. The helo can easily fly 120 mph as the crow flies, so ten miles is a moment in time. We fly with the doors wide open sitting with our feet dangling out unless we have patients. The unobstructed view blazes by with amazing speed and sensations. Along the mountains you could see these extensive trail networks, almost like how I imagine the Ho Chi Minh Trail in Vietnam would appear from the air. This was one of the main ground routes through the area, and a hotbed for the insurgents. The area reminded me of Tucson in the 1940s, but extremely steep and mountainous, a hard area to control because of the rugged terrain and harsh weather conditions.

When we launch like this on a mission you are forced into a meditative projection of what you're flying rapidly toward. You think about the terrain, the casualties, and the best tactics to streamline the problem solving. About what problems are approaching and if there is anything you are not considering. Your senses heighten and time starts getting weird.

We circled just south of the objective. We were coordinating with the Apaches and Kiowas to cover our infil. We were taking sporadic ground fire but something less apparent was beginning to happen. We flew south of the objective for just a short time, listening to the guys on the ground and coordinating with the assault weapons team. Coordinating five aircraft in a fluid situation is not as easy as it sounds, but the effort was clear: get our helo to the casualties as soon as possible. The situation on the ground was changing and growing much worse.

In a very short period of time the report would change dramatically. The radio operator changed voices a few times. We could hear overwhelming gunfire over the radio transmissions. Our headsets were being overwhelmed with information, we were coordinating with the Apaches, the ground team, as well as ourselves.

The reports changed. The tone of the men on the radio spoke more than the facts. Shit was getting bad. Or worse. The number jumped from two to now six casualties. The voice on the ground, relaying numbers and coordinates, told us something more, too. We all heard it.

Fear and impending panic.

We all knew it wasn't going to be routine even by the intensity of the last seventy-two hours. We immediately changed our plan to a leader option, which would put our helicopter into the zone before Jimmy and Stuemke. By this time the voice on the radio had grown emotional, cursing, yelling, tough to understand. I began to really sense that things were out of control. Our new plan was to put lead in, link up, receive trail, start packaging, and call the birds back in for exfil. What this meant was I would hit the ground first with Koa, and then Ski would drop in, and we would get the tactical situation under control and collect the casualties. Then we would call in the trail helo. We would then package and hoist the casualties getting them to the forward surgical team as quickly as possible.

The farther up the valley we flew, the steeper the terrain. The area beneath me looked so familiar, like some arid desert version of the rugged Chugach Mountains where we're often rescuing climbers and injured sheep hunters. We approached the area, all of us scanning the sides of the mountains for our men. We spotted two or three friendlies huddled around a shrub brush. Our helo flew low, quickly approaching the men we had spotted. We readied for the hoist, Koa and me weighting the cable. We connected into the device and disconnected from the helo. With a flick of my thumb we were suspended and ready to lower.

We committed to the terminal area. The altitude was 7,200 feet and the terrain was steep and undulating. I pointed to an area 40 feet below and a hundred meters west of where we initially saw the three men huddled around the steep scrub. This indicated to the crew the exact location I wished to hoist. We did a sharp clockwise circle over the objective, a wisp of purple smoke lingered on the finger out of the corner of my eye. We had been told it had been clear for fifteen minutes prior to going in, but as soon as we came into the circle the enemy fire erupted in a bewildering display of violence.

We were committed as a team. I began to notice the pops,

snaps, and thuds over the scream of our engines and rotors. The only thing you can do is focus on each moment.

Tracers and shit flew everywhere. Changes and chaos continued over the radio.

Koa and I would be lowered to the ground first. In this moment, speed and audacity are our only magic. We were already hooked up on the hoist and suspended. I was outside the cabin with my feet stabilizing us. Koa was facing directly into my chest disconnecting from our internal comms. Although it was obvious, I screamed to him we were taking fire. I had been obstructing his view with my body. In a brief moment I made certain to make eye contact with him and give a nod.

As we flared and began to hoist the area erupted in gunfire. When I say erupted in gunfire, I mean it was overwhelming in every sense. Overwhelming to the point that I couldn't hear the helicopter. Overwhelming to the point that it was clear we had seconds to live, or possibly were already dead.

Percussion and snaps filled the air, a cold void occupied the spaces between.

I've witnessed my share of combat, and what we experienced during those moments is impossible to explain. Hollywood, or any books, this one included, will forever fall short. The gunfire coming through the aircraft looked like chem lights whizzing past. So I knew the rounds were from crew-serve machine guns shooting at us, and bullets were zipping between Koa and me as we clipped into the hoist. In reflection, the horror of what you're witnessing amid something like that can easily overcome you. It is the realm of the subconscious. You're stuck in the moment to moment, and you become removed from yourself.

The bullets popped and hissed by in amazing volume that seemed to grow in intensity. Koa relayed to the pilot and flight engineer, "We're taking fire, get us down! Go! Go! Go!"

I pointed down to where I wanted to go. I was off the comms now. I was disconnected, which is why I pointed. As the helicopter was flying, I keep pointing at that spot and Brandon Hill, the flight engineer, the guy lowering us, instructed the pilot, "Ten right. Ten right. Forward ten. Forward ten. Hold hover."

Hill ran the hoist to the ground, and he ran it fast. There we were, plummeting down, lowered into the red maw of whatever awaited. As we dropped, the continual hiss and pop of rounds came from every direction. I wrapped my arms and legs around Koa in an attempt to shield him from the inevitable. I could feel the inputs of the helo through the thin cable jerking back and forth. This couldn't end well.

Marcus Maris was our aircraft commander, and I'm alive today to tell this story because of him and the other pilots. We all are. His nickname when we operated was Cyclone, and I was Anvil. As a crew we'd decided together to make the insertion. None of us could have imagined how bad shit was about to get. He could see out the right side for the hover, and the sight below was definitely disturbing. Maris and that entire HH-60 crew were solid professionals, not to mention they had some heavy coconuts between their legs. We believed in each other and what we were doing together.

I'd been in life-and-death situations before, but at that moment something was very different. The intensity of the violence around us, blossomed as we continued to plummet to its center. I told myself, *I'm going to die right now*—but at the same time I wanted to make it better for the guys who needed my help below. In those seconds of fleeting horror and panic, the *real* world around me became absolutely *surreal*, forcing me into simple, shrimp-brain thinking. I thought, *How can I stay alive for the next five seconds?* It was every five seconds from then on. I kept thinking, *Well, I'm going to die any moment here*, and as each second ticked away, the world around me became more and more surreal and more and more nightmarish.

Despite the reality and speed we were lowered the 40 feet and it felt like a lifetime. And then another.

Above the hurricane howl of the helo rotor, I could hear and feel steady gunfire. Everywhere. When you're being shot at you hear distinct snaps, and as we neared the ground those percussive snaps zipped around us at a rate that didn't make sense. At the rate we fell, we also made a few rotations on the wire. Add that factor and the pulse of tracers ripping past us, the feeling was only enhanced. If we were not already dead, we were gambling in the space of a heartbeat.

The things I am articulating are in studied hindsight. However, as I stated above, in the midst of living through these moments it is a thing of the subconscious. Whatever we are unknowingly harboring and projecting will become the motives of our actions. The wolves and sheep of our brains orchestrate our actions. Resolve and intent.

You either have those two things or you don't. Resolve and intent. It doesn't mean you've been in combat or rescuing people forever. You could have a young man more switched-on with his resolve and intent than an old grizzled warrior. A young PJ is training all the time to be prepared for mortal situations and is thinking all the time about life and death, but your view of your own mortality changes over time. Think of your own mortality when you were eighteen; now you're a father, and your view on life and death changes. A man can be in the career field for a lifetime, but his views on dying and death will change. They change over time and they change in a muzzle flash or in the pressure wave of an IED blast. We all would experience a shift in resolve and intent in the week of Bulldog Bite. Men can go catatonic with fear. Others will step forward and beyond what they knew they were capable of achieving. War and fear can alter your view of mortality; deep-seated beliefs change in an instant. Your view on mortality becomes a moving map. Unfortunately most in the career field only think about their resolve and intent once or twice as young PJs, but when they get older and have children of their own, a new vision of mortality appears. When you're young you can be somewhat protected from these thoughts. Even when you're young and continually jumping out of aircraft into precarious scenarios, your adrenaline is going, and the reason your adrenaline is going is because there is a very real chance of death there, and that is what gives you that sense of exhilaration. The samurai believed that the moment you set foot outside your home, you needed to live as if your life were already over. Yamamoto said, "In constantly hardening one's resolution to die in battle, deliberately becoming as one already dead. . . . The person without previous resolution to inevitable death makes certain that his death will be in bad form."

I stretched my right foot toward the mountain below, toward solid ground. I ascertained we were getting shot at from at least three different positions by crew-serve fire. The locations and directions were abstract and at the time I could not comprehend their origins. When my right leg reached the ground, everything stopped. I saw a red flash moving at incredible speed come from the edge of the finger where the purple wisps of smoke had just been less than fifty meters away. At that very moment when our boots made contact, the world went orange, blinding orange. An overwhelming brightness engulfed us, simultaneously followed by intense heat and pressure. It was as if our weight on the earth had triggered the violence. The percussive blast and heat sent Koa and I down. Hard.

The rocket-propelled grenade detonated no more than twenty feet from us.

I rose to my knees, perhaps out of disbelief. Reflexively, I unhooked us from the hoist cable. This might sound strange, but I didn't know if I was alive. I felt fuzzy, ears ringing, eyes still seeing the flash, but then Koa jumped up. His own reaction brought me to my senses. He's an incredibly strong and powerful guy, and he leaped to his feet in what must have been a subconscious reaction to get up and fight. I immediately grabbed him, forced him down to the ground with me. If there is a hard rule in war, it's *don't stand up when you're being shot at*. You're going to get ripped in fucking half. I didn't want to see that, so I kept grabbing him and pulling him down, and having him fall on top of me.

We were getting shot at with such magnitude that we couldn't return fire—there was no one we could even see to shoot. Dirt and gravel filled the air, and on top of that we were directly under the helo, in the eye of the storm. Fifteen feet out from the eye, hurricane-force winds whipped vertically, but right underneath the helo, the winds came straight down, hot and recirculating. Extremely hot fucking air. Imagine the strongest fan you've ever felt, blades slicing the air to the point where you cannot physically stand or fight. Now make the air hot. Dragon's breath. The winds alone make it difficult if not impossible at times to stand. And as soon as that yoke of safety in the eye moves past you, the winds will go horizontal tossing anything not anchored in the soil to violently be cast airborne.

There was so much gunfire hitting right where we were lying that at first I couldn't see or hear a thing. Between RPG and the gunfire impacting the ground around us, and the conditions created by the HH-60, the world had become nothing but noise and debris.

Rounds were continually snapping at the earth and air around us. It sounds odd, but in reflection it was difficult to breathe. The helo continued to hover, still above us. This was procedure. They needed to know if we were off the hoist, so they could recover or shear it to pick up forward airspeed and get the hell out of there.

Over our headset I heard, "Comm check, Guardian Angel?!!"

That was the crew calling from above, desperate for some sort of communication, any communication at all. They required verbal indication that we were off the hoist. They needed to know if we were shot up and still attached to the helo, or lying dead and dying disconnected. Concerned about dragging or injuring us on the ground, and unsure if we were off the hoist yet or not, the crew remained overhead. The nerve and resolve exhibited by the crew, with Maris at the helm, is hard to comprehend. They needed to get the hell out of there before it was too late, if it wasn't already. Any moment an RPG could hit the mark and end it for all of us.

When the RPG zipped toward us and detonated my hand was keying the mic. I instinctually and somewhat unintelligibly relayed "Holy shit!" to the crew above. The last thing any of us wanted was the aircraft to come crashing down on our heads.

"Get out of here!" Koa responded.

Rich Joy, the left gunner above, began to engage with the .50 cal. He unloaded 250 rounds of exploding, armor-piercing, and incendiary rounds into active enemy positions. Red-hot casings rained down from the sky, and I was comforted by the percussion of the .50 cal firing and feeling those casings raining down onto us. It felt powerful to have those forces exerting on our behalf. The bullet casings poured down on us, propelled by those hurricane force winds.

Kung. Kung. Kung. Kung.

Hot devils everywhere. Ours and theirs.

I was glad they were killing the people who were trying to kill us, because I couldn't see them and that's the way it works. You couldn't see anything. It's like someone is torturing your loved ones in the next room, and you can't do anything, but then you hear shots being fired, and you know the bad guys are getting butchered, "Fuck them. Fuck you guys." In this way, the heavy fire above us felt good. I could hear it all around us. Our trail helo orbited tightly overhead and was actively engaging targets as well. Knowing our team was returning the love was as comfortable as it was going to get.

At least when I died, I'd know the bastards were feeling it as well.

I noted the exact direction Joy was firing. It was one of the only things we could be certain of. The last known friendlies were uphill at a 70-degree heading about fifty to a hundred yards, but in the chaos, I couldn't even comprehend the distance.

Dust and debris from the rotor wash and the enemies' rounds kicked up a dirt blizzard around us. Koa relayed not to infil any additional PJs due to the overwhelming fire, ensuring that they understood. Our intent initially was to put myself and Koa in followed by Ski. Obviously that wasn't going to happen.

The hisses and pops kept flying and impacting within feet of our position.

Once on the ground it was game on. I hadn't thought we were going to live through the hoist, after the RPG detonated and the continued impacts around us the hands of the world's clock slowed. I noticed the hoist cable lying there. It rested right there beside us, the hook sitting in the dirt and running up to the helo. Shit continued hitting all around us, too intense for us to look out at the vista below. The helo gathered forward speed and rolled off the mountain, into the thin air below. Falling at first—the aircraft itself was too heavy, and at too high an altitude, to fly up; it had to tilt and basically plummet toward the valley floor to get airspeed. I distinctly remember watching as that hook, our lifeline, went dragging away.

Within moments the two 60s joined together overhead in an circular orbit and engaging everything, attempting to tame a tactical situation that was by far out of control.

From at least two or three different places, the DShK crew-serve fire or PKM fire rained down on us. On insert we could see two or three coalition members wearing MultiCam American uniforms, and so we knew those were the good guys. Koa and I were intent on reaching them.

The helos circled above us, engaging everything they could see, but this was a volatile and dynamic situation. We didn't know this, but as we were being inserted, insurgents had overrun the hill. Enemy infiltrated the area where the casualties had awaited us. As the helicopters orbited and suppressed the enemy, Koa and I bear-crawled at a run, up the steep, rocky slope. A few degrees steeper, and we would have required ropes. The mountainside was as close to class-five terrain as you could get. Really steep; thick brush. The mountains towered above us.

When we crested the top, we were ten feet from the small scrub tree where we believed the ground force commander and radio operator were waiting. Two of our men were there. At the exact moment we put eyes on them, another RPG hit, impacting the tree we were headed for, and heat and pressure tossed us both down below.

Stunned and half-lucid we scrambled toward what was left of the base of the tree, where the first guy sat, all but five to ten feet from us. I watched as piss pooled at his legs. The guy had his helmet blown completely off.

He looked up at me, his face was injured from his helmet and the blast. He was bleeding badly from the mouth, and who knows how conscious he was. "Get down! We just took an RPG," he said, as if he was completely unaware of time and space. He winced, then shook his head. "Goddamn. I thought you were gonna die on the way in," he said. "The captain is dead. I'm in charge now."

Koa and I tucked down by this ruin of a tree. The rounds would hit on the other side of the hill, and I could feel the impact of the earth. We were surrounded by chewed-up earth. RPGs would hit the knoll that sheltered us, bounce off, and explode.

Thud.

Boom!

We couldn't talk. Our mouths were so dry, so full of debris and dirt, that we couldn't speak. Koa pulled out some water and took a drink as the barrage of fire continued to zing over our heads. We must have looked as if we were casually discussing the previous Sunday's football scores, but what we were really doing was talking about how we were going to solve the problem at hand and get these guys out. I reasoned, but was by no means certain, that the enemy couldn't support the amount of fire we had been enduring for that long. I felt fairly confident that the enemy was attempting to overrun our position. What we were hearing and feeling, the constant barrage of bullets and rockets, was not harassment fire.

Koa handed the water to me and I took a drink. These guys just stared at us like, *What the fuck?* They were panicked, beyond themselves, and concussed.

Our pilot, Maris, continually asked for updates. Communications were spotty. I relayed we were with friendly forces, but that the tactical situation was not secure. He felt overwhelmingly responsible for us, but the helos were out of ammo and critical on fuel.

A little micro-hill shielded us from what was happening on the other side. Blast after blast shook the ground.

As we got our wits, we oriented ourselves to the known targets around us. Koa then confirmed distance and direction with his trusty old military compass. We passed it off to the radio operator, but he was barely able to get out the distance and direction. He was unable to talk clearly, but finally he managed to get the message off with Koa assisting. Whenever the guy would start to sputter or mess up, Koa would hop on the radio. Koa was very hesitant giving the inputs because we did not have certainty of where the other friendly positions were located on the mountain, making it challenging to control the accuracy of what was being put out on the radio.

We had the wherewithal to talk to the helo, and had them

give us intel on what they knew about the enemies' and friend-lies' positions. At that point they shared with us some un-pleasant news. Both helicopters were all but out of fuel and ammo, so they had to refuel and get more ammunition. This was pretty somber to hear.

As pararescue, we work intimately with the pilots and aircrew. When we hoist down into a situation, whether it is an Alaskan civilian rescue or a combat mission, that thin metal wire could just as well be connected to our hearts. We both knew our guys would do everything in their power to take care of us, as well as the troops we were there to rescue. The reality was that the helos had to leave for fuel, repairs, and ammo, if any of us were going to get off that mountain. The area swarmed with heavily armed insurgents. If we were ever going to get home in one piece, the helos had to return to the FOB.

There is no question that Captain Maris, the aircrew, and the other helo pilots and crew kept us alive up to that point. I knew for certain that Maris would as soon fly the helicopter into the enemy on the side of that mountain as leave our asses. We respected Maris and his decision-making at the controls of the helo to the point that Koa and I could operate with the reckless abandon needed. The only way combat rescue works successfully is that each guy carries out responsibilities. In the midst of combat you have to rely on each other completely. Think of how the Spartans used their shields; your personal shield isn't what saves you, it's the men next to you. Koa and I were operating at the lunatic fringe, the razor's edge of our ability in a dynamic and lethal environment.

Huddled low by the small depression adjacent to the mangled tree Koa continued to work the radio, trying to coordinate fire and get rounds on the targets. My concerns were to locate the casualties. It was obvious we would have to fight our way to them. The assault weapons team, the Apaches, prefer to fly at ten thousand feet, which is three thousand feet higher than where we were. Like a fixed-wing fighter, they need to be able to come in on a direct heading, so as to launch their weapons off the front of their aircraft. The HH-60s can shoot off the sides. That's a huge difference. In this situation it was one or the other. You can't have both types of helicopters hovering over you at the same time, especially in the tight airspace of a high-mountain Afghanistan valley. The fog of war is a very real thing.

The coordination for an air strike from the assault weapons team took about ten minutes. The whole time we were at that location we were taking an amount of gunfire that I couldn't imagine would last. Each second that passed, that overwhelming amount of fire continued, with rounds impacting within feet from us. *Pop. Pop. Pop. Pop.* Nonstop, save for the occasional *boom!* from an RPG detonating yards from us on the other side of the hill.

During those fifteen minutes, we were able to ascertain where the friendlies where and get the call off. Inbound came two Apaches, the Longbow team, each loaded with Hellfire missiles. I saw the Hellfires coming. The Apache has to come from far off—they appear as a little dot until they come closer. You hear the servos and fins on the Hellfire first. You see a puff of smoke, and then you can know death is coming. When one of those missiles flies toward you, you see this white speck, and that speck grows larger and larger. Those white dots were coming right toward us. Horrifying. I could hear the servos on the missile, directing the weapon. *Zip. Zip. Zip.* From the looks of it, we would be dead in seconds.

The first missile passed directly by us. I could have read the serial numbers on the side.

Boom!

Dirt and rock exploded into the air showering us with debris. Spooky. The second Apache was coming up the valley. I saw a puff of smoke come from the sides of the Apache and then another. The Hellfires snaked toward us slightly ahead of their sound, and two by two they passed right over our shoulders in a blinding streak, impacting just over the small hill. Again their percussion and lethality gave comfort to us.

All of this we observed through a maze of tracer fire interlocking around us. The sun was setting and this intensified the luminescence.

Countless rounds zipped across the mountainside with a crazy intensity. Multiple colors of smoke wisps filled the valley.

The first missiles struck with a force that made the mountainside shudder. The two explosions brought death and silence to a handful of the insurgents who were uncomfortably close. After each percussion there would be a void of silence and hesitation, as if everyone questioned whether they were still alive. After the first two hit, the second two missiles cleaned up the enemies directly above us. The idea of our rocket fire so close was horrifying. In the Marine Corps, I had been around plenty of terminal control with aircraft, but I'd never wanted or needed to call fire in that close. I really maintained that singular thought, the whole time since we had first clipped into the hoist: *We have seconds to live, let's make it good. Just make it good.* Now I added a new thought: *Don't make problems. Just solve problems. Solve problems. Make this better.*

At no point did I really think we were going to get off that mountain alive. But the Hellfires extended precious seconds in our favor. Each explosion bought us one thing: time.

Not long after the fourth Hellfire impacted, one of our guys dove over the knoll. The man was visibly shaken. I immediately assumed he was the platoon leader; it was in the way he carried himself and in the way he was speaking.

His mouth was filled with dirt and rocks. Dried tears tracked through the dirt and blood on his face. His hands shook, uncontrollably. And he looked me right in the eyes and said, "You guys got a smoke?"

I reached for my belt. "I've got two red, two green," I said. "What do you want?"

"No. No, man! A cigarette!"

I immediately knew this was the guy making things happen. He would be the one if anyone who knew what the hell was going on. After all, he'd risked everything to crest the hill. Right? It was eerie to attempt conversation with him. Koa continued directing aircraft, while I tried to ascertain the number of wounded and where they were located.

"Where are your casualties?" I asked.

"Right over the hill," he said, gesturing to the knoll behind him, "thirty feet from us."

"Take us to them," I said.

"No," he replied. "No. We'll all die."

I had to trust this guy. It was difficult in that we were in somewhat of a bind. The whole time I was talking to him there were rounds impacting around us, and I could see RPGs detonating and bouncing off the rocks right above. I was talking to a man who wanted only to smoke a cigarette. Through my scattered interrogation, he basically told me that they were black on crew-serve ammo. This was bad news. Really fucking bad news. The reality that the only fire came from enemy weapons forced that cold wet blanket of fear to tighten. If your men don't have crew-serve weapons, you're pretty much useless. You have to overwhelm the enemy and maneuver on them so you can kill them. The battlefield is not like when you're on a shooting range and shooting targets with M4s. You have to suppress and maneuver over the terrain and kill the bad guys. If you don't do it, they will.

Koa and I had basically hoisted into a meat grinder. We were surrounded by heavily armed insurgents, and the Americans we'd come to help were out of ammunition.

Koa and I huddled. Koa asked, "What do you think, Rog?" At this point we had five to ten minutes left of daylight.

We knew we would need to collapse security to the casualty site. We asked the platoon leader if he had men available to move to our position. He seemed perplexed, and reminded us they were out of ammo. The men we were trying to help seemed like ghosts. Everything was in a fog.

"Koa, what do you have for medical equipment?" I asked.

"That's it," he said, tossing me three battle packs. The battle pack is sexy because it's been dolled up with years of refinement. The pack includes wound dressings and tourniquets, airway devices, and needles to decompress lungs, along with coagulant dressings, and fentanyl lollipops. This is a pack for care under fire, and will keep guys alive buying time to get them to trauma surgeons.

Koa had coordinated with Pedro the refuel and reset, and this news made it clear that we would be on the ground for a while. The helos would be delayed. Time was irrelevant.

We directed the platoon leader to get four to six guys to move to our location. It occurred to me that we didn't know their challenge and password. These are words used in combat for identification, to be recognized as friendly. Koa continued working the comms, and I tried to reassure these four guys huddled near us that we would get their buddies out. Our presence seemed to give order to everything for them. Koa and I knew the original plan was to exfil these dudes that night, but we also knew they weren't going anywhere at the moment.

The platoon leader asked, "How do we get out of here? You guys are the experts. Where the fuck can we land a 47?"

Koa assured them that he would pass a "no shit" report of their ground situation, and what the men were facing, to their higher-up at Joyce. These guys were beyond fucked up. The platoon leader muttered, mostly to himself, "Let them know I am going to knock me out an O3 if we get back. Okay?" At this point he was emotionally all over the map. He went from crying to hugging and squeezing us both, telling us they couldn't believe we had flown into this.

Another one of the guys slapped me on the back and said, "Fucking PJs, I don't know how you are still alive! I don't know how you did it. Holy fuck!" he kept shouting over and over again, in awe that we had flown into that shit and lived. They were relieved we were there, as if the situation was now under control.

Our problems were not solved. The incoming fire was relentless; there was no time to celebrate.

Combat is just a traumatic chess match. If you have a crew-serve weapon, a guy with a machine gun, a big machine gun, and you have a bunch of really unlucky bastards off the end of that weapon, there will be rocks and little depressions those troops can hide behind or crouch down below when the heartless bastard with the chain gun opens up on them. Sure, if that beast hits you, the bullets will rip your arm off or do other horrible things to your body and psyche. The most important part is the psyche part—because when one of those guns begins to talk, everyone goes horizontal. Guys dive behind rocks or drop into holes, do anything they can to escape the relentless force bearing down on them. This situation is something we call the OODA loop. OODA stands for observe, orient, decide, and act. This is a way of explaining how we go through the process of reacting to stimulus. This is all about attacking the mind.

The OODA loop is the way of basically staying in the

chess match. The guys under fire can't do anything. And if you did hit any of them, his best friend is lying there ripped in half and bleeding everywhere, spurting blood, fucked up, so he can't do anything. You've limited his choices. And while that is taking place, you send your footloose unsavory friends over to come in from the side. You send a group of guys over to flank and do the job. During the predicament we were in it was probably five men or so. Now our guys are wearing armor and heavy boots, and packing radios and equipment and spare barrels and fucking rucks, food, and water. Our boys are up against agile fighters carrying AK-47s and wearing nothing but sandals and linens. They can move fast as fuck. They are deadly high-mountain athletes up against corn-fed flatlanders.

Once their guys get on the side, with their AK-47s, they will make their move. The guys on the ground can't react to the men coming in from their side, because the crew-serve weapons are limiting your choices mentally and physically. You would think the bastard with the belt-fed weapon is going to kill you, but the men off to the side are the real killers. The bad guys drop in and flank them, covered by the crew-serve fire, they engage guys from an area that cannot be defended. They are going to come prowling in there and shoot guys point-blank and bash the heads in with a rifle butt. The crew-served guys had us pinned down. They were in charge at the moment. I was waiting for the guys to sweep in from the side. And they were. They were flanking us. Those heartless bastards were on their way up over the ridge. That is what it takes to kill people. Our guys had all these casualties right over the hill from us. Now the enemy was coming, they were closing in, and soon would be moving over our position.

We're weighing our options, which have pretty much been reduced to sitting and waiting for the enemy to kill us, or make a break for it and attempt to get to the casualties over the hill and likely die in the attempt. That would not be improving anything.

To make matters worse, the Apaches informed us they were out of ordnance. They were out of chain gun ammunition. They had shot their load. They were done. We needed someone to circle around us, like the circles our helos had flown. In a fight, intimidation always matters. To even fly in close patterns around us would help. But they were out of everything, including fuel. The Apaches reluctantly signed off. They departed off into the sunset, literally. I knew the setting sun and impending darkness was on our side. I discussed this with Koa, reassuring both him and myself. Again the volume of enemy fire could not be sustained, something had to give.

Don't make problems, solve problems. Make this better. Make this better . . . just problems. Solve problems.

As soon as the Apaches disappeared our radios flickered with sound. An F-18 checked in with us. They will customarily tell us the ordnance they have onboard. He was carrying one MK-84. In this instance the MK could possibly stand for "might kill" Koa, me, and the rest of the Americans on that mountain. Calling a bomb strike on your own location is akin to trying to pet a polar bear. The odds you'll live to tell about the experience hover marginally low.

Koa locked eyes with me and asked, "What do you want to do, Rog?"

"How big? I asked.

"Two thousand," he said.

The way I saw it, we didn't have a choice. "Drop it, man," I said.

"Danger close, just northwest of our position," Koa said, as he made the call. He gave authorization. His credit card number, and the expiration date. The whole nine. Koa and I were doing the unthinkable, literally authorizing the pilot to possibly martyr us in the vain attempt to kill the remaining enemy.

The danger close call is really hard to try to explain.

When we set this in motion we knew it was very likely that the MK-84 would be lethal to the majority of us. Our situation was dire. We had no crew-serve ammunition, and we knew the enemy were moving in on us.

Fuck it.

Drop the damn thing. You play the cards in your hand.

We didn't know that the pilot was a different sort of guardian angel. I'll never even know the pilot's name, but I imagine this guy flying five hundred miles an hour, in a dive, positioned upside down so he can see us, and at the last possible second, he rolls his aircraft and releases a ton of death. He's a smart dude, but he's dropping a very dumb bomb. This is not a guided bomb. So in order to deploy it, he's doing dive-bomber shit. They don't need to do that in Afghanistan, because no one has surface-to-air missiles to pose a threat. But fighter pilots have developed tactics and procedures that are tried and true.

We heard the pilot say, "In the pop, danger close, verify."

"Roger," Koa said. "cleared hot." Because this is being recorded, this is evidence of that; this is the pilot and the military covering their asses, then covering them again.

In laymen's terms: This is on you?

Yes. I told you to do it.

Are you sure?

Yes.

There is no going back on that final confirmation.

The pilot says, "inbound," and he's got to come way out of the valley, and turn around and come back. He's finding an IP, an initial point, to come in from. Then, as he is coming in, he wants to see us, so he's marked our location on a heads-up display, and he wants to hit the release point just past us, and bombs away. He's coming at us and says "in the pop" and he's upside down, looking at us, and when he's in the pop, that is when we say, "cleared hot." You only say "cleared hot" when you see him pass you, and he's going to drop death, and then he rolls over, and we're somewhere in the middle.

Fortunately, our pilots are really good dropping these things, and they train all the time. But this is such a dynamic environment to bomb. He dropped an enormous bomb and he was done. Nothing to see here. He had taken off from Bagram, and a few moments after that explosive slipped out from the jet, falling toward us, he would turn back around and head back for debrief and hot chow.

For a moment our reality on the mountainside turned black. As if all the world's disasters struck at the exact moment: an inferno, an earthquake, and a hurricane. For the shudder of one heartbeat the disasters all paused in unison before they destroyed the world.

The bomb hit within a horrifying proximity to us. The combined effects both terrified and comforted. Two thousand pounds of high explosives detonated throwing stones thousands of feet in the air. The blast wave sailed right over our heads, showering us with an overwhelming amount of rocks and debris.

The percussion from the air strike gave us the only lull we could count on.

We lived for one reason: the terrain. I had assumed that if the bomb didn't hit us directly, we were likely to die from the percussion alone.

The bomb hit where the vertices of the ridge above met the top of the valley. Perfect placement. We were terrain shielded and the blast shot down and out of the valley, away from us. The blast wave from a bomb of this size is what kills you. The force of the discharge gelatinizes your hard organs. The wave is powerful and instantaneous. You've seen those pictures of atomic blasts and the movement of buildings. It's that coup-countercoup that creates the damage. The thermobaric pressure generates a wave that ruptures your organs.

With the tactical situation so out of control at that point, the danger close call was all we had. Anybody with real combat experience knows that war is not like the movies.

In real battles combat is like the ocean: extended firefights will ebb and flow. You have to understand and anticipate when the ebbs and flows are going to happen. After a two-thousand-pound bomb hits, and the dust and debris fill the air, and everyone's ears are ringing. Everyone is wondering if they are alive and are asking themselves what the fuck just happened— that is the ebb. So that was when I made my move, with animalistic decisions and movement.

I knew that was my one chance. I set off in the direction the cigarette guy had escaped from moments ago. The direction of the casualties and the ultraviolence. Before I sprang up, I gave a nod to Koa, then took off sprinting over the knoll toward where I hoped the casualties were holding on.

I knew Koa would be right behind me. The whole while we raced over the hill, debris and rocks rained from the sky. For a moment, the gunfire had ceased.

As we moved, I confirmed to Koa to stay on top of the security, so I would start treating right away. We knew our roles and identified where we would attempt to hoist from. Logically that would be downhill from the main source of casualties. Sporadic fire began to pick up. The hiss and pop came from unseen directions. The last light of day dwindled, and the rugged terrain made it all but impossible to know the direction of the enemy positions. We had absolutely no tactical control over what was going on. We had no crew-serve weapons ammo and no one lucid enough to direct. I knew Koa would have his hands full wrangling assets overhead and updating me.

We immediately came up and over the crest of that berm that had shielded us, not only from the relentless enemy fire and the MK-84 blast, but also the horrors awaiting on the other side.

The RPGs and Hellfires had devastated everything.

Bodies, trees, and debris strewn about the mountain. Men screamed and moaned. The air smelled of gunpowder and blood, something like rotten eggs soaked in ammonia. Bushes burned and smoldered. Gear littered the ground. Men with their armor blown off lay scattered throughout what looked like a freshly dug ditch. The earth had been chewed up, and everything was naked and raw, exposed to the marrow.

Out of my periphery directly below I saw Koa take a position. I started seeing casualties. Our troops were strung out over this steep mountainside. We beat the "security" there and I dove in to start treating. Koa worked the communications, and began relaying everything to me. We had a place to defend and hoist from, but the scene was overwhelming in every sense, from the destruction and carnage to the chaos and probability that one or both of us would die soon.

It took me about five to ten seconds to shift into trauma-lane gear, to go from not thinking I would live at all, to questioning if I was in fact still alive, to time to get to work. The entire scene on that mountainside embodied the meaning of surreal.

Koa said, "Get on 'em, Rog."

In some way his words stuck with me because I knew it was on me.

The first guy rested in the middle of a very shallow draw. I decided I would drag everything to him. It just seemed to make sense; the spot appeared to be a little flatter to hoist from and it was downhill from everyone else, so it would be a natural point to drag all the patients down to, and as easy to defend as anywhere else. Koa and I were thinking in unison.

Things just started to click. The two of us were on the same page with everything.

"I'll move the casualties to you," I said. We both knew he would be the center of our casualty collection point. He could coordinate with the aircraft that would get us out. From the spot I would drag all wounded and dead to.

I set to work on the first guy. A blast had thrown his body into a bush, suspending him halfway off the ground. His legs were turned backward; they twitched, and he was gasping loudly for each breath. He was almost gone at this point, his armor blown off his body. Think for a moment about the amount of explosive force it would take to rip a man's armor from his body. Even in normal working conditions, taking your body armor on or off is a painstaking chore that takes muscle and time. The shit is heavy and cumbersome. Now imagine those thick Kevlar plates being blown off you in a fraction of a second.

The poor guy had a gaping triangular wound on his right side, big enough to fit my fist through. I immediately got to work on him. I snatched a HyFin package from my battle pack and jammed it in his side. He grabbed on to me with intensity and force. He wouldn't let go. I struggled to pull free; I beat the hell out of him to get him off me. He seized my jacket, face, and neck desperately, barely clinging to life, pulling and clawing. I attempted to work him, struggling the whole time with his flailing. I jabbed a 14-gauge needle into his chest, first one side then the other, decompressing his left and then right lung. In addition to my other treatments, I gave him a fentanyl pop for the pain. Looking like an oversize Q-tip, with a small cylindrical white lollipop on one end and a marker cap on the other end, this is our modern equivalent to the old-school morphine shots medics gave in wars past. But unlike those old morphine shots, which took fifteen or twenty minutes to kick in, the lollipop becomes effective very quickly, within five minutes.

For some reason I paused with this guy before I treated him; nothing more than a second, but I did stop, to be there for him or for some other reason that I can't explain.

I couldn't sit long. I needed to keep moving.

I took a moment to survey my surroundings. Then I pushed up the steep cliff toward the next casualty, a man absolutely screaming. I could sense the enemy on the move, but I had no idea how close. I sprinted up the ravine, continually taking fire, trying to stay low.

Ten feet up the ditch. I reached the guy. He was screaming.

He lay twisted and on his right side. Blood covered his left arm. An arterial bleed. Where his triceps should have been I found a gaping hole, the muscle and bone basically ripped away. I wrapped a tourniquet on his arm and shoulder, and twisted the band into place.

He was shrieking before I got to him; twisting tissue through the constricting tourniquet did not affect him in any way other than stopping the bleeding. I rolled him onto his back and needle decompressed both sides on him, just as I had the guy a few moments earlier. I had no choice but to use the same needle. I had only two needles and knew I would need more than one.

The light at this point was gone. I worked in darkness, my hands barely visible as I felt over his body, checking to see if I had missed any other injuries. He continued screaming. The temperature was quickly heading below freezing.

Wailing.

Evidence of an airway. And, to the best of my abilities, I could tell he was not bleeding out.

So, on I went to the next guy.

Not far away, I found the next casualty lying on his stomach. He was saying something over and over, and it wasn't until I kneeled at his side that I could hear him. "Your kingdom come, your will be done, on earth as it is in heaven," he said. He continued repeating the Lord's Prayer over and over and over without answering any of my questions. I did a quick triage. He'd taken a bullet through the right butt cheek, and it had come out his right hip flexor. The socket of his hip protruded out of the front and side of his lower stomach area. The wound was massive. When a high-caliber round hits bone, the wound doesn't initially bleed. Instead it turns into a terrible pink mass of meat and froth. Almost as if you'd mixed blood and mashed potatoes; it has that look and consistency. Meat and tissue. The injury doesn't bleed because it is so traumatized. Like pink cauliflower; hideous. You don't even know what to do with it. In no training do they show you what to do with that shit.

The best thing you can do for a shot-up long bone is put on a tourniquet. But if the wound is on a hip bone those are primary arteries, vessels you can't effectively compress. This guy seemed to know that there wasn't much we could do. He wouldn't stop with the Lord's Prayer. I did what I could, but my medical supplies were limited. I didn't have too many options for a wound of that nature. I applied a battle dressing. There was no visible arterial bleed. He didn't have an airway problem. There wasn't much more I could do.

After I worked on him—this is where it gets really confusing—a guy appeared in the gully with me, and he was really trying to lend a hand. I'm not sure if he had medical training, but he was trying to help by telling me everyone's names and what the enemy was doing. I assumed he was on security. He had a 240 Golf, a large, powerful machine gun, and he was on his stomach with his barrel pointed out toward the north.

I kept moving farther up the steep ravine.

My eyes had adjusted to the darkness. But visibility was negligible, and the tracers that lit up the blackness would cause my pupils to contract, so I would struggle again to see. Using night-vision goggles was out of the question. The casualties were strung out twenty to thirty feet apart, surrounded by loose scrub brush in a gully with a nearly sheer incline.

I found the next guy sprawled out on the rocks. His helmet sat beside him, and he appeared to be kicked back and reclining. He mumbled, "Help my buddies. Help my buddies. Help my buddies." He just kept repeating this, and I couldn't see anything wrong with him. I glanced farther up the ravine. What I saw took a moment to make sense of.

There above me, in a mesquite tree, I spotted a body hanging upside down. The first glimmer of the evening moon revealed a shadowed figure, eviscerated and still illuminated by the first of the moonlight.

A rocket blast had inverted him, tossing him into the steep loose scrub, five feet off the ground and facing downhill. His feet were pointed up. With the tree on the uphill slope from me, this made him appear about seven feet above where I first saw him. The exiting wound from a crew-serve weapon had eviscerated him, ripping open his belly. His abdominal cavity was open in the crisp moonlight air.

The man's body shook. He wore a Crye Precision uniform, but was older. I noticed his beard. I thought, *What the fuck?* The rest of the men were young, clean-cut Army guys. Immediately I thought Special Forces, CIA, or a contractor. Obviously a different cat. I approached him to pull him down out of the tree, to at least recover his body, and he immediately started talking. His name was Karl and he said he was cold—we were all cold, but I knew he was revealing more. He was hypovolemic, and bleeding out.

For once my height really mattered.

I reached up for him. His legs were shaking really bad, which made me think he had a spinal injury, but I wasn't going to do anything more for him at the moment. I would take precautions and take it easy, but hanging upside down in scrub brush, exposed to crew-serve fire, was more dangerous than me doing C-spine precautions. I decided I would drag him down on top of me and try to get him bandaged up. I took his arms and pulled him out from the branches, as gently as possible. I did all I could to soften his fall to the rocks. I held his arms and jerked him into me as his legs and body dropped to the ground with a thud. I placed the partially used fentanyl lollipop between his cheek and gum.

He was doing relatively well, but the problem is that when your intestines or hard organs come out of your body, they dry up really quickly, and when they dry out the tissue dies and eventually you will follow. I knew that even if I saved his life there in the field, with his guts exposed, hanging out of his body, he was probably not likely to survive. He might die not of sepsis, but of organ failure later on.

I was going to do what I could to salvage Karl's life. If I could manage to save him he would likely be paralyzed and have a colostomy bag for life. But the guy was still alive, surprisingly chipper, so I decided I would do everything I could. Understanding the reasoning for everything you do in a situation like this is really important. He had a horrific injury, but there were other guys whose situation was even more dire.

Once I had Karl on the ground, I looked at his guts. I needed to get his organs back into his body and cover him up. I started getting mad at myself because I couldn't get his shirt off; at first I couldn't rip the material. There were no more dressings in my bag. I didn't have my trauma shears. I didn't have anything occlusive to put over the wound. I finally managed to rip off a portion of his shirt, and stuffed his intestines back into his abdominal cavity. The fabric would do more than help keep everything in its place—it would, more important, reduce heat and fluid loss.

His legs trembled.

I stared down at his quaking blood-and-bile-splattered pants. "Can you feel your legs shaking?" I asked.

He shook his head.

"Are you moving them?"

"No."

"I'll be back, okay, Karl?" I told him. There was nothing more I could do.

I looked around for more casualties. All the time that had transpired with the patients at this point was maybe thirty minutes. I'm not sure. I could sense no other casualties up the ravine. I decided to drop back down to patient one. I didn't see any security farther up the mountain. Four to six guys from the platoon slowly filtered toward us, bound for our location in between continued sporadic enemy fire. These men were grief-stricken, beyond words. They lay loosely around our casualty collection point, semiresponsive, staring into nothingness.

I assumed farther up were more security, but I couldn't be sure. It was fucking surreal; nothing was certain. The fire continued, slowed only by the night which now enveloped us. Everything remained chaotic; it was tough to really know anything that was going on. Koa and I controlled this one small location, with dead and dying men surrounding us.

We had no outside air support at that point. No Apaches. No fixed-wing fighters. No anything. I ran, half slid, down the ravine, and began working on the first guy again. When I got back to patient one I could tell he was slipping. Koa was still there, continuing to work with the platoon leader and attempting to dial in security. I could hear Koa directing guys where to go. I was still trying to assess the situation and give Koa an accurate patient count.

That's when patient one started coughing blood. I'm wasn't sure what was going on. His pulse raced. I stuck my thumbs in his mouth and opened his airway again. I began pouring my heart and soul into him. I started yelling at the guy, "Come on, motherfucker!"

After about twenty seconds of that, Koa leaned over and said, "Get out of the weeds, Rog."

I didn't want to let go but Koa was right. I checked his pulse again; nothing. I realized the man was no longer breathing. I punched him in the face a couple of times, decompressed him again, and I started cursing at him, I held his face in my hands.

He left this world staring me dead in the eyes.

It took me about five seconds before I could let him go.

That's something you don't walk away from. He had died clutching at me and looking me in the eyes. I really wanted to show respect to him; I don't know where it came from, but at the time this really meant something to me. I brushed my fingers over his face, and closed his eyes. I patted him on the cheek, and squeezed him on the shoulders; I guess in some way, to prepare him to take off. I took the HyFin dressing out of his chest and put it in my pocket. I took the fentanyl pop out of his mouth and put that in my pocket, too.

I pulled the dressing I'd used off him, thinking I might need it for someone else. I had few supplies left. The whole time between the rounds zipping in at us, I could hear men yelling, calling the others in toward us. Someone would yell, "The PJs are here!" or "Doc, over here. Doc!"

I took off toward the man with the left arm shattered and just hanging on. I realized I needed to get guys closer to Koa and the man who had just died in my arms. I kneeled beside the guy with the mutilated arm. He continued shrieking in pain. I reached in my pocket and gave him the used fentanyl pop. "Here we go, buddy," I said, and I began pulling him toward Koa. We came to rest near the first body. I did a quick check of his tourniquet, which was still secure.

Next I moved to the man conscious and praying. He was still praying and I figured good to go. I dragged him to the side of the man with the partially dismembered arm and said, "Keep an eye on your buddy." I thought the task might help keep him occupied. I felt good about it. I made my way back up the shallow, steep ravine. I stopped at the guy who had been kicked back, lying prone, looking up in the sky with his helmet off, the one who had been telling me to help his buddies earlier. As I approached I realized he was talking to me, or himself, and he'd stopped repeating "Help my buddies, help my buddies." Instead, he mumbled to himself like a baby or someone speaking in tongues, and later babbling nothingness.

I dropped down at his side to comfort him, ease him off the rocks. I slid my left hand under his body, to cradle him, and the other behind his head. My right hand disappeared into the back half of his skull. He was missing the back of his head.

His voice trailed off, lost to the darkness. His spirit followed, and he stopped breathing.

I lost myself in rage.

I lost control at that point.

My job was to save these guys' lives, and that was not happening.

I wasn't doing my job.

I was failing them.

I sat him down very gently, and just as I did the first guy, without knowing or understanding my own actions, I squeezed his shoulders and patted him on the face, too. Then, and I can't explain exactly why, I removed one of his patches and slipped it into my pocket.

The adrenaline surging through my body became rage and despair.

I gently set him down and I crawled over to the guy on the 240. This was the guy who had been telling me the names of his teammates and what the enemy was doing.

He was still pointing the 240 out over the dirt berm. My words to him were harsh: "Hey, motherfucker," I asked, "what the fuck? Help me get these guys down!" We were still taking fire. I crawled on top and kneed him in the ribs to get him up, but he didn't move. I rolled him over to find his face blown inward, the entire front of his skull caved in by percussion dirt and rock. *What the fuck? He was just speaking to me, how could I have missed this?*

All emotion slipped from me.

I lost myself.

I took hold of his legs to drag him the twenty feet down to Koa. I wanted get him to the collection point, his body would shield the others. As I pulled him down the embankment, the sling of that 240 Golf caught on an arête, a horn of a rock outcropping. I was insane with horror. I fought and pulled him down the hill. I tumbled down, with his weapon sling hung up on a rock. Crew-serve weapons are heavier than you would imagine, and in the struggle the cumbersome weapon dumped over. The feed tray spilled open wide. Reflected by moonlight, the empty feed tray gleamed. His 240 had gone completely dry. He had died at some point while I was crawling up and down the ravine helping his buddies. He'd lain facing the threat with no ammunition.

I stared at that empty feed tray, and then his body.

As I had been pulling him, his shirt and armor came up over his head, exposing his torso. His stomach and chest were riddled with holes from rock or shrapnel. He wasn't bleeding. His pale skin glowed in the darkness.

I got him down to the collection point. I placed the bodies of the dead in an attempt to shield the living.

I crawled back up to the guy missing the back of his head. I scooped him up and carried him as gently as I could. I know it sounds stupid now, but I didn't want to hurt him. I cannot explain my actions.

During this Koa and I would shout: "Collect your wounded and bring them to us. If you can hear me crawl to my voice."

Halfway up to retrieve Karl, a man was crawling to me, ghost white and dry heaving.

"Help me, Doc, I am cold," he said.

"Where are you hit?" I asked. He lifted up his shirt and showed me a hole on the left side of his abdomen. Dark blood was pulsing out. I wasn't sure if I should decompress him. "Are you having trouble breathing?" He said no, but I could tell he was struggling. I took the needle and decompressed him. He was pale and dying.

He was shot, the hole in the side of him the size of a silver dollar. No exit wound. His entire body quaked with shivering. The night air felt cool, right around freezing, but when you are wounded and losing blood, you shake. The iron in our blood is what gives us the capacity to stay warm; shivering begins with blood loss. This guy had a zombie look. They all had a zombie look, but his was the worst. Even in the low illumination of the moonlight, he was pallid. A bleeding ghost. The moonlight made his appearance that much more horrifying.

I looked at this wound. A dark venous blood poured out of his abdomen. The blood pulsed from the gaping hole, in a roselike pattern. I could find no exit wound. He'd been hit by a .50 cal and the bullet had skimmed off his pelvis and was still lodged somewhere inside him.

I did what I could with what little I had. He died moments later.

I removed his field jacket and continued to Karl. After reaching him I placed the jacket on Karl.

I needed to get him to the collection point, but I couldn't risk dragging him by his feet. "Hang on, brother," I said. I gripped his wrists hard and began towing him, by his arms. We descended the steep slope that way. I moved him to a point just above the other casualties.

At the collection point, I asked Koa for his personal fentanyl pop and I gave it to the man in agony with the partial dismemberment. I assessed all the living and found no changes. I spoke to them as a group. I don't remember what was said.

I started trying to give Koa the numbers we had. I know I was wrong in my count, but I wasn't sure. I knew I had eight Americans, four KIA and four wounded. Koa insisted we had one more, asking, "Are you sure?" He was right. They brought an Afghan national, one of their interpreters, to us. I wasn't even concerned about him, not because he was a terp, but because they just said his lower leg was shot. In the midst of this a lower leg being shot was negligible to treat. He had a tourniquet already on and it was placed well.

Our casualty collection point was very grim. The helicopters were dealing with leaking fuel and undergoing battle-damage assessment. They couldn't come right back in to get us. We were still taking fire, but at this time it was dark. Pitch-black. Below freezing. Men were slowly filtering to us as they could between barrages and exchanges of fire. After the two-thousand-pounder, we had definitely wasted one of the threats, the Dishka that had been pretty much tearing up our position. There were insurgent corpses mixed around in the location and I didn't really understand or compre-hend why at the time. Later I would learn that they had made their flanking maneuver.

Just above the tree we'd seen explode from the RPG, the insurgents had begun overrunning the casualty site when our Hellfires found them. They were beginning to drag guys out when we called in those Hellfire missiles. If insurgents are scared of anything, they are scared of Apaches. Those guys ran like hell once those Apaches started releasing ordnance, they dropped back down in an attempt to take cover, and the effects of the MK-84 touched most of them.

I had depleted the last of my medical supplies. I had been carrying the two or three battle packs distributed across the pockets and pouches on my body. Those supplies had long since been used and reused. I continually searched the injured for supplies.

I began peeling armor off the dead and covering the injured, hoping to provide an additional layer to protect them. The dead provided cover as well. At this point my triage work started dying down as we finally had everyone consolidated. In between treating guys I would attempt to gather loose equipment into piles or toss it down to the collection of casualties. Helmets, NVG's, destroyed weapons, radios, and rucks were strewn up and down the ravine. Guys started asking, "What next, Doc?"

Thirty minutes or an hour passed, with me exhausted but still treating people. They were slowing slipping away on me, and I couldn't do anything more. I began making jokes, trying to keep their spirits up, saying crude shit—just being me. I said something like, "Hey guys, don't worry, man. No one is going to fucking leave us here. Twenty minutes you'll be finger-banging nurses." A stir of strained laughter floated across our moonlit ridge. Karl lifted his arm up and gave me a thumbs-up. It wasn't like he could sit up and cheer. He had no abdominal wall to make noise with. The guy with his arm just hanging on only moaned. The prayer guy with the fucked-up cauliflower

hip, snowed over with fentanyl, and still repeating the Lord's
Prayer over and over, stopped praying after my nurse joke
and said, "I'm married."

I shook my head in disbelief and thought, *You're bringing everybody down, man!* There are people like that in the
military who are so fucking square. *Now is not the time.*

I think I said, "Don't listen to that guy. These nurses are
going to be cute and not too hairy." I was doing my best to dis-
tract them, but this married guy was killing me. *You want to
critique my comedy at this point? It's all I have!*

I am trying to lighten this a bit but the desperation was
opaque.

All I could do—all I could do was tell these guys shitty
fucking jokes. I know I told them more jokes; I can't remember what I said, but I know whatever ever came out of my
mouth was crude. I was just trying to get their minds off what
was going on. Trying to keep them calm, give them hope, and
be there with them in some way.

Their various responses to my jokes caused me to take
note of what I was no longer hearing. I realized that the guy
who had been screaming, the one missing his arm, had fallen
silent. I dove over to him, feeling like even more of a failure.
He wasn't even breathing. While I'd been Mr. Richard Fucking Pryor with my terrible jokes, he was dying. Once I cogni-
tively realized he had stopped screaming I immediately knew
something was wrong. Here I was joking with him, and now
he might be dead. But once I got on him I realized his airway
was obstructed. I opened his jaw and ripped his helmet off. I
was able to dig some dirt and crap out of his mouth. Only with

both of my thumbs in his mouth, holding his tongue down and pulling his jaw forward, was he able to breathe. I had to put both my knees on his chest and put my thumbs in the back of his throat and pull his tongue out so he could get air. He was seizing up and his tongue would block his airway and prevent him from breathing. I searched him frantically, eventually finding an entry hole just below his clavicle and through an unprotected part of his armor. I immediately decompressed both sides of his lungs with a needle I had used many times earlier.

I realized I needed to stay on top of him if he was going to stay alive. I would let him breathe for ten or twenty seconds, then drop him for other things, then return and do the same again. I couldn't believe I had missed him being shot. He had been next to me throughout my efforts. I cannot explain it. The situation had highs and lows, but would never let up.

I was doing everything I could, but it felt like pissing to put out a forest fire.

I did not have to concern myself with anything related to getting us out of there, as Koa communicated the ground situation and relayed everything I requested most of the time before I said anything to him. We were definitely in tune with each other. I didn't need to know every detail of what he was doing, because I trusted he understood the situation and knew what we needed to do. He did.

"Rog," Koa said, "Pedros are inbound, soon as they refuel."

"Hear that, boys?" I said. "Get ready to spit on those

fingers. The nurses are waiting." I made another pass over each of the guys, telling them to hold on, reassuring them, once again, that the 60s were coming.

The sound of those HH-60s coming up the valley should have put me at ease, but honestly it didn't. I might have been joking with the guys about naughty nurses and how nice that hot food and a shower were going to be, but my mind wasn't there itself. I needed to make sure we got these guys out, and there was no way two 60s were getting everyone off the mountain.

A helo circled and kicked out a giant sack of ammo and medical supplies. Missing our location completely, it went tumbling down the mountain, a donation to the enemy. We'd have to risk leaving our position and spend twenty or thirty minutes to drop down the valley to retrieve it, and take even longer to get back.

Brandon and Jimmy came down first, to another barrage of tracers. They hit the ground below us somewhere in the dark. They knew we had three patients in critical condition. The men with me were dead or dying. When Brandon and Jimmy were finally on the ground, we had our much-needed help. But for some reason they took forever getting to us, and I felt they were not up to speed with the intensity of the situation. I perceived their lack of speed as them not being emotionally invested, and this enraged me.

In their defense, they had cartwheeled, ass-over-teakettle, down a ten- or fifteen-foot scree ledge, attached to each other with two different types of rescue baskets. When they reached us, I jumped up in their faces and yelled, "Unfuck yourselves!"

I grabbed Jimmy and put him on the one-armed airway guy and screamed, "Keep his fucking airway open!" Pedro 83 came in and hoisted Ski down with a litter. Koa ran down the scree to assist Ski.

I prepared the patients for the helo flight as best as possible. I stripped them of everything the platoon would value on the ground to link up when we departed: ammo, radios, grenades, and weapons.

As soon as Ski reached the collection point, I brought him up to speed. I directed Ski to Karl and the married, praying guy. We prepared the screaming, now "not screaming guy" first, with Jimmy. I identified this guy as most critical. Within minutes we had him ready to hoist up into the bird with Jimmy.

Immediately after we had Jimmy and his patient ready to hoist, Brandon and I started working on Karl and loaded him into the second litter. By the time Jimmy and the first casualty were in the aircraft, and we had Karl ready for hoist. The crew asked if they needed make another pass around. "No," we replied, "Patient two is ready for hoist." We immediately hoisted Karl into the aircraft. Koa read my mind and sent the helo away to the forward surgical team.

Koa maintained complete control of the situation as we worked to get the casualties out. He controlled the aircraft and flow on the ground. I could hear Koa deconflicting all of that as we handled the patients.

The second helo rolled in; Ski's patients were ready to go. He packaged and tag-lined them up. I yelled to him, "Ski! Go on up, Ski, and send the stokes back down." I had to argue for a moment to convey what I wanted, but he got it. He rose up, climbed into the aircraft, dumped the patient out, and sent the litter right back down to us. I directed the married guy with the hip shot to crawl toward the litter, and loaded him into it as well. I had Brandon secure him and tag-line him up, and Ski received him into the aircraft.

They dropped the empty litter down for us to load the heroes in, and Koa sent that helo off as well. We were alone again. All of our wounded, except for the interpreter, were headed at 130 knots toward those nurses I'd promised were waiting.

We started prepping the heroes, the KIAs, with the help of the platoon leader and the remaining team on the ground. In whatever free time we had we consolidated their sensitive items and redistributed them as necessary. Out of nowhere, Koa said, "Pedro 85 is inbound." We had no idea where that came from. Before I knew it they hovered over us and dropped the hoist. We double stacked two heroes into the litter, tag-lined it up, dumped them in the bird, brought the litter back down, and sent up the next two.

Then Koa looked at me and said, "Where is the terp?"

Shit!

He was gone.

We made a game plan for a quick search. Brandon and Koa went sprinting up the mountain, disappearing into the darkness. All of the sudden a rock stood up from a rice paddy squat out of the moonlight, right next to me. I radioed up to them, "I got him!" Brandon and Koa stumbled back down the hill. Brandon hooked in with the interpreter and up they went.

Before Koa came down the hill to us, for his own exfil, he had some words with the platoon leader, ensuring him of the coordination plan and resupply. Koa and I hooked up and hoisted up into the helo. I would like to tell you that at that moment, two bloodied warriors looked each other in the eyes and rode on Valkyrie wings up to the heavens, but there would be no such magical moment. We were both overcome with the gravity and emotion of the situation, and we weren't finished. There was no celebration, just grief and horror.

We hit the top of the hoist and climbed into the cabin of the helo. Doug and Aaron, two additional PJs from our team, stared at us. They looked as surprised to see us as we did them. They were just performing another rescue in the valley below and were directed to assist us as soon as possible. They also had no idea at what had taken place. Like I said before, that fog of war is a very real thing. It was still sinking in that this was not a lead or trail helo. Everything was still very much surreal, and honestly I did not care. The cabin had no room. Koa and I crawled over the top of the dead.

Once we were safely inside, the cabin doors were shut and the helo shifted and fell out underneath us. Koa laid back and let out a guttural scream. We were falling out of the sky, dropping off the side of the mountain. Falling all over everything inside. I laid among the bodies of men who relied on me. Men who died in my arms.

I wanted to get them off that helo as quick as possible. I

wanted to treat them with as much respect as possible. But there we were all crammed in the back of the helicopter, fumbling, sitting, and lying over them.

We stopped to refuel at FOB Blessing. The flight took longer than I expected. I began to get angry again. There was no room. I could feel the head of one of the casualties beneath me. These men had depended on me over the last two or three hours of their lives, and they died. And now I was sitting on them because I couldn't fit anywhere else in the helicopter. I was face-to-face with my inadequacy and rage.

I'd plugged in to the onboard communications, talking to the pilot, and we were flying toward the FOB. The pilot made some type of light joke; I can't recall it now, it was something slight but it pissed me off. I became enraged and wild. Again, only in hindsight did they know anything of what had happened. I also didn't realize that one of the gunners, in trying to help pull bodies in, had become overwhelmed and fell silent. The lead pilot sensed this and attempted to lighten the situation and get his guy to talk. His banter only worked as fuel to enrage me.

I tried to refocus, but the grief and anger was debilitating.

I yelled to Aaron, "Body bags." He knew what I meant and began scrambling to get the bags out. I figured that when we landed in Asadabad, the quick reaction force was going to be there huddled around the burn barrels, waiting, and they were going to see us roll in with all these mutilated bodies, their teammates, their brothers. Lying on top of and among the remains was so morbid and visceral; I felt my sanity come and go. The mutilated bodies spoke to me about losing myself. We rely on ceremony, clinging to our humanity, and to respect what is lost.

Aaron grabbed some bags and we all went to work, maneuvering around inside the cabin was impossible. Four dead, five PJ's, and one shot interpreter in the space of a small minivan. It's not simple to place a grown man in body armor in a body bag. Blood, bile, and feces covered the floor, making the helo cabin slick.

On approach to Asadabad, I told the pilot to land with the left door away from the burn barrels. We had only managed to place one man successfully in a bag. The pilot put the helo down and we jumped out and finished the job. After landing the crew turned on the green cabin lights to aid our work. We tried to treat those guys with as much respect as we could. Putting the men in body bags and carrying them to the Conex container is something I will not explain. Words fail me.

Tears poured. I was filled with rage. Filled with grief. With disbelief. Disbelief at what I saw. Disbelief and guilt that we had survived.

I was a fucking wreck.

Doug found a bloody wedding ring next to an eyelet in the back as we were moving the bodies. He showed it to me and we stared at it in disbelief. We flew back to FOB Joyce just a few miles away numb and lost. The cabin doors were open. The sights and wind and sensations were hypnotic. The floor of the cabin still slick with gore.

Moments later we landed at Joyce. I directed the guys to clean the floors of the helos. I went inside to the bright fluorescent light and sat down on the ground and shuddered. I was attempting to come to terms with myself. Within seconds I heard another 9-line request come over the radio. In that moment, I knew we would not be allowed to process this until it was over, at another time and on our own terms. Bulldog Bite would last four more days. In all there were more than forty-nine casualties and eleven Americans killed. In a selfish way I would like to believe we saved them all, as well as ourselves.

19

CATHARTIC INK AND SERENDIPITY

At a glance, every individual's own measure of dignity is manifested just as it is. There is dignity in personal appearance. There is dignity in a calm aspect. There is dignity in paucity of words. There is dignity in flawlessness of manners. There is dignity in solemn behavior. And there is dignity in deep insight and a clear perspective. These are all reflected on the surface. But in the end, their foundation is simplicity of thought and tautness of spirit.

—YAMAMOTO TSUNETOMO, *HAGAKURE*

Our team returned to Bagram after the eight days of Bulldog Bite. Dried blood and gore crusted and caked on our uniforms. We'd been marinated in horror and grief; we were beside ourselves and exhausted. We needed to unwind and decompress. We needed to pick up the pieces of who we were.

A public affairs person came into the Opium Den, and

the dude was destitute, at the end of his rope. He had a documentary film crew with him, three guys who had been hanging out on Bagram in an attempt to get their film project off the ground. They were trying to talk to troops who either weren't direct combatants or were guys from the task force, and those guys aren't going to talk to anyone. We were really this perfect storm, not only the odd chance of us having gone through the most intense combat that I can imagine, but them out of desperation asking just the right question, "Who else can we talk to on this base?"

The public affairs guy offered us up to the film crew: "Well, there are these guys called PJs, Special Ops guys who risk their lives to save others' lives as their job; some of the most highly trained guys in the military. We can drive around the base to go talk to them." It had to have been a pretty reflective drive, as these civilians made their way around that whole base, from the Disney World side they were on to the user side of the base. Nothing but Warthogs, Predators, and constant airlift. The business end of freedom resides over there. We'd be out doing workouts on the tarmac in between missions and a Predator drone would fire up with no visible pilot or controller, only a few feet away from us, and start taxiing away with Hellfire missiles on board.

This was the side of the base where the war was happening. On the other side of base you had the Green Beans (a military-contract version of Starbucks), pizza places, markets and shit, salsa night, and CrossFit gyms. A real glimpse of Americana. Fuck all that. I didn't even want my men exposed to Facebook while deployed. I wanted my guys to be able to grow their hair in a Mohawk and war mullets and do whatever the fuck they wanted, like not shower. One of my guys didn't shower for three months. He was stinky as fuck. Living in a steel box with no air-conditioning does that to you. We were treating guys and bringing them into the aid station at Bagram and I would get complaints. "Your guys need to fucking wash, Roger. One, it's unsanitary; and two, it's fucking gross." These were my guys. And I was saying do whatever you want. I believe this, I really do, that you have to leave yourself in order to return. So if you let guys be barbarians, then at some point when they come back they can do a reentry and come back to themselves. But if you want guys to deal with mortality on a daily basis, you don't want to have niceties and air-conditioning and mochas and shit. You don't want them to have a Coca-Cola or cold Sprite on request. You want their reality to be very apparent; war is not your normal life. You want war to be uncomfortable. It needs to be bad to return to what's normal. To go back and forth from comfort to combat is harmful. To project mortal violence or save people from their own mortality, randomly two to three times a day or even once a week, you have to stay in a specific frame of mind. To shift back into a mindset from combat to normal is difficult. So during deployments I would say, fuck it, let's stay in Bizarro World, keep it road warrior. Stay in that mind-set. Keep your gear on. Go work out in full battle rattle until you throw up and leave the gear on all day. Stay in that frame of mind and it's more beneficial to you than to shut it off at the end of a mission and have to return when the call comes. That is what we were trying to do when we'd returned.

The public affairs guy showed up, dejected, trying to get this film crew with him some subjects to film, men of value and backstory. The public affairs guy ran into Kirby, and Jimmy and Kirby said they'd have to talk to Roger about this before okaying it. At this point I think Jimmy and Scott were taking their shirts off and comparing tattoos with the film crew, joking and talking with them, when Kirby came inside and said, "Hey Roger, there are these three guys outside and I think you should come talk to them."

"Well, what the fuck do they want?" I asked.

"They want to tattoo us. They are shooting a documentary."

Hmmm. That's not normal, I thought to myself. *Interesting.* On a human level, the project sounded interesting.

Overcome with sorrow and grief, and at the same time feeling both relieved and guilty to be returning alive when so many others were in body bags, I went outside, prepared to tell whoever it was to go eat shit. But honestly, at the same time something in me was attentive. Subconsciously I might have been remembering how I had felt when Craig's buddy Oliver tattooed me with the Recon jack. I opened the door to the Opium Den. I immediately sensed that the men on the other side were not chumps. There I stood, in front of these complete strangers, and I was still splattered with dried brain matter, blood, and feces, and inside, a grenade of grief.

I approached them and said something like, "Hey, I'm the enlisted guy in charge of the pararescuemen here. We just got back from some pretty gnarly stuff." The three men were Scott Campbell, Casey Neistat, and David Kuhn. A tattoo artist, a filmmaker, and a film producer and lawyer. All friends with an ambitious film project to tattoo men fresh off the field from combat.

This tattoo artist, Scott Campbell, a man I had never heard of, looked at my expression, and he seemed to take in the whole of my being with one intense glance. He turned to his friend and in this soft-spoken manner said, "This is wrong, Casey; let's go home."

They were human beings of value. They had skin in the game. They seemed to be unique, solid guys. I guess in many ways I sensed in them an energy we needed. They weren't on the same gravy train that we were on, and they were coming from a completely different world.

A profound moment occurred there in front of the Opium Den. Not only was Scott experiencing the potential loss of a project, shot down at the doorway of some shitty warehouse in the middle of a war zone, but more profound for me was this loss of an idea or dream happening because of something the man saw within me. In that moment, I realized that I had lost a certain sense of myself. There was something very human about the initial interaction I had had with these three strangers, something that I wanted to hold on to, perhaps something I needed at that exact moment in time. In retrospect, the reflection of myself through their eyes brought me much closer to my own humanity.

I cannot explain it beyond this: I was immediately endeared to these men. Despite the fact that I knew nothing about them or who they were, I gave them a chance.

"Come on in," I said. "My guys are going to be kind of weird. We've been through some shit, and in three more days we're going back out into it."

They said, "No, no, no—we get it." The look that Scott was giving me was *Wow, man.* This is all just my reflection, and this moment has played over in my mind a thousand times. When you're faced with the *now* of realizing your dreams, and when you can fulfill those now, and the moment is here, much of the time you're too taken aback to react, so your response is the collective *fuck.* That was the look on Scott's face that I'll never forget. These guys were so passionate and so full of humanity that they had caught me off guard. Scott's face revealed his trepidation. The look really said, *Whoa . . . I don't think this is the right thing.* All this time you had this dream to make love to the prom queen, and now here she is drunk and pulling you into the backseat of your car. What are you going to do?

In many ways I think I said yes to their project because I knew that it would be good for my team and myself in terms of healing. But, honestly, I was so overwhelmed with the humanity of their gesture to tattoo us and listen to our stories that I couldn't say no to the idea. I didn't know it then, but the experience would shape my reality for the rest of my life.

I opened the door and waved them inside.

"Let's do this," I said. "Come on in."

In hindsight, when I reflect on my introduction to Scott, Casey, and David, somehow subconsciously I think I knew that they could bring us back to our humanity through tattooing. This sounds so fucking weird to say to someone unless you've had a similar experience. We had all survived multiple life-and-death situations over a weeklong period, events that were extremely surreal and graphic. Then someone wants to tattoo us on a military base away from everything? There is something about that that is so cathartic that I simply cannot explain. I want to say that, collectively, I knew that the experience of tattooing and storytelling was going to be that profound, but at the same time it had such context in raw grit that I thought, *We're doing this.* I knew that some of our team couldn't quite understand it at the time, or possibly never. It's all on Casey's footage; if you watch it, I say something like, "Hey, these guys are looking for some legit motherfuckers to tattoo and we're them." I almost got emotional introducing them when they were videoing us because I was so overwhelmed by how the universe was coming back for us. I know it sounds stupid and clichéd, but at the time their appearance and the possibility that they might help us then was beyond powerful.

In all of my crazy military and life experiences, these three civilians dropping in to rescue the rescuers is as profound as any that I've had. I was in the military twenty-five years. I possess a lifetime of combat and rescue experiences, none bearing the magnitude of Bulldog Bite, but in all of my deployments, no one has come to tattoo me afterward. In all of my deployments, nothing like that has ever remotely happened.

So how can I even explain their appearance? Is it just me and my mind that gives it such weight? My imagination? It can't be. Is that God? Grace? Mercy? What is that? Whatever it is, I can tell you this: the magic of them coming into my life then haunts the fuck out of me. I cannot explain it, and of course I'm driven to try to re-create that for others. I was responsible for the guys who were there, and I wanted to try to help foster and create moments that would have value for them. But beyond that I don't know. I have no answers.

Honestly, I was probably looking to validate my own experiences too, my own shallow life, my own weird experiences on that mountain with those men dying in my arms, and at some level I too wanted to feel valued. Somewhere inside me I was probably looking for a sign that the universe gave a fuck, or that what we did was even real, or that all that suffering mattered. I know for certain I was struggling with the fact that I had returned with nothing to show for that experience other than a sense of overwhelming grief, a mountain of survivor's guilt, and isolation. Perhaps I understood that if Scott tattooed me, well then, *that* was real, and then I at least have a time stamp of the time and place.

When it was my turn, with Casey filming, Scott began to tattoo some sparrows on my chest, each with my sons' names. The sparrow is a landlocked bird, and when sailors would get close to home, that's when they would see those birds, a powerful symbol of homecoming and a returning to our humanity.

One of the things I asked Scott, when I first met him, was, "Scott, do you know Oliver Peck?"

His response was funny: "Oh yeah! Fuck yeah, the Pecker!"

"I know him pretty well," I said. "He's tattooed my mom and friends."

That was how we broke down and became closer. Real knows real. And sharing time with Scott was powerful. It had to have been like a junkie relapsing and overdosing. This was life-altering stuff. Literally a tsunami of juju swept over me; I felt like I had to attempt to harness it somehow. Beyond just getting a tattoo. And that's the thing. When you look at a really good tattoo, it's the net result of a lot of juju. Whether it is the secret language of iconography or the way that it was done. There is some black magic in that shit. I'm haunted with the power of that.

What ended up happening was that once Scott, Casey, and David understood the magnitude of what our job as PJs was, and what we'd experienced during the mission, they set their entire project aside and focused on us. They just wanted to give to the team. Scott took out his gear and started working his magic on us.

They didn't care about the filming, it was all about tattooing us. The experience was amazing and, in a word, cathartic. Scott tattooed us over a forty-eight-hour vision quest session of almost nonstop tattooing. As they were kind of wrapping it up I approached Scott for one more piece: "Scott, can you put these coordinates on me?" The team had been throwing really lofty goals at Scott the entire time. And he dealt with their requests with grace. In retrospect, I realize now how we didn't understand that what we were asking him for could take days or even weeks to complete.

My uniform and gear were blood and gore stained. I'd left it all with not so much as a scratch, but my mind reeled from the horrors of days earlier. It's interesting how a tattoo could somehow encompass and make real all that was in my heart and head.

What Scott really needed from us were one-shot simple tattoos, so I'm sure he felt relieved when I said, "Could we do some coordinates and a date on my forearm?" A request like that doesn't take anything for him, but now there is juju in creation. It's just as powerful as if you got your whole chest and torso covered in the Virgin Mary. A series of a couple of numbers and letters can be just as meaningful. It's not the size, it's the meaning and the juju. The context of art is where the magic comes into play. If the imagery supports the context, then the meaning becomes ever greater. The act of getting tattooed after combat is a profound ritual. To have sincerely profound ritual done with very meaningful context? Drop the mic, man. Tell me something more powerful than that, other than love or death? There is not anything more powerful. You've got love, death, and fucking tattoos. That's it. That's the order of things the way they were ordered in my mind at that point. Love, death, and tattoos.

Scott scribbled the date, time, and grid zone coordinates, the DTG used in the military to signify a specific event. So if you and your fighter pilot buddy were flying, and you're in one jet and he's in the other, and he gets shot down, there will be a DTG for that event. It's an identifier. For me it was a concrete way to capture what happened that night on the mountain. Scott scrawled those digits while I was seeking to validate the experiences and connect on a deeper level with the horror of those events. That series of numerals and letters made the intangible a few degrees more tangible. The tattoo turned the memory of the event into something I could see and touch. The tattoo boiled it all down to something I could feel. The context of the tattoo is what is so powerful. There it is: love, death, and tattoos. There is significance, catharsis, and value to that. It's all there on my arm, on my chest, and in my heart.

How could I have turned away from them? How could I not see the promise of healing that would come from those tattoos and the ensuing friendships? I've been told, and have read, and have had conversations with dear friends about this stuff: when you see the way, you see the way. And if you ever look away from that, once you recognize the way, your life will have nothing but despair. You have to have the courage at that moment to shoulder that new path forward. If you're a junkie and you're shooting up and your kids are watching you get high, and you recognize that they understand what you're doing deeply affects you, if you keep shooting up, well, you're going down a dark road. Or—at that moment you were offered the humanity and the grace to say to yourself, *Hey, man, I need to fucking stop. I need to change, despite the pain.*

The healing nature of what Scott, Casey, and David did for us was miraculous as we bonded with them. When they finished tattooing, they packed up their film and tattoo gear and flew back to New York City. We finished our deployment and returned to Anchorage. Back to rescuing wayward tourists off Flattop Peak and picking up the pieces of small plane crashes and sinking boats.

I returned, haunted with what I'd survived and carrying

an unbearable amount of grief and guilt for those I couldn't save. At the same time, I simply could not shake the catharsis I felt being tattooed by Scott after we'd returned from the battlefield.

One afternoon, I asked Jennifer if she could please take the kids to go see a movie. I was struggling that day to keep it together. In those moments I could have reached for my pistol to end the pain and anguish. Instead I went downstairs and dug out a gift Jen had bought me a few months earlier: a shitty tattoo kit.

I sat down and began tattooing my leg. I know none of that makes sense, but it definitely made sense at the time. I was so consumed with sorrow that tattooing myself made sense. Tattooing my own flesh felt like low-hanging fruit on the tree of suffering, for me.

I initially started on the inside of my thigh on my left leg, covering up that scar from where I'd burned myself on my dad's motorcycle. I covered over the burn with my first cherry blossom. I was tattooing over scar tissue, which doesn't really work, but that didn't matter. I was learning the art, and even more important than that, I was beginning down the road to healing. Once I saw the potential for healing and the way forward that tattooing held for me, I had to pour myself into the profession.

You want to validate your experiences with grand events. You place more weight upon random occurrences; the fact that you are seeking things to be what they are forces you on that path. You claim it, and you tell yourself: *It can't be chance, it's God, Yoda, Elvis,* whatever you want it to be, but you place that grandeur, because you're stuck in that moment attempting to process and make sense of things.

But there is another way of looking at these moments of life: pure desperation. Your values relate to your desperation. When I've become desperate, I begin to synthesize meaning out of life, out of very surreal experiences I've lived. And then, that desperation carries me forward on a path with twists and turns and only more moments of serendipity.

Why do we do the things we do? What motivates us? I've said it before: nothing matters more than our resolve and intent, but things happen to us that we need to process. When we accumulate unprocessed events, those memories are never filed within our minds correctly. We seek to find meaning from the trauma, and we project our desperation on random events, finding synchronicity through serendipity and sometimes *grace.*

This is what happened to me with tattooing. An artist has to have something to say. Even if the artist is unaware, regardless, it will project itself throughout the work, subconsciously and powerfully. If the artist is growing in pain, and desperate enough to radiate his voice, his voice will be heard. Nature forces the expression of itself in a self-reflecting affirmation. Pragmatically you're putting in the work, expressing your intentions, and exhausting yourself, and from that, the pulsing rose bathed in moonlight blossoms.

You will interpret a moment as serendipity, but the reality is that you're looking at unprocessed emotional events. So if I'm saying it was serendipitous for me to meet Scott

Campbell, I know I might be making context out of something that isn't there. But in my mind Scott, Casey, and David coming into my life when I needed them most is a beautiful moment of serendipity. Our relationship started the journey toward healing, expression, and moving forward.

20

METAL AND HONOR

When you are listening to the stories of accomplished men and the like, you should listen with deep sincerity, even if it's something about which you already know. If in listening to the same thing ten or twenty times it happens that you come to an unexpected understanding, that moment will be very special. Within the tedious talk of old folks are their meritorious deeds.

—YAMAMOTO TSUNETOMO, *HAGAKURE*

Like a cast iron pan, my life was all seasoning before Bulldog Bite. Whether missions and training in the Marine Corps or pararescue, all of it was seasoning up to that point. Then came the sailing home. All voyages culminate in a release of sorts. But that is difficult, because now, like the legendary Odysseus, when you try to sail home, what exactly are you sailing home to? Because when you arrive you're not yourself anymore.

There is a Zen proverb that says to become enlightened you have to first lose your senses to come to your senses. In other words, you have to lose your shit to come to who you really are. Otherwise you're just this mindless drone on cruise control. We all leave to return. You need to lose yourself to find yourself. In trying to find yourself, you're going home without a home.

A month or two after we'd returned from Bulldog Bite, Joe Conroy, my commander at the time, pulled me aside. He had something to tell me. My entire career I had called him by his first name, and to him I was Roger. Recalling how he dealt with me and the others on our return endeared me even more to him. He understood the significance of what we'd been through—what the team had collectively absorbed. The events seemed to change him dramatically, too. He no longer held my feet to any of the bullshit military fires. "Roger," he said, "on October 25, I need you to go to Hangar 20, and you're going to be one of *the* people to meet the chairman of the Joint Chiefs of Staff."

My commander knew I how much I despised the pomp and fluff of the military, but there he was telling me that *he* needed me to go. As much as I wanted to refuse, I couldn't say no to Joe.

I thought this was the usual gathering of the troops to welcome some top brass. Usually the command will pick a few chumps from a series of units to stand in the green room, before the visiting head honcho steps out to the waiting crowd. He would personally address everyone there, and they have a short private audience with him. I perceived the invitation as a somewhat of a contrived interaction. Of course, with military standards, I was told to arrive an hour before anything was even happening.

I was one of the first guys in the room. I was just sitting, and I could tell the scene wasn't for me. I was still in a very fragile state from everything I'd gone through. You could say I was a broken eggshell, oozing yolk. The others filtered into the room. From my perspective they were the "Airman of the Quarter" or "Soldier of the Month." They'd organized clean-ups on base or canned food drives; one had pulled someone from a burning car that had wrecked right outside the gate to the base. I'm sure in reality these were all good people, but I was in no frame of mind to be in such a place.

I sat, patient as I could, stewing. Thinking. Overthinking. Anger building over the whole scene. Then the PR people rolled in and started giving orders. You have to understand that there are people in the military whose whole job is to make sure that protocol is followed. This is called customs and courtesy. These are field grade officers, inspectors of the highest order, tasked to make sure that everything is perfect for the top brass. They came in and started talking at us. At me. The guy was telling me how I'm going to address the chairman of the Joint Chiefs of Staff. This is what you'll address him as, and this is how you're going to speak, and this is who is speaking first.

And this is where the scene really got fucked up for me. This was T-minus thirty minutes. People were scurrying about setting up all this shit in the room, and in those moments I was a glacier of grief, haunted by that night on the mountain, and these people I don't know were ordering me around like I'm a child. The record skipped when they escorted in this young beautiful woman from the Army. Right there in front of us they were dressing her up and applying cosmetics to her pretty face. Maybe she worked with the publicity department of the military, or what; I don't know. All I know is that the whole thing, at that moment, became too much.

The whole scenario made me sick to my stomach. *Fuck this*, I thought. *Fuck all of this. What am I doing here?* I became angry. Angry at anyone who wanted to take what we went through during Bulldog Bite and turn this into *a moment*. For what? For politics? For publicity?

Fuck this.

I stood up and walked out.

I was so upset. I couldn't go back to the squadron. I climbed into my car and drove to Ski & Benny, a local pizza joint right outside the gate. I ordered a sandwich and sat down, lost in thought. Questioning what I'd done, and what they were doing. Thirty minutes later, deep into my meatball sandwich, and my cellphone rang.

It was Joe.

"Roger, listen," Joe said. "Don't fuck with me. I don't know what is going on, but you need to be here *now*. Get to the hangar. *Now.*"

Reluctantly, I finished up. I drove straight to the hangar, but unlike when I first arrived, the place was packed; it seemed as if the entire base had arrived to hear this guy speak. So I made my way back telling myself, *I'm doing this for Joe.* I didn't want him to have to tap dance for my bullshit.

As soon as I got inside this huge hangar, the kind you can park C-17s in, one of the biggest hangars on our flight line, I heard my name. I heard General Martin Dempsey saying *my name*, and he was telling part of my story in his speech. I heard "and Roger Sparks hoisted down. . . ." He was using me as an analogy for what it means to serve. "Why is he hanging off that cable?" Dempsey asked. "Not for himself. He's hanging off that cable because he understands, if we trust each other and we care about each other, we can get through anything."

I heard him say my name and again I was struck by that sense of the surreal. Everything up to that point, the volume of my life, had been so loud, that even me entering as he said that, and those words, just sounded the same as everything else. *Okay*, I thought, *so he's talking about me.* But then the realization gut-punched me with a sense of anxiety, and at that second, as I searched the crowd for Joe, one of the Secret Service guys grabbed my arm.

"Sergeant Sparks," the Secret Service dude said, "where have you been?" I turned to look at him. This was one of the square-jawed guys with the stupid little ear buds in; using his supersecret service skills he had recognized me, the six feet eight guy, by sight. He grasped me by the arm and started leading me away. "You know," he said, "the general has been waiting for you."

Whatever, I thought.

The agent led me out of the hangar and escorted me to a vehicle, parked and waiting. He opened the door and told me to get in. This was the fancy ride that would shuttle General Dempsey back to Air Force One.

I sat there in the back of this fancy car, waiting and

making small talk with the agent. Thirty minutes or so went by. We heard a roar of applause. Ten minutes later, the door opened and in came the general.

All generals seem to smell the same. The first thing I noticed was the fancy aftershave—something I don't know anything about. Generals are probably mandated to wear a specific kind of cologne, for all I know.

This short, curt man with gray hair and those intense general-type eyes sat down staring at me. He studied me for a moment, reached his hand out to shake mine, and said, "Where *the fuck* have you been?"

He said this, but in a cool and charismatic way. He could have been one of my dad's buddies. I instantly felt at ease. Despite what you think of the politics or whatever was happening at the time, there was something very real about General Dempsey. The man possessed an energy that attracted me right away. Real knows real. I didn't know what to say or how to respond. I was embarrassed and a bit ashamed.

"I work for you, sir. I was doing my job," I said. Then I added, "I'm sorry." I was trying to deflect the question, but I could tell that he'd already assessed that I wasn't sure about his intentions.

After he shook my hand and we got the small talk of out of the way, he said, "You know, I just want you to know that myself and the other men at my level are directly speaking about you. Your name really does get around. I came here today to discuss the details with you personally. We don't have time for that *now* so I just like to say thank you. It's an honor to serve with you." I recognize this is a canned thing that anyone could say, and anyone could have said it, but in that moment, coming from him, the words carried a strange power, only because they felt warm and genuine.

I fumbled my way through a humble acceptance of his words, saying something awkward like, "It was my pleasure, sir." .

Time stopped for a moment in the vehicle with him. I didn't know what to say. Meeting with him was awkward. It made me aware of my grief. "I don't know what any of this means, I know we did everything that we could, and I feel lucky to still be alive. sir."

And that's it.

That is all I said.

All I *could* say.

The general shook my hand again, held it for a moment, and said, "Thank you for your service, Roger. You're an amazing human being and again it's an honor to serve with you!" I hopped out and he headed to his waiting aircraft, and that was that.

I walked back to our section through the parking lot still filled to capacity with cars. Everyone was celebrating something they didn't understand. I found Joe to apologize and went home feeling very alone.

I felt like I had turned my cheek on some kind of collective recognition. When speaking with General Dempsey he was warm and genuine. He was also very sincere, and I don't know for certain if he came all that way to Alaska to specifically speak with me, but I know he genuinely wanted to hear my story. Had I known he wanted the story from the horse's mouth, I still might have left the green room. Honestly, I was not in a state of mind for pageantry. Whether leaving that day undermined hidden intentions or cosmic ju-ju, doesn't concern me. More important, the whole reason I bring this story up is I began to realize that any awareness or recognition honored the moments during Bulldog Bite for everyone involved; I wanted to justify my pain and my sense of grief. I wanted people to understand the lives lost, the battle and ensuing events. I call this closing the gap and I think all combat veterans go through this.

The expression "I feel lucky to still be alive" can really take you for a ride.

Once you've resigned yourself to death—to certain death—and continue completely abandoning your own mortality moment to moment, and death never comes, it is a dark road to come back from. It brings survivor's guilt and a rational gap that holds you like a broken record. You will carry over each of those moments that passed by, and you will toil with that gift, I assume for the rest of your life.

Recognition cannot change that, but closing the gap, creating awareness opens it up for collective perspective and growth.

21

THE TIGER'S SMILE

Worth gradually wanes. If there were a shortage of gold, silver would become treasure, and if there were a shortage of silver, copper would be valued. With changing times and the waning of men's capacities, one would be of suitable worth even if he put forth only slight effort.

—YAMAMOTO TSUNETOMO, *HAGAKURE*

The military had lost or denied an awards package for my actions during Bulldog Bite. The men I worked with had no time for someone grappling with these things. I knew the grief I carried was a burden to the team and myself. In life you turn tricks or get the pimp hand. I was always happy to take mine on the chin. At some point you let go of validating your grief and pain through the military itself. I knew the answers wouldn't come from where the problems originated. During this time I knew I had outgrown whatever it was I had been seeking through my military experience. I occupied myself with painting roses bathed in moonlight in my dingy garage. The universe will find a way to express itself.

I owe a man named Verdie Bowen for many things, not only for his efforts, but for the time and closure he would give my father and me. Verdie, the director of Alaska's Office of Veterans Affairs, caught wind of my story from a staffer in United States Senator Lisa Murkowski's office at some point in 2011. Then, when he read a story Mike Dunham wrote in the *Anchorage Daily News* about a possible Silver Star, he went into overdrive. Feeling that my action merited more, he submitted a package for the Service Cross. That came back denied because some element of the application was incomplete. Verdie wouldn't relent. He met with all of Alaska's top brass and relayed momentum and support.

So many people were stepping up and trying to help. When the award package came back, it had been downgraded from the Service Cross to the Silver Star. I owe a lot to Verdie, but not in the way you would think.

Tim O'Brien, author of *The Things They Carried,* is one of my favorite writers. He's a powerful storyteller; I consider his work among the best of modern war literature because he uses his writing as a catharsis for his experiences. As far as awards are concerned, O'Brien says the only thing true about awards is that some did less and got more, and some did more and got less. That is it.

In the aftermath, the acknowledgment validates your own pain or your own grief, or perhaps recognizes the collective suffering of combat.

I think the more that we experience the lessons of this world, the more that we can reflect on their beauty or their horror, when it's all really just one and the same thing. I've absorbed a lot of experiences, I feel very lucky for the opportunity to share my stories and attempt to find meaning

One of the men who died on the mountain that night in Afghanistan was Jesse Snow, and for his actions he received a posthumous Silver Star. His father, John Snow, organized an amazing ceremony for his son. Thousands of people attended; the crowds filled the Wright-Patterson Air Force Base museum. At the event John somehow learned that PJs had been involved in his son's last moments.

John Snow was a career military man himself, an AC-130 gunship guy, so he knew what PJs were, and realized he hadn't heard the full story.

If your son was killed in action wouldn't you want to speak with someone who had been there at his side in his last moments? John immediately set out to get to the bottom of it. One of the first pararescuemen he reached out to happened to be my indoc proctor, Robby Bean.

"Do you know any of the PJs who were involved with Bulldog Bite?" John asked.

"Oh yeah," Robby said, "Roger Sparks. Here is his cell phone number."

John texted me out of the blue. I got a message something along the lines of "Thank you for bringing my son's body home. I would love to speak with you if that would be okay." I immediately found a quiet spot and called him.

My first thought ran ice through my veins: *Who among the dead was his son?* as tactfully as possible I asked him this as my mind reeled: *Did the Army tell you what injuries your son died from?*

John replied, "Jesse Snow. My son Jesse. He was shot in the back of the head."

The night replayed in my mind and time stopped.

Blackness and vertigo . . . Head injury . . .

Moonlight . . . holding the man asking for me to help his buddies. I'd cradled him in my arms.

Blackness . . .

His *patch*? I remember removing his patch.

His armor . . . the helo.

I came back to myself. The connection with the man on the phone was immediate. We talked for some time and exchanged contact information. After I hung up I stared at the wall with adrenaline coursing through my veins. I felt immense love and pain. I had his son's patch at home in a cedar box in my sock drawer. At times I would hold it and think of the moments it represented, feeling it and knowing the moment was real. The conversation with John opened a chasm larger than my comprehension. At some point I placed the patch in a simple black frame. It was not mine and I knew I had to return it.

John said he'd like to meet me, but traveling from Alaska is not only expensive, my work and the time away from my family would be difficult to manage. I could never afford to fly down to his house from Alaska on a whim. A short time after we made contact over the phone, a strange bit of synchronicity occurred. I had been disqualified from pararescue activities because I'd sought treatment for grief and post-traumatic stress. To be cleared for full duty I had to fly to Ohio be evaluated by the head shrinks at Wright-Patterson AFB. I would be staying less than three miles from where John Snow and his family lived.

John invited me to join him and his wife for dinner. I was overwhelmed by the gravity of this, but I knew I had to go, not only for myself but for Jesse's family as well. During the day I met with several behavioral health professionals. Many would ask, "So what are you doing tonight?" I think the gravity of my response had the doctors worried and mystified. Either way I knew the formality of the shrink visit was secondary to meeting Jesse's family and sharing my experiences with them.

Imagine the look on the doctor's face when I said, "I'm going to meet the family of one of the men that I just told you about. I need to return something that I took from their son and at the time couldn't understand." Perhaps all of this was to allow John and his wife to feel closer to Jesse? Later that evening I arrived at their house. The weight of the visit was overwhelming. I had carefully placed Jesse's patch in the frame on the front seat of the rental car. When I got out of the car to meet them I purposefully left it, feeling its presence the whole time. We exchanged pleasantries with our emotions building. John's wife made an amazing meal with garlic bread and manicotti, the exact way my mother is famous for. As we sipped the wine we discussed details about our lives. I slowly began to feel like a child in my own home. The situation became so familiar to me I felt as if I were speaking directly for Jesse.

Midway through dinner I said, "I need to give you both something, but I don't know what to say. When I was with your son that night I took something from him. At the time I couldn't explain it."

I pushed back my chair. "Excuse me but I need to get something from the car." I came back and said nothing as I handed Jesse's mother her son's patch, in a frame, coated in dried specks of blood.

When Jesse's mom held the frame, I said, "This is as close as I can bring you to your son." The intensity of the moment was too much. I had to look down at the ground as tears ran down my face. After a moment I looked up and she was walking down the hallway with Jesse's patch against her chest. I apologized to John. With tears is his eyes, he gave me a loving hug. John drove me to Jesse's plot, not far from their house. I stood there with John beside his boy's grave on a warm evening, feeling bewildered and comforted at the same time.

When I returned home to Alaska I started turning tricks again. I fell right into place on the alert schedule. On top of the weekly rescues we were also preparing for an upcoming deployment. In the end, Verdie's efforts paid off. The package for the Silver Star had been approved. Out of my own selfish and fragile emotions I had distanced myself from the meaning of it all. The deployment loomed closer. We set the date for the Silver Star ceremony to be two days before we departed for the Horn of Africa.

My father had been fighting lung cancer bravely for almost two years. He fought intensely to hold on to his vitality and strength. The VA flew my mother and father up to Alaska for the ceremony. The globetrotting of air travel beat him down even further. My father was very weak and ill. He could not walk when they landed in Anchorage. I had my buddies grab a wheelchair from the base hospital. He would not miss this for anything and in many ways he had been patiently waiting for it. When we had a private moment he told me how proud he was of me and that he would be starting hospice treatment when he returned home. My father always did things on his terms. This changed the tone of our time together. To me the ceremony became a moment to close the gap and share the events that took place, as well as to celebrate my father's life and the things he had instilled in me.

Karl Beilby was one of the casualties I had treated during that surreal night during Bulldog Bite. He had been in contact earlier with Verdie providing statements for the awards package. He requested that if I ever had a ceremony he must come and speak during the event. I met Karl at the visitor center of the base to get him a visitor pass. I was extremely nervous. The last time I had been with him was on the side of that mountain. I needed him to validate my emotions and grief. I needed him to share in the awe of violence we witnessed. My teammates Koa and Jimmy also flew up from the Lower 48 to attend. We all gathered to speak with Karl and shared a private moment directly before the ceremony began. Eventually Karl took to the podium. There he was, living and breathing and recalling the events of the night. It took everything I had to keep composed while he began talking about that night, thanking me and our team.

"I've been in many firefights," he said during his speech. "This was the mother of all firefights."

The time together with my family, teammates, and Karl was amazing. After the event Jennifer prepared a great meal in our home and we all had a fine evening, connecting and finding meaning.

It would be one of the last times I would see my father alive. He was proud and I made sure he knew that his strength and love for me was a reflection of the way I had lived my life. I deployed two days later.

22

A WARRIOR'S CREED

Tis not the creed that saves the man; but it is the man that justifies the creed.

—INAZO NITOBÉ, *BUSHIDO: THE SOUL OF JAPAN*

The sixteenth-century samurai Miyamoto Musashi retired to a cave to live the life of a hermit. There he penned *The Book of Five Rings*, another work that I've studied and admired. I seemed to be headed toward some sort of similar destiny, retreating to my own cave of sorts, the sacred space where I tattoo. On one wall I have the American flag, on another that iconic movie poster of De Niro from *Taxi Driver*, where he's pointing two pistols at the camera. The image comes from one of the most realistic scenes of combat, in the final five minutes of that film, a movie which I would ensure men I deployed with had watched. Also, near the doorway to our house hangs a copy of the Japanese poem by an unknown author, "Warrior's Creed."

As I readied for retirement I poured much of my energies into tattooing. I fell in love with the idea of tattooing as catharsis. I struggled with the medium, and thanks to Scott Campbell, and our friendship, the process has been healing. I would like to say I believe the most important aspect of a tattoo is who is doing the tattoo and what context the artist has to the person receiving the gesture. I know that is not a practical business model, but to me, the people and intentions involved are more important than the image or the outcome.

We make our own meanings. I've noticed, how people caught in life's transitions are pulled toward tattoos. Getting a tattoo is a way for people to reclaim themselves.

Honestly, when I began tattooing myself, I wanted to express and heal myself, despite the outcome. What I have learned over time was that we have to heal others to heal ourselves.

Contrary to that Japanese notion of tattooing called *irezumi*, which means to soften, we are the ones who have gotten too soft with modern living. Comfort has become the goal and a status symbol of Western culture. To grow we have to be aware of and rebel against these tendencies. A line I've lived by is, "Beware of comfort." We're compromised with our passions, and too civilized. We turn away from vulnerability, discomfort, and struggle. Our inhibitions have made us weaker.

I have spent my life fighting against those inhibitions and I challenge you to do the same.

I found insightful parallels between the ideas written in the *Hagakure* and the experiences of my own life. When reading those ideas it always struck me as a powerful affirmation.

I was always eager to share what I gathered with the men I worked with. For example, before doing a risky jump into a remote Alaskan riverbed, in the middle of the night, no lights, no ground party, burdened with life-saving equipment, below the minimum exit altitude, for your own good you need to be okay with dying. You shouldn't be contemplating that stuff on the ramp of the aircraft. I would show you a quote or two, en route, to remind you "when you leave your house in the morning, just consider yourself as already dead." Those words are timeless and relevant. With a job so intimate to mortality that's some of the best advice I can give you.

The Warrior's Creed wasn't something that was learned; it was something inherent to my life. I embodied so much of the ideology before I knew it was an organized philosophy. It has become increasingly palpable through each of the continuing experiences and ordeals.

When you've accumulated trauma and you're subconsciously scarred by those moments with something like post-traumatic stress, I believe many of our problems come from the inability to articulate them. Your experiences outweigh your ability to process them. So you feel isolated. It's challenging to process memories and find meaning in the horrors when you return to a world so consumed with distractions. Things don't get easier when you've made a career out of combat, and each time you come home it feels harder and harder to return. The arbitrary rules of Western culture seem to make less sense with the truth in your heart.

Why would you not turn away and isolate from the vacant neon sign of our culture? The reality is all so opposite from what you've seen when you look behind the curtain and live with those experiences. When you find little value and only the heartache, you just turn away.

Whatever happened in the way that I grew up, all those subtle and intangible events, I can only tell you that things happen the way they need to. The metamorphosis from that experience, the experiences on the mountain that night, to fill up my own soul from that moment or the residual moments is to transcend and articulate the voice of the world.

With the images I paint and tattoo I'm trying to express that metamorphosis. I'm attempting to capture that transcendence from experience. This is what I believe. This is about the collective good, and the energy that causes a flower to bloom. This is the message I want you to take away from my story. The cultivation of experience, and importance in creating something of value for ourselves and each other. I would hope my story forces you to contemplate your own life, and create some sense of value out of your experiences, because that is what interests me in sharing my story.

The friendships and the adventures that have blossomed from my experiences are the true gift of my life. I'm working again with my friend Rudy Reyes and a team of combat divers. We have helped form and develop an organization called Force Blue. Its mission is to utilize the experience, training, and skills of combat divers working closely with leading ocean conservationists. We are attempting to raise awareness to save the coral reefs, the oceans, and ourselves. The power of dichotomy is a strong element within the organization and has a healing effect on everyone involved.

My work with Force Blue, through more serendipity perhaps, led me to the filmmakers Bobby and Sara Sheehan, and I began working with the two of them and another nonprofit organization called Healing Our Heroes, to bring the latest in stem cell therapy to veterans like myself who have suffered combat-related injuries. I would be one of the first in the organization to receive the stem cell therapy. First on my knee, and later systemic injections. My son Oz has also received treatment, and two weeks after his first treatment, began connecting syllables in promising and miraculous ways.

Where I thought I might be retiring to a cave of solitary and contemplative existence, I've found a renewed sense of service and belonging in my life through tattooing, Force Blue, and in helping combat veterans with Healing Our Heroes.

If my story is a catharsis or thesis of those tenets for those wishing to overcome the adversity they face in their life, then it has value, beyond the entertainment.

There are those stories we cannot or won't share. Most of our collective story will always be unspoken. The act of sharing my experiences with you in this form has been a struggle. I'm uncomfortable being exposed. We all are. I don't share my life with you out of a sense of bravado, because I think that people who really experience combat don't posture. The guy who you never thought was in the military is the guy who probably did the grittiest stuff. It's not the guy beating on his chest and wearing the muscle T-shirt. That guy is still living it, trying to prove himself and his experiences. The guy that has really seen the horror, he's just trying to put himself together and find value. You know what he gets into? He gets into gardening. He doesn't continue to posture and act like he has the answers. Tenderness comes from pain.

There was a famous athlete my dad used to really admire. He was this giant Hawaiian Olympic power lifter. When he wasn't lifting weights he gardened. True power is in dichotomy. And maybe that is the point of my story, the power of that dichotomy. I can be this warrior, but in essence I am just that young boy scared about never walking again. To be strong, you must first be gentle, and appreciate weakness. Understanding violence is out of balance until you know mercy, love, and grace. The only healthy way of the universe is to find the dichotomy in the middle. Samurai culture wrestled with these ideas. They talked about it in their texts with calligraphy and the fine arts. Some were strongly opinionated and said the fine arts belong to the weak, but those who gained respect and experience, they spoke of art and creativity with reverence. So grit your teeth and be as tough as you want, but at some point you'll need to find balance through dichotomy. I hope you find it.

That is humanity's story. We all struggle to tell our stories. Stay the course; it is only through our own devoted practice, that the mysteries of the world are brought to light. To express through my own art, a young man dying in my arms, blood pulsing from an abdominal wound, as a rose bathed in moonlight is gentle and beautiful, despite the emotion. The power of dichotomy is palpable.

Many of those who were masters of Bushido, at some

point would go into art, whether it was calligraphy, writing, or painting. I suspect they were attempting to make sense out of their experiences. At some point I might have led myself back to art, but I don't know that for certain. When you're desperate you take risks. Until you're uncomfortable, you'll never know true growth. My relationship with tattooing and art is, for me, a way to express those things that cannot be explained. To that end, I do my best to be sincere; to be honest with myself and the people in my life, and in all those ways the things that I might represent to other people.

Surviving combat left me with a heavy heart and survivor's guilt. After those experiences it was hard not to feel life was nothing but chance. After many dark hours and struggle I came to a deeper understanding; something much more satisfying in regard to my experiences. Our resolve and our intentions are the magic of our lives. They have command in the space of chance. It is wise to meditate upon these daily. Make them conscious and deliberate. Strengthen and direct them toward your dreams. There's much more at stake than happiness and comfort. It's our families, our humanity, and if we are lucky the ability to sail home to ourselves.

Understand that to overcome anything, when we are faced with unsolvable problems, all we really have is our resolve and our intent. Be selfless and prepared. Whether you are aware or not, the wolves circle us. The alpha wolf stands outside your door waiting.